Leisure and Tourism

Harish Bhatt
B.S. Badan

CRESCENT
PUBLISHING CORPORATION

[*The responsibility for the facts stated, conclusions reached and plagiarism, if any, in this book is entirely that of the Author. And the Publisher bears no responsibility for them, whatsoever.*]

Leisure and Tourism

First Published : 2006

ISBN 81-8342-009-5

Published by :

CRESCENT PUBLISHING CORPORATION
4831/24, Prahlad Street,
Ansari Road, Darya Ganj,
New Delhi - 110002
Ph. : 23272541, 23257835
Fax : 91- 011- 23257835
e-mail : campusbooks@hotmail.com

Typesetting by :

Arjun Computers
Delhi - 110051

Printed at :
Roshan Offset Printers
Delhi

Preface

Leisure is a major activity which fulfils an important role in contributing towards the quality of life of the people. The term 'leisure' not only encompasses participation in active sport, but also children's play and informal recreational pursuits such as walking. The provision of leisure facilities has been going through a period of transition with the private sector becoming more involved in the leisure industry.

Tourism is the activity of all those visiting an area for leisure, business or family reasons, including day visitors. The tourism, leisure, recreation and sport sectors enhance the life of people. The economic and non-economic contributions that they make are recognised and supported from local to international levels.

Economic, demographic and social trends shape our consumption of leisure and tourism. Whilst there were some radical changes in leisure development during the 1990s e.g., the development of leisure parks and eating out places, tourism has tended to develop broadly along established lines, although short-break holidays and urban tourism in former industrial cities a new phenomenon that emerged in the 1980s have consolidated and expanded.

The issues and opportunities of leisure and tourism industry are elaborately described in the present volume. Besides students and researchers, policy makers, managers and working groups of leisure and tourism industry will find this of utmost use.

Harish Bhatt
B.S. Badan

Contents

1

Leisure, Sports and Tourism

The tourism, leisure, recreation and sport sectors enhance the life of people. The economic and non-economic contributions that they make are recognised and supported from local to national levels. New Zealand has developed a dynamic tourism industry which is environmentally, socially, culturally and economically sustainable. The tourism industry has developed an industry strategy that provides leadership and guidance for the industry (including at a regional level) but, at the same time, allows individual businesses to make their own decisions. This industry strategy is grounded in a solid information base which enables industry members to understand mega-trends and to exploit technological advances.

The tourism sector and public agencies monitor all aspects of sustainability with a cost-effective, integrated system of tools and processes. Fragmentation of the industry is addressed through better co-ordination and cohesiveness within the industry, facilitating better flows of information which, in turn, contribute to sustainability at all levels of

the industry. The tourism industry has resolved the dilemma of the late 1990s of different visions for the industry by achieving a balance between mass tourism and added value tourism.

The tourism industry and its stakeholders recognise that its competitive advantage in international markets lies with New Zealand's unique features: the natural environment (high quality environment, scenic beauty); a young dynamic image and sense of space, emptiness and freedom which are energising and revitalising; the people (the warmth and hospitality of New Zealanders, freedom of cultural expression); and Maori identity (a unique, living indigenous culture).

While emphasis on New Zealand's unique features as a competitive advantage implies a finite capacity for some activities at some sites, it may be possible to export some of New Zealand's other tourism, leisure, recreation and sport-related competencies without undermining national or regional competitive advantages. New Zealand's tourism industry is recognised nationally and internationally for its innovative products and services that build on a quality infrastructure.

New Zealand's tourism, leisure, recreation and sporting sectors are well prepared and positioned to take advantage of national and international demographic changes. It is recognised that leisure, recreation and sport activities and industries interface with the tourism industry and that they share many aspirations and points of common interaction (particularly in relation to local government and planning). Consideration has been given to areas of overlap and the sectors understand the nature of the links and are endeavouring to enhance them.

Leisure, recreation and sporting pursuits of New Zealanders are part of the wider overseas tourism experience and are linked with tourism. The interface occurs at sites where tourists and New Zealanders meet when New Zealanders are at leisure, so that site planning for leisure, recreation and sport is important. Since most New Zealanders spend their leisure time in urban areas, urban experiences provide the context for much tourism, leisure, recreation and sport activities - although the "great outdoors" still plays a significant role. The contribution that leisure activities, recreation and sport make to the New Zealand economy, the wellbeing of New Zealanders and to a vibrant culture and sense of identity are recognised and supported.

Aspects of New Zealand culture contribute to the tourist experience and are another site of intersection between the tourism, leisure, recreation and sport industries. It is recognised that there is an infrastructure that supports leisure, recreation and sport in the domestic environment which is not related to tourism. The sector is able to also keep sight of the leisure, recreation and sport infrastructure that differs from the more economically-oriented tourism aims and is able, therefore, to accommodate non-tourism aspects of leisure, recreation and sport, and to meet the needs that are specific to sustaining each area.

Hence, recreation, leisure and sport are recognised as much wider than "holiday" experiences. They include experiences and activities associated with outdoor recreation, sport, the arts, gambling, entertainment, leisure facilities, libraries, museums, media leisure and recreational shopping. A wide spectrum of New Zealanders participate as providers/producers of, and participants/consumers in, these leisure, recreation and sport experiences and activities.

Research on tourism, leisure, recreation and sport will better serve the needs of users and an "information culture" is well established. There will be better communication between research providers and users. Research providers will be able to better conceptualise research issues in ways relevant to users, and will have increased ability to present their research to the industry in ways that facilitate uptake by users. All stakeholders actively seek to understand the motivation of individuals to be involved in these activities and seek to adapt their systems and practices to better meet these needs.

Research will also include a comparative global dimension which provides understanding of how New Zealand is perceived overseas. Users will have greater ability to absorb and use research information and businesses will be better informed. There will be greater investment by the private sector in research and development.

One of the characteristics of the tourism, leisure, recreation and sport industries is that the level of basic information which could underpin planning and decision-making in these industries is low. Enhanced information capacity and flows are required so that the sectors have the information necessary to support them. This includes not only data and access to it, but also better analysis, understanding and use of it. Tourism, leisure, recreation and sport should become "information rich" industries through an enhanced knowledge base, leading to informed management and greater co-ordination at the individual operator, industry, regional and national levels.

The development of a core of skilled people who are able to utilise research and technology in order to contribute to the development of these sectors will also be important.

The changing nature of domestic and international markets: To better inform tourism, leisure, recreation and sport management the sector requires data on, and an understanding of, the changing nature of supply and demand, the changing nature of markets, understanding of international and mega-trends, sustainability issues, leisure behaviour and motivations.

How to manage the sustainable development of tourism through understanding domestic and international customers and host communities: To facilitate the development and exploitation of new markets and achieve increased yields the sector requires information that will increase its effectiveness and efficiency. This includes knowledge of who customers are, understanding of and capacity to cater for customer.needs, knowledge of what customers want in a tourist experience, information on customer numbers and ethnic mix, understanding of the impacts of numbers and mix for host cultures and communities, knowledge and understanding of the impacts of different types of tourism on host cultures and communities, the ability to identify and exploit new technology, and the most appropriate institutional and regulatory frameworks for this.

Ensuring the long term sustainability of tourism, leisure, recreation and sport industries in New Zealand by understanding the role of people as both providers and consumers. There are potential economic, social and community benefits from the industries themselves—on the other hand, New Zealanders participate as consumers of the products and services provided by these industries.

Ensures the long-term sustainability of the natural and built environments—including those environments that are attractions in themselves, as well as environments that these industries impact upon.

Sport tourism

Sport tourism is a growing phenomena. It is becoming more and more popular in academic circles as well as in the marketing of tourism experiences. Connections between sport and tourism are not new, one can trace the link back to ancient times. The excitement surrounding this tourism niche is growing in popularity. This unit will provide an overview of sport, tourism and sport tourism, as well as look at the components of sport tourism products.

Sport tourism refers to the experience of travel to engage in or view sport-related activities. There is general recognition of three types of sport tourism: Sport Event Tourism, Active Sport Tourism and Nostalgia Tourism. One other growing area of interest is Business or work related sport tourism. We will first take a brief look at where sport tourism has come from.

There are two perspectives from which we can look at the foundations of sport tourism, an economic perspective: viewing sport tourism as services and an anthropological perspective: viewing sport tourism as a human experience.

From an economic perspective sport tourism is seen as services. Sport tourism services include services specific to sport but also those that are tourism driven such as transportation, accommodation and food/beverage. Services can be broken down into two areas:

— destination services: transportation, accommodation, meals, beverage services

— services specific to the sport industry: sport equipment suppliers, sport tour operators, sporting event services, halls of fame

The anthropological perspective discusses sport tourism as a human experience. It is an unique experience which may result in or involve one or all of the following:

— evoking emotions and feelings

— improving skills or fitness

— developing relationships

Sport tourism as the interaction of two systems. The economic system in relation to tourism, and the cultural system in relation to sport. Each one has its own set of activities and involvements. The link between the two is through the interconnection of sport facilities, tourism media and sport media. Both systems can involve sport and tourism, when the two come together they créate this niche in the tourism industry.

Sport or tourism are not adequately described as industries; they are activities in which people engage. Sport is about an experience of physical activity, tourism about an experience of travel and place. The sport product is not the activity itself; nor is the tourism product equal to its vehicle of destination. Rather, 'their value is a function of the quality and quantity of experience they promise'" So sport tourism involves the experience and the place or destination. It is more than just the experience itself. It is more than just being at a place. It is the combination of the two. It is a combination of both sport and tourism so let's define those two areas.

There is no universally accepted definition of sport. There are cultural differences, historic variations and perspectives from different fields such as sociology or economics that vary as well. To highlight this let's look at the difference between the North American and European point of view. The North American perspective often views sport as a pursuit that:

— requires complexity of physical skill and vigorous physical exertion;

— involves some form of rule-governed competition;

— and has organized and structured relations but keeps a sense of freedom and spontaneity non-competitive sport activities are usually described in North America as recreation.

In Europe today definitions of sport are generally broader, accepting that a process of value differentiation has developed a wide range of models of sports. The Council of Europe (1992) definition of sport is: "All forms of physical activity, which through casual or organized participation , aimed at improving physical fitness and mental well-being, forming social relationships, or obtaining results in competition at all levels"

The sociological point of view in contemporary society expands the meaning of sport by professing: what people declare to do is sport. Differences are apparent in definitions and in concepts surrounding sport tourism. Experiences in sport and tourism are personal, this adds a difficult dimension in trying to capture a specific definition. If one travels to a certain location at different times in their life the experience will be different, each person sees a destination in a unique way, the significance of both sport and tourism will be different for each. Let's keep exploring.

Sport tourism has become popular for a number of reasons. Its positioning in the marketplace, economic forces, social forces, changes in technology and the global development movement all contribute to the emergence of this tourism niche.

Dr. Charles Pigeassou discusses the positioning of sport tourism in relation to the social meanings of both sport and tourism. Sport tourism appeared when both tourism and sport had a significant place in the economic and social environment of society. Economic and social factors played a role in the evolution of sport tourism. To take this idea further, the roots of sport tourism grew from the emergence of a leisure society (where individuals have free time, discretionary income, access to travel, etc.) and from the coming of a consumer society (economic forces -purchasing power, the ability and desire for consumption). Without these ingredients sport tourism may not have emerged in its present state.

For participation in sport tourism an adequate amount of money is needed. The affluence of families today is higher than it has ever been mostly because of type of employment and how people work (more time for leisure). Improvements in technology have also led to more disposable time for many. For most Western societies the economic changes have increased the amount of time and money available to individuals, motivating them to take part in sport tourism.

The consumer society with its emphasis on leisure and self-realization is a shift from the strong work ethic that permeated society not more than fifty years ago. Sport has a greater societal influence in part due to this value change. Examples include the sport clothing boom, now sportswear is not only used for participating in sport but fashionable. Sport is also engaged in not only at the highly competitive level but many individuals take part for the sake of taking part - decreasing the barriers for participation, it is no longer only for the elite athlete.

Along with other technological advancements, new methods of transportation have also increased the popularity of sport tourism. Increased accessibility to automobile and air transportation has increased travel in general. With increased access to modes of transportation, the accommodation and food and beverage industry emerged and flourishes. More recently innovations in media technology, television and internet, have increased sport tourism's popularity especially in spectator sport.

Sport equipment production has also contributed greatly to the popularizing of sport. Because of these many innovations, the accessibility to travel and sport has increased its appeal and availability leading to a rise in popularity. At the same time that sport tourism was emerging other global movements were also emerging that had/have direct implications for sport tourism. The area of development has become a strong global force and of increasing importance. It is crossing over traditional boundaries and being embraced by industries that were not in the past, considered to be compatible. Some development issues related to sport tourism include:

— support for the development of tourism (sport can draw tourism to an area)

— local and sustainable development approaches through sport tourism

— economic enhancement activities (facility and infrastructure development)

Sport tourism is seen as an instrument for development. Sport is seen as a method for developing tourism in new forms and to new markets. It is also seen as a catalyst for local and sustainable development which can enhance economies. Social, economic and technological factors along with the global development movement have all contributed to its popularity. Knowing the factors that have contributed to its popularity may help in understanding the dynamics of the industry and in turn help in managing and marketing sport tourism activities.

Now let's explore the features of sport tourism to ensure a clear understanding of the dynamics between sport and tourism and how the two fit together.

The two major features of sport tourism are:

— tourism (a destination, the idea of journey and travel away from home are necessary), and

— sport (socially identified activities in sport and leisure sport, including physical activity participation, viewing, nostalgia or business).

The link between them is that the object and aim of travelling are determined by the involvement in some aspect of sport. Sport tourism includes many types of 'sport activities' not all of which may be traditionally thought of as sport. There are the traditional physically active inclusions such as competing in a competition and taking part to stay fit, but there are also cultural sport activities which may not be so apparent (visiting sports halls of fame, attending seminars). Volunteer activities, attending sport events, visiting sport heritage attractions are all areas included in the cultural aspect of sport tourism.

There are four major reasons for involvement with sport tourism, those who:

— travel to participate (athletes, participants)

— travel to watch (spectators)

— travel to celebrate, worship (nostalgia)

— travel to participate in sport administration activities - work/business (coaches, scouts, journalists, media)

There are many different kinds of sport tourism products (offerings). A few include:

— *Products for Individual participation in sport travel* - international bicycling and snowmobile tours,

— *Products for Sport team travel* - long-haul destination sport tours with matches against local opposition,

— *Products for Attending sport events, museums or attractions.*

These are just a few of the sport tourism offerings. From spectatorship to active involvement, attending or participating in events to visiting sport museums or facilities, there are many types of sport tourism along with a multitude of offerings. We will look at the components of the sport tourism industry as a whole, then investigate aspects of demand and then take a closer look at sport tourism products.

COMPONENTS OF THE SPORT TOURISM INDUSTRY

Sport tourism incorporates many different components. The main components include:

— Consumers

— Transportation

— Destination Services

— Primary Attractions

— Secondary Attractions

— Information Services

— Politics

— Sellers of travel

— Travel infrastructure and services

— Destination promotion

— Media outlets

Sport tourism is seen as a system because these components work together in running the industry. The sport tourism system is closely tied to the tourism industry system. The difference lies in that the destination attractions are focused on sport activities. Gunn produced a model of the key functional components that make up the dynamic and interrelated tourism system, upon which the *Sport Tourism System model* is based. The major difference of the sport tourism model is that it puts politics at the centre.

The consumers at the top are considered to be the demand generators, the remaining elements are supply related. The tourism system is delicate. It is highly dependent on the sport tourists' economic health to provide revenue. Many companies form alliances to gain market advantages making sport tourism a volatile business environment. Government policies can impact the system just as new attractions, promotional campaigns and innovative technology. Policies on taxation, regulations for building, zoning, and many more governmental influences affect sport tourism.

Many of the components in the system serve residents and tourists alike. Because of this there may be competing demands and hence suppliers may not be as successful in meeting the needs of both groups. If suppliers concentrate on one group they may be more able to provide for the needs of their customers. However, if suppliers choose to concentrate on one group over the other friction and frustration may result. For example, if tourists are the focus residents may be left out in the cold.

An example comes to mind of Bondi Beach, Australia just outside of Sydney. Bondi Beach was the beach volleyball location for the 2002 Summer Olympic Games. There was some upheaval in the community because of the need for space near the beach. Shop-owners in one strip of shops located right on the edge of the beach had to vacate their shops in order to accommodate the Games. With such a mega-event the priority is of course the sport tourists, with the spill-over effects felt by locals.

Consumers - many complex factors are included in purchasing a sport tourism experience. Motivations, attitudes, and constraints are all a part of the process. There is a decision making process that the potential sport tourist moves through, from finding out about the opportunity and gathering information to evaluating the option and purchasing it. Of course this process is a very intricate and well orchestrated dance, one that marketers must understand in the development of their products. The supply of information is very important at this stage in the process. The more information the consumer has, the more likely the opportunity is to be purchased and experienced.

The sellers of travel are the intermediaries - who link the consumer to the other elements in the system (transportation, accommodation and attractions). At this stage sellers do not really care which opportunity the consumer buys, just that they do purchase something. There is a range of experiences available and they try to match consumers with the appropriate sport tourism opportunity.

Some of the main travel intermediaries include tour wholesalers, tour operators, retail travel agents, and electronic intermediaries.

The internet has grown in importance as a method of informing potential sport tourism consumers. Sixty-nine percent (69%) of frequent U.S. travelers use the internet to plan for travel.

Transportation - includes all modes; automobile (rental or private), airplane, ship, train, bus, etcetera. The most preferred transportation mode in the United States is private automobile by far (77%) and air travel is second at 18%. The most prevalent factors for choosing transportation are convenience and cost. European data may differ due to the cost of fuel and especially the level of service of other types of travel. Rail service is more reliable and reasonably priced than in North America.

Travel Infrastructure and Services - include those involved in the supply of infrastructure for moving people around. Many times the infrastructure is governmentally supplied (airports, docks, roads, utilities, safety services etc.). If it is in good repair and working well it goes unnoticed, however, if it is not then frustration for the traveler is probable (long waiting lines at airports, poor road conditions, etc.). A tourist from Northern Montana was reported as saying that he would no longer travel to Saskatchewan even though he loved the beautiful province, great fishing, breath-taking lakes and wilderness. He had been traveling there for many years but because the road conditions were absolutely horrible, he was no longer going to visit. Infrastructure can have a major impact on the generation of tourism.

The destination services involve suppliers who offer accommodations, food, beverage, entertainment and related products. Accommodations include many forms from hotels and bed and breakfasts to campsites. Many hotels provide fitness areas and pools. Some food and beverage establishments are directly related to sport activities as Toronto's Sky Dome restaurant and the old Ponsonby "Pot" pub in Auckland, New Zealand. Entertainment and related products could include services by the hotel (massages) or dinner theatre entertainment.

Primary attractions - are the activities that bring sport tourists to participate, organize or watch. We will look closer at the types of primary attractors later in the discussion of the categories of sport tourism. The significance of destination in sport tourism is important to note. Destination plays an important role in terms of the sport tourism experience. In order to have certain sport activities take place the destination must have certain features, natural or man-made. To ski, mountains or hills are necessary, a race track is needed for car racing.

The sport tourist is also looking at the environment in a different way. For example when mountain or rock climbers drive through the mountains they are looking at the potential passes and crevices to climb through to make it to the top. A runner may be looking for potential running routes, paths through parks, access through fences when moving through cities or natural areas. The sport tourist is looking at the environment with their sport(s) in mind. How conducive is the environment to their sport(s)? This also involves the spectator. Where can items with the logo of their team be purchased?

Sport tourists look for the opportunity to meet players, to get the best seats. For the sport tourist wanting to visit museums and see the great sport sites (nostalgia) they are searching for locations where great events took place or where a player grew up, the essence of the person, place or past event. With these in mind it is a different type of experience than from one who is not a sport tourist. A person traveling without the sport aspect in mind may not be concerned with many of these specific sport related ideas.

Secondary attractions - are usually those which have little to do with sports. They are alternative activities that take place outside of the sporting activity. They may include attending movies or shows, shopping, etc.

Destination promotion - involves the many information suppliers at the tourist destination. They provide information on-site and try to draw tourists to their attraction. CVB's (convention and visitor bureaus in North America are well known for their involvement in disseminating local tourism information through visitor guides), sport associations, tourism promotion boards, sport leagues and teams all may be a part of this element.

Information services - spread the knowledge of sport tourism opportunities to all potential consumers, the media, television, internet, radio, newspaper, and magazines.

Politics - the centre of the model is seen to affect all aspects of the system from interoffice politics to the political policies of the country. Politics are ever-present and must be recognized as playing a part in the workings of the system. To exemplify this idea read the following example where politics and sport tourism met.

Sport Tourism Models

There are many specific sport tourism models. Each has a unique perspective and helps in looking at the industry from different angles.

The Sports Tourism Phenomenon Model

This model integrates sport tourism motivation with destinations and settings that serve sport tourists. It includes:

— sport tourism motivations (self-actualization, competitiveness, formalized sports and informal sports)

— destinations (resorts, tours, cruises, other attractions and events)

— and settings that serve sport tourists (human-made settings, economic setting, cultural setting, social setting and natural setting)

It also identifies other types of tourism that may contribute to sport tourism (ecotourism, festivals, heritage tourism, social tourism, etc.) At the centre of the model is 'focus sports' (competitive or recreational, participant, official, or spectator) which is the hub of the model. A closer look at the bolded words in the model (tours, cruise ships, resorts, other attractions and special events) tell us where sport tourism takes place at, within, or on. Each of these settings have unique characteristics. For example Cruises - one could join a golf cruise where passengers set tee times at ports of call.

The Sport Tourism Definitional Model

This model classifies sport tourism activities into either sport tourism (where sport is the primary motivator for travel) or tourism sport (where sport is incidental to the travel). Under each of these is 'hard' or 'soft' categorizations of the endeavour. This model classifies sport tourists by the activities while traveling and by primary or secondary motives for sport. The left is sport tourism, right tourism sport. A further breakdown of the activities is seen in the hard or soft classification, which deals with the level of intensity or frequency. Examples are given in the model.

A Conceptual Classification of Sport Tourism: This scheme is quite broad and inclusive. It uses two categories as the base:

— physical activity - environmental or interpersonal

— place - natural or manmade

A grid of eight segments is derived. The grid allows one to plot the position of different sporting activities in different tourist settings according to the nature of the activities and the geographical resources in which they take place. It treats both the sport and tourism aspects with the same importance.

Intensity of Involvement in Sport Tourism

This model relates to the level of intensity of involvement in sport tourism. Simplified, it delineates those who are heavily involved in sport tourism and those who may have other interests. It includes both a demand circle and a supply circle.

The demand side shows the involvement of sport tourists in the event, contest or competition and has four dimensions.

— The inner most circle is primary involvement - essential for the activity to happen, the athlete, participant, they have the greatest intensity of involvement in the sport. Sport museums, hall of fames, stadiums, sport speakers, instructors, natural sport challenges, and various human-made attractions are also included here.

— The second circle is secondary involvement - those active in the sport but not playing, officials, organizers, coaches, statisticians. The activity could take place without them but it would change dramatically.

— The third is spectator involvement - spectators and supporters, not essential for the activity to take place. They demand the services but may have alternative activities that draw their attention.

— The fourth includes those who travel to the destination for other leisure related purposes.

The supply side includes six levels of suppliers in the circle.

— The first - those participating in the activity, without them it is not happening, they are at the heart of the supply and the demand circles.

— The second circle - organizers, managers, promoters, marketers of sport tourism opportunities. They serve as the links between the sport and other tourists. Sport organizations and associations, sport commissions, and local, regional and national sport ministries are also included.

— The third include tour operators or travel agents who get tourists to their destinations, they also supply accommodations and culinary choices.

— The fourth are seen to be retailers, sellers of equipment, memorabilia, and other attractions as well.

— The fifth - themed restaurants, hotels, vendors, food and beverage establishments not necessarily dependent on sport tourism for their revenue.

— The sixth a very important component but a small part of the scheme - providers of infrastructure, roads, airports, utilities, health and safety services, government support.

The types of sport tourism are endless. In 1991 the Sports Tourism International Council, presented their Categories of Sport Tourism. The main headings that opportunities were broken down into include: attractions, resorts, cruises, tours and events. Pigeassou breaks experiences down into active and passive forms. Take a look at the many types of sport tourism opportunities and how one might understand them.

Recreation and Leisure Tourism

Recreation and leisure tourism whilst ensuring that facilities are provided where they cater for the needs of the local population and visitors, on a sustainable basis. In Cambridgeshire and Peterborough the total value of tourism in 1999 was £754 million and the total number of actual tourism related jobs supported 21,530 people. Increases in the overall spending power in the Plan area as well as growing leisure time and mobility are likely to put increased pressure on existing and new tourism, leisure and recreational facilities. These pressures may need to be managed to ensure they do not damage the facilities people have come to enjoy.

Leisure and recreation cover a wide range of activities, from informal activities, such as walking and cycling, to organised sports such as football and cricket. Cultural recreational activities, such as visits to historic places, museums and galleries are also included. These activities can benefit the local economy and improve the health and well being of the population.

Tourism, recreation and leisure strategy creates a positive framework for plans and proposals relating to tourism, recreation and leisure. At the same time it identifies criteria so that provision will be targeted to sustainable locations, to meet local needs and to support economic objectives. Proposals will be subject to assessments of environmental capacity and measures needed to manage the impact of increased tourist numbers.

Cambridge, with the University and its colleges, is a major generator of tourist and leisure activity and the local economy benefits considerably from the jobs and income it creates. However, the concentration of tourism on a relatively small part of the City causes congestion and problems for the people that live and work in Cambridge. If not carefully managed, tourism may also detract from the environment that tourists are coming to enjoy. The aim is to achieve tourism that is sustainable and accessible to as many people as possible.

Cambridge City Council should assess proposals for tourism against a locally agreed strategy of positive management and selective development, working in partnership with local communities, businesses and government agencies. Tourism in Peterborough, the market towns and North Cambridgeshire has not, in the past, contributed so significantly to the economy as in Cambridge and it's immediate surrounding area. Particular emphasis should therefore be given to the promotion of tourism to the north and east of the Plan area and in the nine market towns, many of which have riverside attractions and historical associations.

Peterborough City Council should explore the opportunities for developing quality tourism projects and key cultural facilities within the City. Informal recreation provides enjoyment and exercise for many people, which contributes towards the health and well being of the population. The countryside provides an important resource for people to undertake informal leisure pursuits such as walking, cycling and horse riding.

Opportunities for increasing recreation and access will be concentrated on urban fringes and in conjunction with the new settlement. There may be roads that would be suitable for designation as 'Quiet Lanes' under the Transport Act 2000. These are country lanes where walkers, cyclists and horse-riders are given priority and traffic speeds are reduced. Other quiet recreational activities that can be encouraged include angling, sailing, and nature watching.

Country parks provide opportunities for a range of informal recreational pursuits and for nature conservation. This is important for Cambridgeshire and Peterborough which otherwise has limited open countryside areas for informal recreational use. Walking and cycling are the two most popular participant sports in the country. The flat landscape of Cambridgeshire and Peterborough is well suited to cycling which offers a sustainable way of enjoying the countryside with significant health benefits.

The County Council will produce Rights of Way Improvement Plans to steer the recording, protection, management and improvement of the Rights of Way network. Green Wheel' cycle network have been successful in providing recreational routes convenient for residents of Peterborough and the surrounding villages. The Fens Cycle Tourism project links 'the Green Wheel' to Fenland towns and forms part of a national SUSTRANS route. Similar projects should be encouraged, to further expand the network of safe rural/urban cycle routes for recreational purposes.

Open spaces, such as commons, public parks, pocket parks and playing fields have a vital role in meeting the leisure needs of the population by providing recreational areas near to their homes. Such facilities provide general health benefits for those that use them and also contribute to the environmental quality of the area. Therefore they should normally be protected. There will be cases when it may be beneficial to move such facilities in order to achieve better access and amenity.

A local assessment of need to be undertaken by the Local Planning Authorities should be used to inform decisions and demonstrate whether substitution or replacement would provide a qualitative gain for the community. Local Plans should set out the requirements for areas for informal recreation and leisure taking account of local need.

Water-based recreation

The waterways and water bodies of Cambridgeshire and Peterborough are an important resource for recreation and tourism as well as providing areas for wildlife and nature conservation. Local Planning Authorities should encourage proposals for using waterways for tourism and leisure uses, including the use of river systems to provide a sustainable mode of transport. In doing so they should take into account any environmental impacts from, for example, pollution, congestion and noise, which could have an adverse effect on nature conservation and quieter forms of recreation.

The Environment Agency is producing Waterway Plans for all navigations for which it has responsibility. Within the Structure Plan area they provide a framework for development of navigation and water-related recreation for the River Great Ouse and the River Nene. The plans cover a range of issues, including improvement of facilities, access both to and adjacent to the waterway, enhancement of biodiversity value and improved navigation infrastructure.

The Middle Level, which is not under the control of the Environment Agency, forms an important link between the Nene and the Ouse where additional recreational use could be promoted subject to there being no adverse impact on drainage functions. The proposed link between Milton Keynes and Bedford will provide a much improved route between the waterways of the Midlands and those in the East of England, opening up the potential for increased recreational use of the waterways of Cambridgeshire. This likely increased usage and the economic benefits it will bring should be taken into consideration in planning increased provision of waterside facilities such as marinas and temporary moorings and associated facilities.

The capacity of waterways is an important factor in considering whether development proposals should proceed. Circumstances and usage will change over time. The local authorities will need to take account of existing and forecast usage in drawing up and assessing proposals. There may also be opportunities to advance proposals which can relieve points of congestion by working with other bodies, such as the Environment Agency and the Middle Level Commissioners.

New or improved tourism, recreation and leisure development should:

— maintain or increase employment opportunities;

— meet the needs of local communities as well as visitors;

— be accessible by a choice of sustainable transport modes;

— protect or improve the local environment, landscape and residential amenity;

— strengthen and diversify the local economy, particularly in Peterborough and North Cambridgeshire.

Role of Nature in Receational Tourism

Nature tourism is a sufficiently broad term that it can be applied to a broad range of different landscapes and tourism destinations. It should be stated that although the term nature-based tourism places focus on the natural aspects, it is recognised that the natural environment contains cultural components, and therefore, although not always stated, cultural aspects are included in discussions about nature tourism. Many terms exist that describe different types of nature-based tourism. These terms attempt to differentiate nature travel by more specific factors. There are many subtle and sometimes ambiguous differences between all of these terms, which make identifying specific and comprehensive definitions for all of these nature-based tourism terms difficult and time consuming.

Nature plays a primary role in attracting tourists to specific destinations, so in this sense most tourism may be described as nature-based. Nature-based tourism can occur as mass tourism to destinations compatible with high volumes of people, such as beach resorts, touring, and cruise vacationing. Nature-based tourism can also occur as special interest tourism with destinations such as nature observation in a forest, fishing in a stream, or canoeing in a lake. A group of nature tourism visitors may all have a more specific common interest, such as enjoying hiking in mountains.

These visitors will choose locations where this is available, making it possible to market to them a collection of destinations that meet those criteria. By adding a motivation component, it is possible to see that the types of visitors who choose special interest tourism are more likely to possess motivations that will support the goals of sustainable nature tourism. Beach tourists may be motivated by relaxation and entertainment. This does not imply any interest in learning about the special natural features of the area, nor any responsibility to ensure that their vacation maximises positive impacts to the environment and surrounding communities while minimising the negative ones. Nature-based tourists are usually motivated by education and personal enrichment.

The motivations of the latter are closely correlated with objectives of a more specific form of special interest nature-based tourism, called ecotourism. A specific type of nature-based tourism is ecotourism. It is nature-based tourism that involves education and interpretation of the natural environment and is managed to be ecologically sustainable. For tourism to be ecologically sustainable, there must be an appropriate return to the local community and a contribution to the long-term conservation of the resource.

A distinction exists between nature-based tourism and ecotourism. Nature-based tourism is a broader term, concerned in general with the enjoyment of nature (which may or may not contribute directly to nature conservation). For a specific nature-based tourism experience to qualify as an ecotourism experience, more specific criteria must be present (than those defined by nature tourism), such as an identifiable contribution to conservation (recall that not all nature tourism automatically contributes positively to conservation efforts). Because the term has different meanings, it is difficult to state exactly all the criteria. Adding to the confusion is the opportunistic and sometimes inaccurate use of the term in marketing.

The terminology is sometimes liberally applied to a range of businesses, products and services (even though a large difference can exist in the sustainable efforts made by these companies) because marketers and advertisers know it appeals to the consumer's desire to support environmentally friendly products. Most ecotourism definitions address some combination of motivation, philosophy, conduct and economic benefit to conservation. Butler identifies ecotourism as: a) an activity, b) a philosophy, and c) a model of how to approach the environment. Ecotourism is a word with many meanings. Some use it to attract visitors to their business, others use it to define a combination of interests. It encompasses both nature-based and recreational tourism.

There are many theories and concepts associated with ecotourism, and its true definition is only understood by those who are aware of these concepts. Hopefully, this confusion will change in the near future. There are various definitions of ecotourism, most of which have to do with combining the travel industry with an ideal that emphasizes conservation and preservation of the wilderness in which people spend their vacations. The Ecotourism Society defines ecotourism as "responsible travel which conserves environments and sustains the well-being of local people".

Although this is a loosely constructed definition, the truth is that ecotourism has different connotations to different people in their varying relationships within the ecotourism industry, from tour operators to conservationists, to actual tourists. The World Wildlife Fund, who has a vested interest in the ecotourism industry in terms of wilderness protection for habitats and various species present, believes "the term ecotourism refers to any travel to or through wilderness areas that has minimal impact on the natural environment and its wildlife while providing some economic benefits to local communities and the area's indigenous stewards". Ecotourism incorporates many different activities that individuals enjoy in nature, usually that are more physically active than the typical vacation to a resort where one is pampered and is determined to relax.

Ecotourism tends to incorporate activities such as hiking, camping, observing wildlife in its habitat, mountain climbing, and water sports of different kinds. Water sports will be the focus of this proposal, specifically kayaking, canoeing, and white water rafting. The typical person who is interested in ecotourism and has taken to participating in these activities are "in their 30s and 40s, with more travelers above that range than below it.

Women are as active as men. Most enjoy above-average incomes and educations, and have traveled widely already to more conventional destinations. Now they are looking for something different". These travelers are in search of something different for this vacation, as they have already experienced the typical vacation. They seek a more active and modern alternative, which is met in ecotourism. Not only is it a physical challenge, in most cases, but it is also a chance to learn respect for nature, and for some, a chance to do some self-reflection, inspired by the beauty of their surroundings. There are some definite trends that have been occurring over the last thirty years, and especially the last decade, that indicate that ecotourism is becoming an increasingly popular option for travel.

Tourism is the world's fastest growing industry, and this includes ecotourism. Statistics indicate that "tourism grew by nearly 300% between 1970 and 1990, and is expected to grow by half again before the end of the century. In 1991, 450 million international travelers generated more than $3 trillion in tourism revenues. About 15%, or nearly 68 million, of these travelers participated in nature-related trips" . Although not all of these "nature-related" trips constitute ecotourism, it does show an increasing interest for outdoor activities, and possibly, education. The growth of ecotourism, specifically, is indeed a reality, although, as we stated before, ecotourism has many different definitions.

It is estimated by the "World Tourism Organization, based in Madrid, found in one recent study that global spending on ecotourism was increasing by 20% a year-about six times the average rate of growth for the tourism industry. Although prescriptions and guidelines have emerged to promote successful implementation, standardardized or widely-utilized methods to identify the potential and gauge the progress of ecotourism sites have yet to emerge. In this situation, the availability and application of a framework with which to define and evaluate the functions and status of ecotourism at the site level may assist in understanding gaps between ideal prescriptions and ground-level failure, and encourage and facilitate the achievement of goals for ecotourism at an operational level. Throughout the 1980's and 1990's, widespread environmental interest fostered trendy "environmental opportunism" and encouraged loose uses of the pre-fix "eco". Promotion of ecotourism, with or without a hyphen, and in the absence of a clear indication of meaning, often resulted in use of the term being little more than a marketing tactic to give businesses an apparent green edge on the competition.

However, at the same time, world-wide, a growing expanse of land and sea has come to be exploited to cater to the demands of an expanding number of people seeking nature for pleasure and it has become clear that such tourism ultimately relies on the availability and quality of natural areas and, therefore, must be considered alongside strategies for maintaining and protecting nature. Those at the forefront of ecotourism research and development now provide definitions which address the fundamental goals of conservation of natural areas and local development. In ecotourism, natural areas and local populations are united in a symbiotic relationship through the introduction of tourism.

Ecotourism is viewed as a means of protecting natural areas through the generation of revenues, environmental education and the involvement of local people. In such ways, both conservation and development will be promoted in a sustainable forms (all malleable and contested concepts). Unfortunately, on the ground, distinction between ecotourism and other forms of tourism are often not evident and are widely debated. Discrepancies are a result of the variety of different perspectives and criteria used to distinguish ecotourism. These include the motivations for initiating ecotourism (e.g. as a conservation strategy, a business venture, or as part of an environmental education campaign), the motivations of users, the presence and scale of environmental, social and economic impacts, and the presence and quality of services offered. Proponents of ecotourism have attempted to overcome such differences by developing valueladen ethical principles as criteria for distinguishing ecotourism.

Ecotourism, requires embodiment of "intrinsic rather than extrinsic values" reflecting a "biocentric rather than homocentric philosophy". In addition to ascribing to environmental ethics, tourists themselves are described as "purposeful" and "environmentally responsible" travelers. However, such descriptors do not address the functions of ecotourism and what it is expected to achieve, nor do they lend themselves readily to measurement and evaluation. In addition to a definition of what ecotourism is, there should be consideration of what is to be achieved through ecotourism.

In a symbiotic relationship between local populations and protected area resources or biodiversity, local residents act as stewards of the natural resources and, in return, they benefit from protected areas through sustainable harvesting, integrated and multiple use zones, and protection of important resources such as water catchments. Often, the relationship between local communities and resource use, particularly in the peripheral locations common to many ecotourism sites, is one where dependence on resource exploitation is high and, thus, attempts to regulate or prohibit resource use may be unrealistic and antagonistic to local people.

Livelihoods based on activities such as slash and burn agriculture, cattle farming, hunting, fishing, wood collection, timber harvesting and mineral extraction require substantial amounts of natural resources (water, trees, game, minerals and, most of all, land and soil) to sustain large populations. Implementation and enforcement of use restrictions may foster confusion and resentment on the part of local people accustomed to using such lands and resources. In such situations, local people may become opponents of tourism and undermine its operation.

Such obstacles to the success of ecotourism can often be countered by involving local people in planning and management processes, whereby they have some control over and agreed-upon access to the resources they require. Even so, it is quite possible that in some circumstances local people may not welcome tourism at all and that view should be respected, but in many developing countries and in peripheral locations in socalled developed countries, tourism is often seen to be one among a limited number of development options. Relationship indicators are measurable variables which may be used to reflect antagonistic or symbiotic links between people and resources.

An evaluation employing such indicators can provides insight into the challenges and possibilities for local development, capacity building, and ecotourism. The characteristics of communities will influence the extent to which ecotourism affects social changes and attitudes towards tourism and conservation. For example, social and familial cohesion may encourage the spreading of positive attitudes (if an individual benefits, it may be viewed as a benefit to the broader community), in contrast to a community where individuals are only concerned for their own personal benefits.

Furthermore, communities already exposed to outside influences, exogenous technological advances or other forms of change, will likely respond differently to development opportunities than populations which have not experienced such changes. Similarly, characteristics of ecosystems reveal a natural area's capacity to withstand activities such as resource harvesting, which may be required or desired by local communities. In addition to the benefits which may accrue from protection of resources, local residents may receive a variety of benefits from becoming host communities for ecotourists. By participating in ecotourism, communities can receive tangible economic, infrastructural and social benefits - benefits which are less likely to leak out of the community if participation is local.

In turn, experiences of tourists may be enhanced by opportunities to interact with local people. If positive attitudes to ecotourism are to be fostered, residents living in or adjacent to a protected area should be receiving economic and social benefits or compensations which will support or complement their livelihoods. Local economic benefits from ecotourism have been documented both in the form of increased employment opportunities and incomes, community sharing in the distribution of revenues, and compensations. Thus, the introduction of ecotourism can encourage socio-economic development, if it is desired by the community.

External judgments and assumptions about the benefits of development, however conceived, should be avoided. Whether increased economic activity or changes in the educational system of a rural area are needed or desirable may be a point of dispute. Such a perspective emphasizes again the importance of involving members of destination communities as stakeholders in tourism planning and decision making. The interrelatedness of people-resource-tourism relationships is likely to be evident in the attitudes of local peoples: if local people are already disgruntled about resource-use restrictions from protected area regulations, it is likely that this negativity may influence attitudes towards tourism development. However, communities should not be encouraged to become solely dependent upon ecotourism: rather, ecotourism ideally should complement other activities and help to diversify an economy. Tourism of any type should not be viewed in isolation and its development should be considered as part of a broader plan for the use of resoucres.

The challenges in developing such plans should not be underestimated for reasons as diverse as the fact that powerful interests may benefit from the absence of a plan and governments in some locations have withdrawn from many planning functions in favour of the operation of an unfettered market. The contributions which ecotourism can make to biodiversity and the integrity of natural areas are as important as the potentially positive affects on adjacent communities. The provision of environmental education through enhancement of opportunities to appreciate nature is fundamental to the success of ecotourism.

Biodiversity and natural areas can provide this service in return for economic revenues which can contribute to protected area conservation. Many people who travel to natural areas do so specifically to indulge in experiences with nature, regardless of what activities they choose to do. It is the responsibility of the managers of a protected area to ensure the quality of the available natural experiences and to work towards instilling 'transformative values' (values which, through a learning experience with nature, yield greater environmental awareness, appreciation and respect for nature.

Protected areas can be viewed as natural laboratories, living museums, retreats, havens, and outdoor schools, and provide unique, interactive opportunities for promoting environmental stewardship for both locals and visitors. Education, through passive (in the form of reading materials, maps, signs, information centres) and perhaps active interpretation (such as guided tours, talk groups, theatre), if not too intrusive and depending upon program objectives, are forms of tourist management in themselves. They also can add to the visitors' experiences, direct people towards appropriate behaviours and, again, encourage appreciation of natural areas which can result in environmental advocacy. Tourism revenues can make a substantial contribution to the costs of managing protected areas.

There are many other factors apart from those at the site-level, which influence the capacity for effective environmental education and revenue-capturing. National and regional policies will dictate the limits of possible contributions from tourism revenues and the quality of support available to implement management strategies. Often it is not possible to earmark revenues which must be remitted to central governments and are not returned to the protected area responsible for their collection. The development of positive relationships between people, resources and tourism is very unlikely to occur without implementation of effective policies, management strategies, and involvement of a wide range of organizations, including NGOs and, in developing areas, conservation and development assistance agencies.

The qualities of protected area policies and of those who are employed to carry them out may influence everything from the extent of resource exploitation which occurs, to the amount of revenue generated and the quality of interpretation. NGOs, research teams and conservation and development-assistance agencies have important roles to play, particularly in rapidly-developing tropical countries where funding for the preparation of management plans or community development programs may be insufficient and personnel with the necessary knowledge, skills and training may be lacking. Such agencies may assist in developing data bases for natural areas and also can provide opportunities for education and local capacity building through the hiring and training of local people.

Ecotourism should be regarded as being more than tourism to natural areas and should be viewed as a means of combining the goals of resource conservation and local development through tourism in a synergistic fashion. This means that care should be taken to ensure that the goals of tourism development do not interfere with the goals of protecting natural areas and biodiversity. Ecotourism should function under the premises that, among other things, natural resources are finite and their appreciation and protection can be fostered through education, and the presence of supplementary sources of income from tourism will encourage residents to become stewards of their environment.

Ideally, local populations may become advocates for protection of their natural resources and take pride in the unique surroundings which attract outsiders. If planning and decision-making do not involve local populations, then ecotourism will not succeed, and may even be detrimental to local communities. Many interrelated processes influence the potential and success of ecotourism within a protected area and links between natural areas, local people and tourism have been highlighted in this matter. When agricultural direct marketers view their business as a tourist attraction as well as an agricultural enterprise, many new sources of information and opportunity become available.

A visitor to a farm or ranch who wants a farm or rural experience as much as to buy agricultural products is a tourist. The number of visitors to farm outlets who are interested in a farm or ranch experience is increasing. Some of the most successful direct marketing operators recognized the potential of selling a farm or ranch experience early. In a study of agritourism in New York State, 63% of the 17 farm tour enterprises contacted had increased in size between 1986 and 1991. All but one of the remaining enterprises had stayed the same size. Over 3/5ths of all visitors were school children who paid admission for the tour. Admissions for children ranged from $.50 to $1.75 while the typical adult admissions were $2.50 to $3.50.

Catering to 'agricultural tourists' is especially important at direct farm marketing outlets that are located farther away from urban centers. More distant farm outlets will have to offer more than just products to stay competitive as new farm outlets spring up near major urban areas. One way to stay competitive is to understand what visitors are looking for in a farm experience and to provide services that appeal to visitors. Understanding visitors is an important step towards dealing with them and marketing to them. A couple of important trends have shown up in recent tourism studies. Aside from growing as an activity, tourism is changing shape. People are taking more short vacations rather than one long vacation each year. There is a growing interest in vacations that involve doing or experiencing. Hence, the growth in the "new" tourisms: ecological, cultural, heritage and agricultural tourism.

Other trends affecting tourism are the increase in the number of two earner households and the increasing interest of the populace in the environment. Tourism is an activity that involves a large array of retail and service businesses. The sectors most affected by tourism are hotels and other lodging facilities, eating and drinking establishments, and amusement and recreation facilities such as theme parks and ski resorts. One of the largest expenses in these industries is salaries and wages for employees. Often these employees are from the local area. However, for some businesses that are highly seasonal, employees may come from outside.

Some communities worry about relying too heavily on tourism. Some of the negative aspects of tourism may include the highly seasonal nature of employment, the low average wage level in tourism related industries, the congestion and increases in prices of products and real estate that tourists can cause. However, well managed tourism can complement other economic activities in a community. One positive aspect of tourism is its ability to bring new money into the community. Multipliers in industries that serve tourists are relatively high because wages and salaries are such a large part of the industries' total expenses.

The impacts of tourism can be increased by selling local products and by helping local people retain ownership of businesses that serve tourists. Agricultural tourism is particularly high in impacts because the labour used, business ownership and the products sold are usually local. There are two basic ways for a community or a business to increase revenues from tourism. Either increase the number of visitors or increase the amount that each visitor spends. This is why local chambers of commerce have devoted so much of their resources to attracting more visitors to the area. In an area that may have limited visitor accommodations, attracting day visitors may be the most effective strategy to pursue.

However, in communities that do have hotels and other lodging, convincing visitors to stay overnight is the most effective way to increase visitor expenditures. Not only do such visitors spend additional money on lodging, they eat more meals in the community and have more time to shop in local stores. In most surveys of visitors, shopping is one of the most popular vacation activities. An effective way for individual businesses to increase their sales to visitors is to offer a range of products and services that will keep the visitor at their outlets longer. Many grocery stores are arranged to slow shoppers down because typically the longer a person is in a store, the more they are likely to spend. In the study of agricultural tourism in Cochise County, 81,450 non-local visitors spent close to one million dollars and generated $1.9 million in sales impacts in the county. While the average expenditure per visitor party was $58, overnight visitors spent $130 per visitor party.

Tourism Planning and Biodiversity Conservation

Both tourism planning and biodiversity conservation planning lend themselves to a bio-regional approach. It is important to promote valuing of natural resources and tourism assets for inclusion in national accounts. The importance of tourism has to be promoted at a national scale. One of the challenges that governmental tourism agencies face is that usually they are low priority compared to other government bodies. Tourism agencies need to do a much better job of understanding and demonstrating the importance of tourism to national and regional economies.

"Use-it-or-lose-it" conservation strategies aim to achieve their goals through strictly controlled access to ecologically significant areas and resources - and tourism is a key component in this approach, giving value to the natural resources, including biodiversity. Since there is the need for communities to appropriately value their resources, local education in the environmental and tourism fields are urgently required. It is very important to recognise the need for a symbiotic relationship between biodiversity conservation planning and tourism planning. Most countries around the world still do not dedicate enough effort towards the conservation of biodiversity, perhaps because they haven't recognised the value and usefulness of this effort. Keeping the biodiversity resource base means enhancing the tourism attractiveness of a country.

Unfortunately, in many developing countries, any change proposed in favour of an improvement in the conservation of biodiversity is interpreted as an obstacle for development. The sustainable positive impact of biodiversity within a comprehensive regional development strategy that considers overall qualitative benefits and not merely quantitative economic gains within a partial sectoral focus is still not understood by the population at large, nor by many politicians. It is important to recognise that many rural communities located in some of the most attractive ecotourism destinations are characterised by extreme poverty. Many government development plans don't consider their involvement in tourism activities, especially ecotourism, as an option to alleviate poverty.

Thus, it is very important to insist on promoting ecotourism to governments as an important tool for rural poverty alleviation programmes. There is a generalised lack of information on the environmental impact of the different economic activities on biodiversity and of mechanisms to evaluate and monitor this impact. The key factor for success for Costa Rica's tourism sector is sustainability as much of tourism activity as of natural resources. The State plays the role of coordinating entity and regulator of projects and programmes that provide incentives to the communities, and also promotes and generates a real need for a sustainable model as part of environmental, business and local participation schemes.

Tourism activity is one of the most important ways of valuing biodiversity and backing its conservation. National and foreign tourists are counted among the National System of Conservation Areas (SINAC's) main clients. It is they who currently generate the greatest amount of resources for the institution. With the aim of using tourism as a positive tool for the management of the protected wilderness areas (PWAs), SINAC has defined as its general policy facilitating sustainable tourism development based on responsible practices of planning and management that are in accord with actions for conserving the country's natural and cultural heritage.

Tourism in the PWAs seeks to prevent environmental damage, foster the satisfaction of visitors, provide support to the monitoring of sustainable tourism and is interested in contributing to the country's local economies. This is a good example of a clear objective in planning to use tourism as a tool for natural resource management. In South Africa, taxing pollution and subsidising products and activities with less environmental damage (including ecotourism), as well as altering interest rates to encourage certain land use patterns are economic mechanisms that are efficiently being used by the government. In Mexico, the Ministry of Tourism (SECTUR), in coordination with the Ministry of the Environment (previously SEMARNAP, now SEMARNAT), the Commission for the Knowledge and Use of Biodiversity (CONABIO) and several other institutions from the public, private, social and academic sectors, published in the year 2000 a National Policy and Strategy for Sustainable Tourism, which represents a good inter-sectoral effort and contains valuable guidelines and action plans. In UK, a good example of striving to alleviate poverty is the British government's Department for International Development (DFID's) pro-poor concerns and their interest in funding tourism.

Promote and strengthen the decision making process and the standardisation (norms) process in a participatory manner, especially at the local level. Build up institutional capacity of the environmental authorities for follow up of environmental impact assessment and application of prevailing norms. Apply integrated land use planning at a regional scale, taking into consideration the local communities' opinions. Within the framework of the national tourism strategy, establish a sound ecotourism policy of an inter-sectoral nature that will provide viable options for biodiversity conservation and sustainable development especially at the local rural level. Concentrate efforts on mid and long-term development policies without being pressured by periodical changes in government administration.

Foster the use of taxes, subsidies and interest rates to reduce the negative environmental impacts of economic activity and enhance the positive effects. Making loans more easily available is a key point, in which the government should also participate. Both biodiversity conservation planning and tourism planning and development are complex, interdisciplinary and inter-sectoral phenomena, thus appropriate interaction and integration is even more so challenging. There is an overall need to develop effective inter-sectoral mechanisms that will ensure the harmonious interaction among all stakeholders and a symbiotic linkage between biodiversity conservation planning and tourism planning and development. For this reason, practical and dynamic coordination bodies (whether they be called commissions, committees, councils or agencies) for ensuring this appropriate interaction must be set up.

These bodies should include genuine, fully empowered representatives of the different stakeholders or sectors: government, private tourism sector, NGOs, local communities, and financial institutions. Although it is difficult to have the tourists themselves in a committee of this sort, their input should be sought. Inter-sectoral cooperation for the appropriate, sustainable and interactive development of tourism and biodiversity conservation planning must occur at the local, national, and international levels. Jurisdictions and responsibilities of the different agencies, authorities and organisations should be clearly defined and complement each other. Government representatives in these inter-sectoral coordination committees should at least come from the ministries (or equivalent government or para-statal agencies) dealing with tourism and the environment, and it is convenient also that the ministries dealing with agriculture, fisheries, and education be included.

Sometimes it is not necessary to create a new entity. A preexisting body may be strengthened so as to develop a mandate of cooperation and non-duplication - one which is legislated, if need be. In a number of countries, these inter-sectoral coordination bodies have been established, with varying degrees of success. In every case it is important to first create the appropriate political environment between government departments (tourism, environment, agriculture) before bringing the other sectors (NGOs, tour operators, local communities) together. The role of NGOs is vital, and should include local, national and international NGOs.

Bilateral and multilateral development aid agencies (where appropriate) should collaborate, but always serving the local and national interests of the corresponding country. There must also be environmental education for those who are taking decisions, both in the fields of conservation and tourism. In Australia, CRC is a network of Cooperative Research Centres in Australia, one group of which is dedicated to sustainable tourism. The Sustainable Tourism CRC is a very effective model of how universities can work with government and the tourism sector to develop and implement a research agenda that works for all three groups. Housed in universities throughout Australia, the research is undertaken by academics but directly responds to the needs of government and industry. It helps all facets of the sustainable tourism industry to become linked.

In Chile, in 1994, an entity called the National Commission for the Environment (CONAMA) coordinated through the President's Secretariat was created. In Costa Rica, this country has successfully integrated the management of national parks, wildlife and forests into a single organisation, the MINAE's (Ministry of the Environment and Energy) SINAC (National System of Conservation Areas). The system is made up of eleven Conservation Areas that comprise 25% of the entire country, providing a good scenario for inter-sectoral synergy.

Strengthening of inter-sectoral coordination is achieved through clear mechanisms for participation of the private and state sectors for planning tourism: e.g., the National Accreditation Commission for the Certification for Sustainable Tourism (CST). In Costa Rica, communities have formed associations and cooperatives in different places throughout the country that have, as their main activity, local tourism. Private reserves, which at the moment total more than 100, and cover 1% of the national territory, rely on ecotourism as their main source of revenue. They carry out their activities in coordination with, and backing from, the Costa Rican Tourism Institute (ICT) and the MINAE, in the case of ecotourism, and in the case of agrotourism projects, with the ICT and Agrarian Development Institute

(IDA). The Belize Tourism Industry Association (BTIA) was formed in 1985 to bring together tourism-related interests to meet the challenges of the industry and act as an important link between the public and private sectors.

BTIA has chapters in each district of Belize, and includes a broad range of individual members from all areas of the industry as well as representation from associations such as the Belize Hotels Association, Belize Tour Guides Association, Belize Tour Operators Association, Belize Ecotourism Association and others. A perceived weakness of BTIA is that it functions more like a membership-based organisation rather than an umbrella organisation. As the latter, it would be able to function more directly as an advocacy for the industry. In Canada, there are a number of senior level government committees which are designed to enable united action across the country, in the various jurisdictions which have independent authority over resources.

In Canada, the Canadian Tourism Commission (CTC) developed their vision and mission tapping into the direction of a 20-member team of industry experts, then presented them to industry stakeholders, provincial and territorial governments, and destination marketing organisations, to get consensus on a shared vision and mission, and to encourage a unified Canada perspective. In Canada, the Biosphere Reserve Ecotourism Initiative is one of a number of tourism partnerships in the CTC Product Club Programme. The Ecotourism Product Club is a partnering programme between individual Canadian Biosphere Reserves, local communities and the private sector.

The goals of this partnership are to: encourage and package sustainable tourism opportunities based in nearby communities and tapping into the resources of the Biosphere Reserves; and help communities value protected areas through demonstrating that economic benefits can emerge from ecotourism. Strengthen the coordination of tourism and biodiversity conservation planning government policies at both the national and local levels. Foster the participation of biodiversity conservation planners in meetings dealing with tourism planning and, conversely, the participation of tourism planners in discussions of biodiversity conservation issues. Tourism needs to be involved in biodiversity and biodiversity in tourism.

Create dynamic and practical inter-sectoral mechanisms (e.g. committees) for effectively coordinating interaction between biodiversity conservation planning and tourism planning and development. Ensure that these committees have representatives not only from the government sector, but also from the tourism industry, NGOs, local communities and the universities. Nations around the world have growing economic needs and generally growing populations. However, their land area normally remains the same and this produces many conflicts regarding use of the land and its resources.

Utilisation of land for tourism is becoming an increasing trend in many countries. It is important to ensure that national development plans contain a set of development guidelines for the sustainable use of land, water and natural resources. The development of a diverse tourism base that is appropriately integrated with other local economic activities should be promoted. The only type of tourism which should be permitted in ecologically relevant and fragile natural areas is ecotourism.

Ecotourism provides viable economic alternatives for other activities which are less sustainable—and many times downright destructive to the environment—, such as uncontrolled logging, extensive animal husbandry, mass tourism or mining. This may bring about conflicting interests of water supply and other vital resources between tourists, the needs of the local population, and intensive agriculture. For this reason effective national zoning plans for land use are urgently required (and of course, effective enforcement of those plans).

Ecotourism should not be seen as a panacea or as a monoculture in a given area, but should be considered a complement for other sustainable economic activities that make wise use of the natural resources. All relevant stakeholders should be involved in the development of sound management plans for land-use. Means for providing the organisation, facilities and enforcement capacity required for effective implementation of those management plans should be put in place. In Australia, in the Shark Bay Region of Western Australia, the 1995 Shark Bay Regional Plan coordinated a World Heritage Strategic Plan, several tourism strategies and several fisheries management strategies.

In order to effectively manage future development and use, the Department of Conservation and the Ministry of Planning worked together to ensure that their planning was complementary and there were no areas of conflict as regards use of land and coastal zones. In Costa Rica, the Conservation Area is an original national regionalisation structure created by MINAE (Ministry of Environment and Energy) and SINAC (Conservation Areas National System). A Conservation Area is defined as that territorial unit governed by one and the same strategy for development and administration, where there is interaction between private activities (including tourism) and state activities on issues of management and conservation of natural resources, and where sustainable development solutions are pursued jointly with civil society. In this way, SINAC's administration covers all of the national territory (including protected areas) where exploitation of biodiversity activities and natural resources in general are promoted and regulated. Each area has a set number of protected wilderness areas (PWAs), including buffer zones.

There is coordination between state institutions and civil society that carry out activities in the areas. In Costa Rica, as for protected areas, SINAC in coordination with NGOs, has widely invested in the promotion of the different and numerous PWAs in the country and in bettering the infrastructure for attention to the public. This effort has had its positive impact, as was shown by a recent survey on tourists ' perception on international tourism but more so and especially on national tourism, as reflected by the growing number of visitors to the PWAs. In Costa Rica, both in conservation areas and protected areas the ENB (National Biodiversity Strategy) establishes a line of action and top priority activities according to five-year planning periods, where the tourism sector is a key factor.

In the Strategy, ecotourism with ample participation by civil society and in coordination with the government, is visualised as the top priority tourist activity to be developed and strengthened for conservation and sustainable use of biodiversity. Ensure that tourism planning is undertaken as part of the overall development plan for any area (including its land-use plan), and not undertaken in isolation. Focus on ways in which different interests can complement each other within a balanced programme for sustainable development, enabling the different stakeholders to work alongside each other. Minimise negative impacts of tourism on the natural and cultural environment and promote tourism as a tool to protect important natural habitats and conserve biodiversity in accordance with the Convention on Biological Diversity.

Ensure that, wherever tourism occurs or is liable to occur, the corresponding land-use plan should include a component of tourism land-use, carefully zoning the areas as regards the type of tourism that should take place: high, middle or low intensity. The inclusion of natural areas (and provisions for their conservation) is a vital element of any zoning plan. Ensure that the only type of tourism that will take place in vulnerable and fragile natural ecosystems follows the principles of ecotourism, considering it a viable option for minimising negative impacts and promoting positive environmental and socio-economic contributions. Ecotourism should always be carried out with the active involvement of the local communities.

Foster the creation of links between natural protected areas and other ecotourism destinations by means of biological corridors that will amplify biodiversity conservation to a larger regional level. In every case, tourism should pay attention to the "triple bottom line": economic, environmental and social factors must be attended to simultaneously. This implies the need for integrated management and the adoption of an ecosystem approach, as advocated by the CBD.

Continuous management of tourism is just as important as proper planning and development. It is imperative to provide incentives for the wide range application of environmental management systems. The only viable relationship between tourism and nature conservation is a symbiotic one. It is not enough to have a situation of coexistence and certainly nobody benefits from a conflictive relationship. Tourism management needs to form part of biodiversity management planning. The allocation of land uses must be carefully coordinated and inappropriate activities that damage ecosystems should be strictly regulated. This may be done only by strengthening and developing integrated policies and management that cover all socio-economic activities in the different ecosystems, including terrestrial, coastal and marine zones.

Management solutions are also needed for simple, but persistent, problems such as litter. It must be emphasised that enjoyment of biodiversity and natural areas is not only for rich foreigners, but for all national inhabitants. Ecotourism is made up of visitation by both national and international tourists. The former component is usually more sustainable than the latter if a sufficient standard of living exists in the country (i.e. domestic tourists possess the financial means to visit, and consequently support, protected areas). The different sectors must understand the tourism market for cultural and natural heritage products, and how this is linked to tourism's ability to support conservation through product demand. Understanding the experiences and products tourists are looking for, enables protected area managers to tailor certain aspects of the destination for the desired type of tourist.

Accurately forecasting the amount of anticipated visitors enables planners to lobby for and develop sufficient infrastructure. It is important to demonstrate how the private sector can implement environmental management plans, using low cost methods first, and then use any left over money to retrofit, making the tourism facility more sustainable. It is necessary to show the large hotel chains that environmental management brings a profit.

Using environmentally friendly techniques saves money for hotels and all other tourism service providers. In Australia, a national agenda to support sustainable tourism (including ecotourism) as a tool for conserving biodiversity and for better use of natural areas. The National Tourism Strategy was formulated in 1992 to, among other goals, enhance community awareness of the economic, environmental and cultural significance of tourism. The Strategy's environmental goal is to provide for sustainable tourism development by encouraging responsible planning and management practices consistent with the conservation of Australia's natural and cultural heritage.

In 1994, within the framework of this strategy, the National Ecotourism Strategy was published also by the Department of Tourism. In the strategy, integrated management of biodiversity resources and sustainable tourism, with ample participation of civil society and in coordination with the government, is considered as the top priority for national development. As part of sustainable tourism, Costa Rica seeks an activity where there is better distribution of resources in the different regions of the country and direct involvement of rural communities, while at the same time minimising negative environmental impacts. In Cuba, following the 1992 Earth Summit, where Cuba was one of only two countries to obtain the highest rating for implementing sustainable development practices.

The government set up a National Programme for Environment and Development and created a series of new institutions to continue along a course of sustainable development. The new institutions include a National Commission on Ecotourism, made up of tourism officials, environmentalists and scientists, created to ensure integrated management of biodiversity resources and tourism activities.

The conventional mass tourism is still the mainstream of the tourism industry and it is quite probable that this situation will prevail for some time. For this reason it is vitally important to aim our attention on mass tourism, striving to apply measures to make it more environmentally friendly and minimising its negative impacts on biodiversity. We should not consider only ecotourism linkages with biodiversity conservation, but also linkages of mass tourism, especially the effects of big hotels on the environment and how their design and operation can become more environmentally friendly. At a global scale, perhaps providing a number of ecolodges is not going to make much of a difference- ultimately we have to affect the larger tourism industry.

This means we have to consider how to improve the environmental record of very different items like airlines, airports, big amusement and theme parks, golf courses, and sports stadia. Training to develop skills of hotel owners and operators to understand what sustainable tourism is and education about best practices are vital activities. There is a need to strengthen and to revise legislation so that this approach is well understood and widely disseminated. Environmental legislation should act as a motivation force, and also as a base for certification. Also, a widespread educational campaign so that tourists will be demanding environmentally-friendly hotels is urgently needed.

Tourism shouldn't be only market driven. In Africa, for example, people feel bad about tourism use proscribed to the community. A cause for conflict arises when developing nations are told to be sustainable whereas western countries can have the huge hotels. It is vital to disseminate codes of ethics for conventional tourists, which will serve as a tool for alleviation of negative impacts. The effects of negative impacts are frequently long term and not always obvious in the short term. Saving water and energy by reducing the number of towels used in hotel rooms has become a cliché - but only because notices have made a difference in hotels around the world.

In analysing mass tourism impacts, both new tourism facilities and preexisting tourism facilities must be considered. In the former case, the application of minimal environmental standards for siting of new tourism services and facilities is urgently required. In the latter case, methods for improving the operation, making it more environmentally-friendly, should be applied, through retrofitting or adding new, more appropriate technologies. In every case, the benefits to the tourism sector (market demand, economics, effective management) must be persuasively demonstrated.

It is not a matter of sanctions and pressuring, rather encouraging the tourism sector to become more environmentally friendly (which will result in economic benefits for them). For example, water heating in many conventional hotels around the world is currently very inefficient and costly, so that wide use of alternative energy sources should be more than welcome by mainstream tourism operations. Also, many traditional beach destinations are experiencing a loss of repeat visitors because of water pollution, so that more environmentally-friendly practices are definitely in the interest of beach resort owners and operators. Cruise ships cause enormous environmental damage.

It is estimated that they discard many thousands of tons of untreated waste into the oceans of the world every day. Strict regulations have to be applied to this type of destructive tourism. In Australia, for the 2000 Olympic

Games the Sydney Organising Committee for the Olympic Games (SOCOG's) mission was "to deliver the most harmonious, athlete oriented, technically excellent and culturally enhancing Olympic Games of the modern era". SOCOG used its best endeavours to set a new standard of environmental excellence for organising and staging a large sporting event. To this end, SOCOG was committed to strict environmental guidelines, guided by the principles of Ecologically Sustainable Development (ESD). Environment was considered by the organisers as the "third pillar of Olympism".

Among the major environmental achievements were: the SOCOG Environment Programme was established in 1996, early enough to allow sufficient time for staff to be integrally involved in planning; carrying out of the Olympic Greenhouse Challenge, a major project to assess the greenhouse impact of the Games for minimising greenhouse gas emissions; a programme of environmental education (including a waste education plan) as a component of staff training; an environmental specification for sponsors, licensees and suppliers; an integrated waste management solution; packaging and foodware specification to control inputs into the waste stream; an Olympic Results Information Service (ORIS), an electronic system which reduced the huge amount of paper required to provide media with results; saving water and energy at all Olympic buildings and facilities; facilitating access of spectators through public transport, resulting in energy conservation and pollution and greenhouse gas avoidance; Olympic merchandise had minimal packaging and minimised the use of PVC.

Enforce current environmental laws, regulations and norms on waste management, air pollution and monitoring devices. Overcrowding, misuse of natural resources, polluting of air and water, the construction of infrastructure and facilities, and other activities associated with tourism, all produce impacts on the environment. These impacts may be not only physical, but also cultural. Negative impacts of tourism vary according to the nature and number of tourists, the type of physical facilities and the way tourism is managed. The individual tourist normally has a relatively small impact. Problems arise, however, if the number of tourists is large or the resource overused. Thus although tourism can be a lucrative source of revenue for a country, a tour operator or a specific destination, it can also represent a cause of serious damage to the environment, including the biodiversity resources.

Tourism impacts on the environment are manifold: impacts on geological exposures, minerals and fossils; on soils; on air and water resources; on vegetation; on animal life; on sanitation; on the cultural environment; and aesthetic impacts on the landscape. These different impacts, which are actually manifestations of change on the environment, rarely occur singly and their ecological effects are usually very complex. There are different ways of minimising negative impacts of tourism: through widespread environmental education of tourists and the tourism industry, through strict enforcement of laws and regulations, and through effective visitor management. Visitor management begins before arrival, then occurs on the ground at the site, and finally after the visitors leave through continual communication.

The process of environmental impact assessment (EIA) is one of the most effective methods for determining whether a project will be sustainable, and if so, for developing safeguards to ensure its continuing sustainability. EIA aims to ensure that the likely outcomes of any development (including tourism developments) are addressed at an early stage so that disastrous environmental and social consequences can be avoided. EIA applied to tourism projects should play a crucial role in government-decision making in every country. Zoning, a vital component of land-use planning, is the process of applying different management objectives and regulations to different parts or zones of a specific area.

Zoning is a tool required in any land or water-use plan (including marine, coastal and fresh water areas) and should always be used to regulate utilisation of the land and water resource over the long term. Zoning should be applied at all the different levels: national, regional and local. In the first case, zoning plans should be carried out by government authorities at the highest (e.g. federal) level. In every case, zoning must be comprehensive, considering the different socio-economic activities (obviously including tourism, when it occurs), but also natural areas which should be left undeveloped. Zoning plans should solve conflicts of interest with water supply and other vital resources, including biodiversity.

Understand that some areas of relevant biodiversity should be conserved for their own value and that not all relevant biodiversity zones should experience visitation. Biodiversity has is own value. As regards tourism, it is important to have a zoning scheme which should cover the different possible tourism activities. Obviously, in ecotourism destinations (especially in protected areas), there is nor room for this zoning category. But, even in the case of mass tourism destination areas, planning should endeavour to minimise negative impacts, including pollution of air, water, and soil resources. The different zones indicate where and what type of physical infrastructure and services should be provided, by means of a clear categorisation of modality and intensity of land use, striving in every case to minimise negative impacts on the natural and cultural environment, as well as optimising the ecotourists' experience. Zoning also indicates to us where facilities, activities or services should not be developed.

In essence, a zoning scheme shows the development suitability of the different portions of a site. Those activities which are carried out in each zone are normally mutually exclusive (and often conflictive), so that zoning decisions must be taken very carefully. Allow diversity through wise zoning of tourism activities, providing tools so that people (both locals and tourists) can decide upon which zone they fit into (or they prefer to visit) and then follow the regulations related to their zone. Environmental carrying capacity is the capacity of an ecosystem to support healthy organisms while maintaining its productivity, adaptability, and capability of renewal.

Tourism carrying capacity is a specific type of environmental carrying capacity and refers to the carrying capacity of the biophysical and social environment with respect to tourism activity and development. It represents the maximum level of visitor use and related infrastructure that an area can accommodate. If it is exceeded, deterioration of the area's environmental resources, diminished visitor satisfaction, and/or adverse impacts upon the society, economy and culture of an area can be expected to ensue. The principles of recognising that a range of livelihood concerns are important, and supporting systems that enable local people's priorities to be incorporated into tourism decisions, can be generally applied. Some study shows that growing numbers of tourists would like more meaningful contact with local communities, including informative interactions.

Diversifying to meet this demand could provide low - cost economic opportunities for local people, creating a more rounded and sustainable tourism product. Envision ecotourism as a motor for local sustainable development and a job generator. It is vital to reach agreements between tour operators and the community so that the community is a member of the organisation and has ownership over the process. The local community must come to value nearby natural areas (including protected areas) before it will protect them. Management and stewardship by the local community is an important part of education and vital to the long-term survival of the resource. It will also contribute to raise pride regarding the local heritage.

In many rural areas around the world, local inhabitants have shifted from being hunters to serving as park rangers or ecotourist guides. Ecotourism projects should strengthen community organisation. Always apply participatory planning and self management principles to tourism development. Ensure that traditional local resource managers are given statutory rights over the areas that they manage. People need clear legal rights over the area that they live in before tourism which benefits them and conservation can take place.

Encourage capacity building and empowerment for local communities. Foster links between all-inclusive resorts and local enterprises, e.g. local food suppliers, daily market place, local excursions, etc. Promote symbiotic relationships between big hotels and smaller tourism suppliers, including small lodges. Avoid isolation or enclaves and have tourists be in contact in social and natural environment (when desired by community). Recur to social scientists and anthropologists (especially those with long local experience) for advice in developing activities and products that will be acceptable and useful to the entire community, e.g., participatory dances and ceremonies, local arts and crafts, regional foods, etc.

The product needs to move beyond being a simple merchandise, serving the tourists as being part of their travel experience. If they are in agreement, foster the active participation of indigenous people in the ecotourism process in such a way that they obtain tangible socio-economic benefits and also, they contribute to the ecotourist's experience. Minimise traveller impact on local cultures by offering appropriate literature, briefings, leading by example, and taking corrective actions. Develop educational and environmental awareness campaigns and training programmes among the local communities that also include understanding what tourism is about (including positive and negative effects of tourism in local communities).

The best ecotourism guides usually turn out to be the local people (with the right training). Give opportunities to the local people for communicating to the tourists their traditional perception of their environment. Carry out training programmes for tour operators who are working with the local community in order to minimise cultural shock and negative impacts. Diversify tourism experiences. Consider ethnic tourism and agrotourism as excellent complements of ecotourism and conventional tourism. Define whether employment or ownership will give the greater beneficial impact to the community. Encourage both direct and indirect benefits from tourism, e.g. selling of handicrafts, local language teaching, etc. Encourage and/ or facilitate financial support (especially micro-credit schemes) to communities over realistic time periods. Soft money will be a useful tool for economic support but it needs to come with a programme of education based on financial management.

Ensure that independent and financially sustainable community businesses are supported by government promotion of tourism. Simplify forms for obtaining micro-credits. Micro-creditors still need to be paid if the business fails. A safety net needs to be developed. Develop schemes for identifying environmental and social capital (what could be termed 'environmental/social economics'). Transfer consumptive and non-consumptive values to general national accounting. Recognise that tourism is a foreign exchange activity, therefore communities promoting tourism should be eligible for international financing at the same.

In the future, certification should appropriately link tourism with biodiversity conservation, and should be performance-based. Biodiversity (including conservation, maintenance, and enhancement), socio-economic (comprising gender issues , level of participation of local people, and benefit sharing), and cultural criteria must be considered in every certification scheme. It should be recognised that many certification programmes are currently unreliable (resulting , e.g. in lack of training in hotels). The Mohonk Agreement is an agreed framework and principles for the certification of ecotourism and sustainable tourism, which was unanimously adopted at the conclusion of an international workshop held at Mohonk Mountain House, New Paltz, New York in November 2000. This agreement contains a set of general principles and elements that, according to the workshop participants, should be part of any sound ecotourism and sustainable tourism certification programmes. Participants came from

20 countries and delegates represented most of the leading global, regional national, and sub-national sustainable tourism and ecotourism certification programs, conservation and environmental organisations, and others with expertise in tourism and ecotourism certification and environmental management.

2

Planning for Leisure and Tourism

Leisure is a major activity which fulfils an important role in contributing towards the quality of life of the people. The term "leisure" not only encompasses participation in active sport, but also children's play and informal recreational pursuits such as walking. The provision of leisure facilities has been going through a period of transition with the private sector becoming more involved in the leisure industry.

Whilst this does have the affect of broadening the range of facilities available, invariably these are aimed at the more affluent market e.g., Multiplex Cinemas, Theme Parks and new concepts in leisure provision involving accommodation such as Center Parcs. These have changed the way in which recreation was perceived in the 1980's. Such changes have helped to fuel a demand for a wider range of recreational facilities. Within this framework the provision of sports pitches, parks, children's play areas, informal open space and allotments will continue to be an important element in enhancing the quality of life of the people of Nottinghamshire's Mansfield District. The provision of these facilities has traditionally been the role of the Local Authority. However this role is changing, with more emphasis being increasingly put on the private sector as providers.

The 1994 Deposit Nottinghamshire Structure Plan Review defines "Tourism" as being the activity of all those visiting an area for leisure, business or family reasons, including day visitors. It defines tourist facilities as broadly comprising of the following:

— tourist attractions;

— tourist services including information facilities, car parks and toilets;

— tourist accommodation.

Although existing sports pitch provision in the District is more than the minimum recommended levels, as suggested by the National Playing Fields Association, there is an uneven distribution of such facilities. This does not give ready access for all the District's population to sports pitches. In particular there is a paucity of sports pitches in eastern and western Mansfield, which includes the wards of Leeming, Cumberlands, Lindhurst, Ladybrook, Broomhill, Sherwood, Ravensdale and Titchfield.

The East Midlands Council for Sport and Recreation, in its previous publication "Taking Shape" identified that there is also a shortfall of golf courses within the District. The District Council is looking to increase the amount of public open space, where finances permit, in order to improve the urban environment and the quality of life enjoyed by Mansfield residents and visitors.

There are numerous allotment garden sites within the Plan area which in the past adequately served adjacent residential areas. However development has created a possible need for new sites in the Oak Tree, Kings Mill and Forest Town areas. The East Midlands Tourist Board has estimated that in 1990, over £144 million was spent by tourists in Nottinghamshire, little of which was spent in Mansfield District. This can be attributed to three specific factors:

— poor regional image of the District;
— lack of hotel accommodation;
— no major tourist attractions.

Throughout the District opportunities exist to create major areas of open space. These include land at Sherwood Colliery and Litton Road and will often be provided in association with development proposals. With the closure of the collieries within the District, this has created the unique opportunity for recreational facilities on areas previously used for tipping. As a consequence, this authority will encourage the provision of recreational facilities, particularly utilising these tips e.g., at Sherwood and Warsop collieries.

The provision of children's play space facilities particularly in densely populated areas, is important with regard to the quality of life for young children. As a consequence, the Plan will look to increase provision, particularly in the Mansfield Woodhouse, Warsop, Ravensdale, Titchfield and Oak Tree areas of the District. In order to help alleviate the shortfall of allotment gardens that has come about as a result of the growth of specific areas, the Plan identifies the possible need for sites in Forest Town and Oak Tree.

In order to greatly increase Mansfield's contribution towards attracting tourists to the region, the Plan identifies a broad range of hotel sites to increase accommodation. It also highlights a number of other opportunities to help broaden Mansfield's tourism base. In all, the Local Plan recognises that there is an overall deficiency of major recreational facilities in the District. There are, however, major opportunities to address this problem, e.g., disused colliery tips. These offer large areas which can be used to provide recreational facilities for the use of not only the District's population, but also well beyond its boundaries.

Major areas of public open space and local parks provide an important facility, over wide sections of the urban area. All of these areas contribute towards the communities that they serve usually within a half mile radius. Where developments can be proven to enhance such facilities, then they will receive favourable consideration by the District Council.

Both local parks and major areas of open space provide important sports facilities, children's play equipment and informal recreation areas. It is essential that their provision is continued. The location and topography of such facilities often make them desirable for alternative forms of development. The Local Plan will protect them from such alternative development. Only small-scale developments that would enhance the facility for recreational use e.g. the provision of changing facilities, children's play equipment or facilities for the storage of recreational or grounds maintenance equipment, will be viewed favourably.

Major areas of public open space and local parks are defined as those which are regarded as having considerable local importance e.g. Oak Tree Common or, have been established for such a long period of time that they have become an integral part of the local landscape e.g. Yeoman Hill Park. All existing playing fields, play areas and incidental open space in the Plan area contribute towards the well being and quality of life of the communities that they serve, usually within a quarter mile radius.

Public open spaces can often be subject to pressure for development and are, therefore, protected from development by this policy, except where at least one of the above mentioned criteria can be satisfied. Replacement facilities are defined as being of a size and consisting of features similar to the lost open space.

Leisure and Ecotourism

The term ecotourism was used and was defined very broadly as "nature, adventure and cultural experiences in the countryside". Ecotourism, which is based on the unique natural features and traditional cultures of destinations, is intended to conserve resources while providing benefits for local communities. It has a special role to play in strengthening international understanding and rebuilding the images of affected countries. The Worldwide Fund for Nature (WWF), for example, has defined ecotourism as "any travel to or through wilderness areas that has minimal impact on the natural environment and its wildlife while providing some economic benefits to local communities and the area's indigenous stewards."

There is broad agreement on ecotourism's basic characteristics—or at least on what these characteristics should be, as there is often a gap between ideals and practice. Ecotourism generally: is nature-based (visitors are mainly interested in observing and appreciating nature and traditional cultures in natural areas); contributes to biodiversity conservation; supports the well-being of local people; involves responsible action by both tourists and local people to minimize negative environmental and sociocultural impacts; requires the lowest possible consumption of non-renewable resources; stresses local ownership, as well as business opportunities for local (especially rural) people. Ecotourism tends to be modest in scale. It is also likely to be operated by small or medium-sized companies that specialize in leading - and providing accommodation for - small groups in natural areas.

The World Tourism Organization has estimated that "nature travel" - of which ecotourism is one form - generated about 7% of all international travel expenditure in 1997. According to the World Resources Institute, at the beginning of the 1990s tourism overall was growing at a rate of 4% per year and nature travel at a rate of 10-30%. These figures are supported by a 1997 survey of tour operators in the Asia-Pacific region, who were experiencing annual growth rates of 10-25%. World Tourism Organization estimates show global spending on ecotourism increasing by 20% per year, about five times the average rate of growth in the tourism industry as a whole.

One element affecting demand for nature-based tourism is the increase in environmental consciousness worldwide. Nature films and publications have made destinations which are of special environmental interest much more widely known than they once were. The economic value of tourism-related activities is difficult to assess. Many types and sizes of enterprises are involved. Some of them engage in other activities as well. Tourism-related products and services can also be subject to considerable seasonal fluctuations. By some measures, tourism-related activities make up the world's largest economic sector. World Tourism Organization figures indicate that these activities account for over 4% of global GDP, and that their combined direct and indirect contributions to global GDP are over 11%. Tourism-related activities provide over 200 million jobs.

The World Tourism Organization defines international tourists as those who stay at least one night but less than 12 months in a country other than the one where they usually reside, for purposes mainly other than conducting activities that will be remunerated within the country visited. Most of the sources used in compiling these "facts and figures" follow the World Tourism Organization definition or a similar one. Within this definition, however, tourism may take vastly different forms - ranging from mass travel, to adventure or wilderness treks, to religious pilgrimages, to cultural or educational visits, to sports and ecotourism. Both domestic and international tourism have important direct and indirect impacts on many other economic sectors.

Tourism is one of the world's fastest growing industries. The number of international tourist arrivals in 2000 was over 698 million. This represented an estimated 7.4% annual increase, the highest growth rate in nearly ten years and almost twice the increase reported in 1999. Although all the world regions represented in World Tourism Organization statistics received more tourist visits in 2000 than ever before, the highest growth was in East Asia and the Pacific, where there were 14.3 million more tourists than in 1999, an increase of 14.7%. The number of domestic tourists within countries is more difficult to measure, but is often estimated to be up to ten times the number of international visitors. The industrialized countries of the Americas, Europe and Asia are the main destinations of international visitors. Nearly 58% of international tourist arrivals are

European residents and more than 18% are from the Americas. However, there has been substantial growth in the number and diversity of tourists from other parts of the world.

In terms of international departures, East Asia and the Pacific is the fastest growing region. In many countries tourism has become the major source of foreign exchange earnings. According to the World Tourism Organization, tourism is one of the top five export categories in 83% of all countries and the main source of foreign currency in at least 38%. As a source of employment and poverty alleviation tool, tourism plays an essential role in many countries' economies. Nature-based tourism is especially important in developing countries, for example those lacking significant industrial, financial or resource extraction industries.

While tourist visits may be concentrated in critically important conservation areas, often these areas do not benefit economically from tourism -or not to the extent required to protect the ecosystems on which this type of tourism depends. The IUCN considers most of the world's park programmes to be underfunded and to provide only a minimum of resource protection. Tourism in these areas can have destructive effects (e.g. trail erosion, wildlife harassment, poaching, road damage and sewage runoff). Many parks cannot undertake adequate visitor management.

In some countries the scope of the ecotourism industry is limited by the financial non-viability of park agencies. Measuring ecotourism Figures on ecotourism are incomplete and difficult to obtain. Before an industry sector can be measured, that sector needs to be clearly and objectively defined. Besides the definitions above, two general viewpoints are associated with the evaluation of ecotourism: "aspirational" (i.e. concerned with what ecotourism should be) and "phenomenological" (i.e. concerned with products that are presented as examples of ecotourism, many of which are far from the idealized image). The diversity of ecotourism ideas and products, as well as an ongoing debate with respect to definitions, render measurement-taking extremely difficult.

The many stakeholders (e.g. governments, the tourism industry, park management, social and environmental NGOs, organizations representing indigenous or traditional inhabitants) can make defining and measuring even more complex. Regarding the "aspirational" aspect of ecotourism, most of those involved are idealists, at least to some extent. But how can aspirations be measured? Small-scale local operators or groups do not have the ability to hire market survey consultants. Most tourism trade associations do not consider the current volumes of ecotourists large enough to justify major investment in market research. As ecotourism can be highly controversial, with very vocal NGOs and indigenous people, for example, presenting their opinions, a great many operators may prefer not to offer ecotourism.

No in-depth studies have been carried out to determine the extent to which travel decisions by nature tourists are based on ecotourism principles. However, at least two such studies have been initiated. The Inter-American Development Bank has included a regional South American study in a US$ 1.8 million bid, to be released by the Brazilian government as part of the Proecotur package (US$ 200 million to support ecotourism in the Brazilian Amazon); and the World Tourism Organization has undertaken a European market survey.

Ecotourism is often equated with "nature tourism". This can distort figures indicating market size. Studies concerning nature tourism have shown that up to 50% of all tourists would like to visit a natural area (e.g. a national park), which suggests a very large potential market. But these tourists do not necessarily want to travel in small groups, learning about wildlife and culture with a local guide. Ecotourism seeks to increase local control over tourism's effects by stressing that local communities and business owners should be considered a vital part of an ecotourism programme. One of the principles of ecotourism is that local people are to be informed in advance of all the possible consequences of tourism development, and that they must formally consent to tourism development in their area.

According to the World Bank, ecotourism is one of the three types of tourism most amenable to community-based initiatives. These niche markets provide especially desirable "customers" for culturally or environmentally sensitive areas: i.e. visitors who typically spend more and stay longer at a destination than the average tourist, generating a higher yield but with less impact on the life of the community and on local culture and the environment. Community-based tourism can generate a sense of pride in the local population and make funds available for maintaining or upgrading cultural assets (e.g. archeological ruins, historic sites, traditional crafts production). It may also provide some of the best opportunities for "pro-poor tourism", which takes the needs of impoverished local people into account in the planning of tourism development.

Ecotourism can have both direct and indirect economic impacts on a community. Direct impacts are derived from money spent directly by tourists, for example at a restaurant; indirect impacts occur when the restaurant purchases goods and services from other businesses and pays its employees, who can use their wages to buy other goods and services. If the restaurant obtains goods or services outside the local area, the money has no indirect impacts on this area - it is "leakage". By their nature, certain projects have an unavoidably high leakage rate.

In many African countries nature-based tourism is the first or second most important foreign currency earner. However, there is often severe leakage since so many products used in tourism, from safari vehicles to guidebooks, are imported. Ecotourism's economic contribution to local communities needs to be evaluated based mainly on the success of local vendors. The types of products and services most often offered to ecotourists by local community members include food (e.g. from stands, restaurants), vehicle rentals, taxis, guided visits, recreation (e.g. using horses, boats, rafts, bikes) and crafts. Vendors are crucial to the success of any ecotourism venture and its ability to benefit local communities.

Frequently their businesses are quite small. Owners may need some encouragement or capital assistance to get started. This could be provided by NGOs or the ecotourism industry. The economic contribution of ecotourism to local communities can vary tremendously, depending not only on the nature of the project but also on the destination's characteristics. In Belize over 40% of local people in the vicinity of Hol Chan Marine reserve feel that they benefit from the reserve economically. In the nearby village of San Pedro there are small local businesses such as hotels, bars and clothing shops.

On the other hand, Tortuguero National Park in Costa Rica, is characterized by all-inclusive lodges where visitors pay in advance, travel by boat to view wildlife in remote wetlands, and then return to the lodges, which are not owned by local people. Less than 10% of local households are estimated to benefit economically from the park. At Tortuguero there is no small-scale economy of any kind to provide services or goods for ecotourism projects. Locals mainly survive through subsistence fishing. There is little diversity of goods in local communities long dominated by large-scale banana plantations or cattle raising.

The greater the number of micro-enterprises in a tourism area, the more likely it is that a significant percentage of local people will benefit. In areas where there are few small businesses, leakage can be reduced by instituting lease fees, land rental fees and other per-person use charges, and making sure they go to local residents. Successful efforts to encourage community entrepreneurship are based on local cultural needs and value-added approaches to local products, such as improving packaging and design. Ecotourism-related goods and services can provide local people with supplemental income, but they are also of importance in creating new jobs. For example, private nature reserves and eco-tourist destinations are being developed in Africa.

The reserves are generally established primarily for conservation purposes (rather than hunting) and are increasingly viable economically due to tourism income. The average African private reserve, which creates 457 months of employment per year, is an important source of income in a local community. In the case of other types of ecotourism projects the number of jobs created may be low. However, in rural areas even a few new jobs can make a big difference. One of the fundamental problems with respect to environmental protection is the difficulty of putting a value on the environment and on resources such as scenery or biodiversity.

Ecotourism helps create a direct commercial value for environmental protection through entry fees charged at national parks and protected areas. Well-regulated protected areas, like the Galapagos Islands (Ecuador) have created significant local and national-level benefits from entry fees paid by nature and ecotourism companies on behalf of their clients and from license fees for tour boats. In 1998, Galapagos entrance fees totalled US$ 4.3 million. Over the years, such fees have enabled Ecuador's national park service to manage the islands by limiting visitor numbers, requiring high-quality guide services by local people, controlling which islands are visited and which trails are used, and providing some support to park management. It is important to set fees high enough to cover the expenses of proper park management. When entrance fees are too low, the government may be subsidizing tourism - and its attendant impacts. Because of its scale and global extent, tourism inevitably has important environmental impacts.

At the same time, it depends heavily on natural resources such as beaches, mountains, rivers, forests and biodiversity. Threats to the environment therefore threaten the tourism industry's viability. The growth in tourism worldwide presents a significant threat to cultural and biological diversity. Ecotourism, despite its environmentally friendly goals, can also have negative impacts if it is not managed correctly. Ecotourism projects have especially high potential environmental impacts owing to their nature, as they are typically located in pristine or fragile ecosystems. Such areas often have a high degree of biodiversity (one reason they are desirable for ecotourism), but also tend to be extremely vulnerable to environmental damage.

Even more than other forms of tourism, ecotourism risks damaging the environmental assets on which it depends. Among the potential negative impacts to which ecotourism developments are vulnerable are overcrowding, erosion, deforestation for increased access and construction of facilities, loss of biodi-versity and habitats, increased competition for scarce resources, and increased waste and pollution in areas with little or no capacity to absorb them. Ecotourism also has the potential to create positive environmental and social impacts. Indeed, it is this potential that has attracted so much attention to the concept of ecotourism.

Potential positive impacts include the community benefits mentioned above, as well as the opportunity to develop tourism in a way that minimizes negative impacts from the start - without the crowding, sprawl and environmental degradation so often associated with mass tourism. Since ecotourists are often more tolerant of simple or rustic facilities than average tourists would be, tourism income can be increased with lower capital investments than those required for mass tourism developments. In some cases, ecotourism can support capital improvements over the long term. Most ecotourism takes place in national parks, wildlife reserves and similar protected areas established to serve environmental conservation goals. The motives for ecotourist travel are a natural fit with the aims and management philosophy of park agencies.

However, tourism—including ecotourism—can degrade environmental quality through overuse, unplanned access to sensitive sites and inappropriate use levels. Ecotourism depends on the long-term sustainability of natural resource management by government agencies. Inadequate financial resources for national park and protected area management can result in overuse, environmental damage, and reduction of ecotourism's potential benefits. Ecotourism therefore focuses not only on activities but also on environmentally and socially desirable results: conservation of the natural resources being visited, and contributions to the well-being of local people. Efforts to generate these benefits have been the primary objective of ecotourism programmes for over ten years.

During this period it has become clear that some concerns still need to be better addressed, such as: land tenure and control of the ecotourism development process by host communities; the efficiency and fairness of protective measures for biological and cultural diversity; the need for more precautions and monitoring when operating in especially sensitive areas; indigenous and traditional rights in areas suitable for ecotourism development. If ecotourism is to become a successful sustainable development tool, adequate funds will be needed to allow planning and long-term management of ecotourism destinations. The size and nature of the ecotourism market should be sufficient to make government funds available to conserve areas, both cultural and environmental, for ecotourism development. Fees and taxes need to be used for resource protection and visitor management.

No tourism destination (particularly an "ecodestination") can prosper in the long term it is overcrowded, dirty, environmentally degraded, and threatened with the loss of its biological and cultural identity. Ecotourism has developed during the last ten or 15 years as both an industry and a form of sustainable development that conserves natural areas and sustains the well-being of local people. As a concept, it aspires to achieve sustainable development results in all cases. But ecotourism products have become numerous enough to be considered a market segment with sustainable and unsustainable characteristics.

Ecotourism has been widely used (and often misused) as a market label in a variety of circumstances. Nonetheless, the strong orientation of the ecotourism field towards the evolution of principles, guidelines and certification based on sustainability standards gives it a market niche strongly associated with sustainability. During the 1990s, dozens of conferences were held to discuss ecotourism principles. A variety of definitions emerged worldwide to describe this new phenomenon. In 1991, The International Ecotourism Society (TIES) coined one of the first and best recognized definitions: "responsible travel to natural areas that conserves the environment and sustains the well-being of local people." While there are certainly lessons to be learned from good and bad examples of all kinds of tourism development, a genuine analysis of ecotourism should probably be based on projects formulated to follow ecotourism principles.

Efforts to set sustainability standards for the ecotourism industry are less than ten years old. For those interested in understanding how sustainability can be achieved, analysis of projects developed with ecotourism principles in mind will likely produce the most interesting and consistent results. While ecotourism is in nearly all cases nature tourism, not all nature tourism is ecotourism. Rarely has the mainstream cruise line industry, for example, defined itself as ecotourism—despite its dependence on natural resources. While more work needs to be done on cruise lines' sustainability standards, it would not be accurate to analyse them as an ecotourism industry. It is important to recognize that any discussion of the sustainability of the tourism industry is very new. Tourism was not included in the global dialogue on sustainable development that took place at the time of the Rio Summit, resulting in the formation of the UN Commission on Sustainable Development

(UNCSD). Only in 1998 did UNCSD address the sustainability of the tourism industry. In general, international discussion of the tourism industry's sustainability is still a very immature process that needs more expertise and fuller commitment from governments, industry and the development community. The process of establishing principles for ecotourism in the 1990s primarily took place at conferences, attended for the most part by academics and NGO representatives.

Usually there was little involvement by industry members. This resulted in a variety of principles and standards that may or may not be applicable in practice. The International Ecotourism Society (TIES) found that guidelines offer a practical participatory tool for coming to consensus directly with industry members on sustainable development practices. The guideline development process was studied by TIES in the early 1990s to help determine how best to get a variety of stakeholders to adopt sustainability principles.

TIES then adopted a standardized approach to the development of ecotourism guidelines. First, best practice information is gleaned from industry members through surveying. Second, participatory multi-stakeholder meetings (involving researchers specializing in impacts on natural areas and local people, industry, NGOs and communities) are held in Northern and Southern locations. Finally, international review takes place, helping ensure that a wide variety of viewpoints from many nationalities are incorporated. TIES has completed this procedure for nature tour operators, ecolodges and marine ecotourism. Efforts to certify ecotourism are at the earliest stages of development.

Certifying ecotourism businesses involves gathering data on their environmental and social performance and then verifying these data. Difficult issues arise when trying to establish measurable benchmarks for principles that are highly qualitative. Efforts to certify ecotourism businesses have been led by Australia, which established a research programme in 1994 and launched a federally funded initiative in 1996. It is the only ecotourism-specific certification programme in the world. International nature-based businesses began to thrive in the 1980s with the growing interest in outdoor travel and the environment, spurred by excellent new outdoor equipment for camping and hiking and events such as Earth Day. Nature-based tourism companies from San Jose, Costa Rica, to Katmandu, Nepal, proliferated. This created a significant opportunity for local entrepreneurs and nature guides.

International tour operators and their ground-based counterparts offering trips to the Galapagos Islands, Costa Rica, Kenya and Nepal - among other destinations - saw rapid market gains in the 1980s and early 1990s. These companies began to realize that they could take the initiative to conserve the environment by sponsoring local conservation groups at the destinations they visited or raising funds for local causes. So many individuals with unique ideas and creative approaches were involved in the early days that it was rare to see ecotourism carried out the same way twice. Today many ecotour operators around the globe are working to create well-planned, interactive learning experiences that introduce small groups of travellers to new environments and cultures, while minimizing negative environmental impacts and supporting conservation efforts.

These service providers can be local or international. They range from seasonal community-run and family operations to medium-scale outbound operators with yearly revenues in the millions of dollars. Of course, many companies operating throughout the world offers what is falsely labelled as ecotourism. Sometimes these companies even receive aid from governments because of their purported environmental standards. The damage being done by companies that relocate indigenous people in order to build golf courses (under the guise of ecotourism) has clearly been considerable.

It is difficult to quantify what percentage of the market is seeking to meet sustainability standards. The argument over how beneficial the ecotourism industry is, or how harmful it can be, is therefore difficult to resolve. It is likely that this industry will have both sustainable and unsustainable components for years to come. Whether or not this overrides ecotourism's potential benefits is a matter of opinion, but without question there is a continuing need to closely monitor how the industry is evolving, particularly in rural areas and among peoples that lack genuine land and other legal rights.

Overall, the part of the ecotourism industry that is seeking to achieve green standards is developing its own ethics and has used highly individualistic approaches to achieve sustainable development results. At present, the ecotourism industry is still dominated by small to medium-sized, owner-operated businesses that seek to improve their sustainability record only if the owners themselves have a strong sense of the importance of social and environmental goals for their businesses.

The challenges ahead for improving the green performance of the ecotourism industry will primarily involve a process of working with small, individually owned businesses that operate in remote areas and helping them find solutions to the difficult problem of working profitably in areas that often lack the full range of government services or oversight. Governments have an extraordinarily important role to play in developing ecotourism, yet their role is complex and must be defined by a variety of agency players.

Several countries have adopted specific ecotourism strategies. The first national ecotourism plan in the world, prepared by the Australian government in 1994 and, is the most important example of national ecotourism planning. In Australia, the decision to formulate an ecotourism strategy was made in response to growing international interest and the increasing profile of Australia's natural environment as a tourism attraction. Working on behalf of the federal government, a small team undertook a literature review and proceeded to public consultation, which involved local government agencies, natural resource managers, tour operators, tourism marketers, planners, conservation and community groups, developers and indigenous Australians.

In Brazil, the government decided to address the environmental threat of rapid tourism growth by establishing the Interministerial Ecotourism Task Force in the early 1990s. A technical cooperation programme was developed for the Amazon region and signed in 2000 by President Cardoso. The Inter-American Development Bank (IDB) loaned US$ 13.8 million to establish a framework for implementing the investments necessary for the nine Brazilian Amazonian states to responsibly prepare themselves to manage selected ecotourism areas. This loan package, called Proecotur, is a pre-investment for a major US$ 200 million initiative to develop the country's Amazon region for ecotourism.

Community-based ecotourism (CBE) is a growing phenomenon throughout the world. The CBE concept implies that the community has substantial control and involvement in the ecotourism project, and that the majority of benefits remain in the community. Three main types of CBE enterprises have been identified. The purest model suggests that the community owns and manages the enterprise. All community members are employed by the project using a rotation system, and profits are allocated to community projects. The second type of CBE enterprise involves family or group initiatives within communities. This is based on voluntary participation. The third type of CBE is a joint venture between a community or family and an outside business partner. At present there is a large demand, especially in Latin America, for assistance to communities seeking to develop local ecotourism products.

The Nature Conservancy's Latin America division reports that of their 60 local NGO affiliates, 36 have requested assistance with ecotourism feasibility studies. This is just one example of what is well-known throughout Latin America: ecotourism has been chosen by thousands of communities in the region as their preferred development alternative. The NGO community has a role to play in assisting local communities with viable sustainable development projects. However, inadequate expertise and understanding of the ecotourism product has led to inappropriate assistance patterns. The most important new trends in development assistance include better pre-assessment of community needs and community readiness; a full analysis of land tenure and other legal issues relating to long-term access to the political process; training that is more targeted at community needs; research on the market for community ecotourism, paired with efforts to develop appropriate linkages to the global marketplace; and development of improved systems to protect communities from competing land uses, such as logging and oil exploitation. One of the key issues in ecotourism today is the extent to which this portion of the global marketplace can actually represent a different kind of responsible commerce.

Ecotourism can be a form of commerce in which local people actively participate in the formulation of social "contracts" that go well beyond standard business formulas. Given that the great majority of ecotourism businesses are locally owned and that socially conscious owners are frequently involved, communities can achieve more than the *status quo*. The involvement of NGOs and the development assistance community can frequently help reverse top-down business patterns. Participatory decision-making processes can make a difference. These processes are being used increasingly, even in regions where communities have been sidelined in the past.

Certainly no new economic development system can completely transform the social and political context of a people or region. Finding genuinely equitable formulas for responsible commerce between cultures, and between those in the North and the South, can without question be challenging. But honest efforts to find increasingly equitable approaches to the development of ecotourism continue. The natural and cultural resources with which the Caribbean region is blessed have made it the world's most popular warm weather destination.

The fact that it is very fortunate to have tourism as a development option could be taken as the starting point for an extensive discussion concerning tourism's costs and benefits. All indications have been that the region's dependence on tourism for economic development - if not survival - is likely to increase in the immediate future, as other economic sectors encounter a hostile competitive situation. The good news is that Caribbean countries have a comparative advantage in an industry where world demand has been almost unlimited, and where this region has demonstrated creditable industry performance over the years. The bad news is that 1) the Caribbean faces fierce competition as the world's premier warm weather destination, and 2) regional tourism plans have been more focused on "growing" than on "developing" the industry, and therefore countries must address several environmental and social problems in addition to possible loss of market share.

In Caribbea, ecotourism has been recognized as a viable form of sustainable tourism development. Its capacity to generate economic benefits by contributing to the protection of natural and cultural resources (and involving local communities) has made ecotourism an alternative form of tourism, especially in protected and remote rural areas. Ecotourism is not a new concept in the Caribbean. With a generous tropical climate, landscapes that range from volcanic mountains, lakes and limestone cliffs to lush green hills, man-grove swamps and forests, not to mention our well-known sandy beaches and astonishing coral reefs (including the world's second and third largest barrier reefs), our region had been welcoming visitors in search of this natural world well before the term "ecotourism" was coined.

At the time it was recognized that "despite the growing importance of ecotourism and a general concern for the protection of the environment, the Caribbean region has, with the exception of a few countries, not made any serious efforts to examine the potential which this type of tourism may hold for the region or to capitalize on any advantages which the region possesses." In 1993, the Caribbean Environment Programme evaluated the competitiveness of ecotourism in the Wider Caribbean. Difficulties distinguishing between visitors interested in ecotourism activities or traditional activities were explained. These difficulties make it almost impossible to ascertain the economic benefits to be gained from ecotourism.

Regarding the institutional framework necessary for developing ecotourism, the study concluded that "although institutions are being established in the countries with the specific purpose of looking after tourism activities and/or the environment in general, the majority do not consider ecotourism as a section of the framework, but only as a part of their programmes." In general terms, the most important reasons for not developing ecotourism were identified as the lack of qualified staff, infrastructure, legislation, facilities and institutional setup. With respect to the future, countries showed evidence of having more willingness than concrete or real plans. It would not be fair to say that the situation existing almost ten years ago still exists today.

Some progress has been made, but not as much as could have been, given ecotourism's enormous potential in the region. Progress is more evident in countries where ecotourism has been integrated as an important tool in national plans. Belize, for example, has established a system for collecting information on visitors to natural and heritage areas, both in terms of numbers and motivation. Most of its accommodations are distributed throughout the inland country and cays, in small hotels or guesthouses. Bonaire has one of the best managed marine national parks, which has put it on the map as one of the best diving destinations in the world.

In some other countries, despite the recognition that ecotourism is the best alternative for tourism development, separating it from more traditional forms of tourism has not been easy. Dominica, the "Nature Island of the Caribbean", is struggling between the ecotourism potential of its natural and cultural resources, which include the Morne Trois Piton National Park, and the high-impact cruise tourism that makes use of its ports every week. There is also the controversial issue of whether a larger airport should be built to facilitate the arrival of long-haul aircraft. It is expected that orienting the tourism industry towards more sustainable development would facilitate resolution of the conflict between traditional tourism and ecotourism.

Provision of a sustainable tourism framework for all tourism operations, not only those in protected or rural areas, would allow ecotourism to find its own dimension in the Caribbean and to be seen as a true option, not a merely a response to the market. As a region that moves around tourism, the Caribbean has taken steps to define regional sustainable development guidelines. All stakeholders are playing their roles. The regional work carried out by entities such as the CTO, the Caribbean Hotel Association (CHA) through its subsidiary the Caribbean Alliance for Sustainable Tourism (CAST), the Association of Caribbean States (ACS), the Caribbean Natural Resources Institute (CANARI), the regional programmes of international entities such as the Pan American Health Organization (PAHO), and the environmental and development activities of the United Nations (e.g. those of UNEP and UNDP) have been complemented by different sized efforts in different areas at the national level.

A Regional Sustainable Tourism Policy Framework, prepared by CTO and approved by the Ministers of Tourism of the organization's 33 member countries, would facilitate the establishment of the Caribbean as a Sustainable Tourism Zone by harmonizing ongoing individual and regional initiatives. Under the guidance of CAST, hoteliers in the region are seeking certification by Green Globe 21, an international environmental management and awareness programme, in recognition of their commitment to implement environmental management systems. Throughout the Caribbean region, initiatives deserving recognition have been taken by individuals, communities, governmental entities and NGOs.

Southeast Asia is one of the world's fastest growing areas with respect to ecotourism development. There is a trend away from overcrowded beaches and resorts to more nature-based tourism. According to one Thai study, 30% of foreign and 67% of domestic tourists can be considered ecotourists. Malaysia has estimated that 10% of its tourists are ecotourists or nature tourists. A variety of coastal ecosystems are available in Southeast Asia for development of coastal ecotourism.

Diving is the most important activity; others include canoeing and those activities normally covered under marine ecotourism. According to the Professional Association of Diving Instructors (PADI), Malaysia, Thailand and the Philippines are important areas for the potential growth of scuba diving in Southeast Asia. Sabah in Malaysia, for example, has already experienced healthy growth in diving in recent years, with 15,000 to 20,000 overseas divers annually. Coastal resources in Southeast Asia are important sources of food for local villagers. Coral reefs provide half the animal protein in Indonesians' diet. While traditional harvesting has little impact on reefs, a minority of harvesters use harmful methods such as blasting or cyanide.

This is still a problem, for example, in both the Philippines and Indonesia. The demand for aquarium fish and live corals has aggravated reef degradation. Coral reefs are also affected by pollution and sedimentation from mining and other industries. Mangroves are cleared for shrimp and fish ponds, overlogged for timber and charcoal, and converted to land for housing and industries. Southeast Asian countries have systems (ranging from recently initiated to well-established) to protect their coastal resources in designated areas. Legislation exists but enforcement is often lacking. Thus, in practice marine protected areas are exploited.

For example, the Philippines and Indonesia have environmental laws but these are not enforced adequately. Biodiversity conservation is urgently required as damage to coastal resources becomes critical. In Indonesia, 6.49% of reefs are in excellent condition and 24.28 % are in good condition. Reefs in western Indonesia are in the worst condition, compared with those in middle and eastern Indonesia. In the Philippines, 5% of the reefs are in excellent condition and 70% in poor to fair condition. Mangroves have suffered a similar fate. In Indonesia, they were reduced from 4.2 million hectares in 1982 to 2.7 million in 2000.

Historically, coastal tourism in Southeast Asia began with a low impact on coastal resources and generated benefits to the local community. But as demand has increased, unplanned or uncontrolled development has contributed to environmental degradation (e.g. at Pattaya Thailand), Boracay (the Philippines) and Kuta (Indonesia). Some rehabilitation measures have been taken, including use of planned integrated resorts. As the trend is towards more nature-based tourism, reefs and mangroves are seen as potential resources for coastal ecotourism development.

Increasing pressure on coastal resources arises from the subsistence requirements of local communities, biodiversity conservation and recreational demands from tourists. It is in this context that coastal ecotourism can play an increasingly important role. Although the private sector has often been associated with abuse of the ecotourism concept, there are some examples of good practices in coastal ecotourism involving environmental planning and social responsibility.

These include the Sea-Canoe operation in southern Thailand and two resorts operated by Ten Knots in El Nido, North Palawan in the Philippines. These tend to be unique, high-end operations. Although not truly community-based, they are trailblazers compared with other private companies. Marine protected areas are normally developed for biodiversity conservation, with protection measures to ensure conservation while allowing maximum compatible usage. In the face of continual destruction of resources in marine protected areas, one approach has been to develop community-based sustainable tourism. CBST is based on two concepts: community-based management, and alternative livelihood.

According to the community-based management concept, regulatory power over natural resources is placed in the hands of resource users and stakeholders. Alternative livelihood focuses on providing a sustainable income, so that coastal residents need not resort to overfishing or use of destructive methods. If properly established, managed and promoted, ecotourism can generate increased income for coastal villages. The results are improved if ecotourism activities coincide with marine sanctuaries and other protected areas.

Community-based sanctuaries have therefore been developed in Indonesia and the Philippines, with strong links to community-based ecotourism as an alternative livelihood. This has operated through various projects on biodiversity management (e.g. the Biodiversity Conservation Network in the Padaido Islands, Indonesia), conservation (e.g. Conservation International in the Togean Islands), reef management (e.g. COREMAP in Indonesia) and coastal resources management. Continuous injection of funds is normally required in order to bring a community-based ecotourism project to a critical level of self-sufficiency before it becomes fully successful. Other approaches to protecting coastal resources and developing coastal ecotourism at the same time include adoption of villages by resort operators and patronage of villages by live-aboard vessels. Scuba certification agencies, airlines, hotels and equipment manufacturers can also support environmental agencies that contribute directly to the local people, in order to eradicate destructive fishing and ultimately save coral reefs.

Development of coastal ecotourism is not an easy undertaking. It requires investment, skills and marketing. However, it is suitable for small-scale enterprises, which are often thought to provide the maximum benefits to the local community in that facilities and services can be easily provided by locals. The small-scale enterprise is sometimes seen as community-based tourism. In the Gili Islands off Lombok, Indonesia, the success of a small-scale enterprise depends on a local entrepreneur, who can initiate, sustain, and act as diffuser for the rest of community. At one stage of its success, the government resettled the small-scale enterprises of Gili Trawangan to a defined area with individual lots. Thailand has had a national commitment to ecotourism since 1993, beginning with the carrying out of studies and cooperation among agencies involved in tourism.

Ecotourism policies and guidelines were made available subsequently, with many policies and plans placed under the responsibility of different organizations prior to 1998. Ecotourism's potential was recognized and it was included in the tourism plan for 1998-2003. Ecotourism is one of the components of the National Tourism Master Plan 2001-2010. Thailand, the leader in ecotourism development in Southeast Asia, is noted for its hill trekking, scuba diving and nature tours, which started in the mid 1970s. Thailand has the greatest number of protected areas in Southeast Asia.

All parks are under the Royal Forestry Department (RFD). From 1993, marine national parks were managed separately from terrestrial parks but still under the RFD. Up to 1999, there were 21 marine national parks along the Andaman Sea and the Gulf of Thailand. They received about 2.5 million visitors, a third of whom were foreigners and fewer than 15% of whom stayed overnight. The RFD's responsibilities include resource protection and development projects. However, there are constraints on their responsibilities and efforts, including inadequately trained personnel, lack of proper management, and lack of adequate facilities for visitors.

The thin line between conservation and tourism has become an issue, as the Tourism Authority of Thailand (TAT) provides funds for the RFD to build additional tourist facilities in 19 protected areas. The marine parks in southern Thailand are a top priority for development because of their strong potential. Last year entrance fees doubled for foreigners, but for Thais they remain low and have not changed. The increased fee provides ecotourism revenue.

It is also part of a wider strategy to reduce the number of tourists, whose impact on the parks is beginning to be negative.

For example, the popularity of Phuket as a tourist destination has affected marine parks from Phangnga Bay to the Surin Islands. During the peak season, the Similan Islands are overcrowded due to live-aboard tours. Encroachment by neighbouring villagers and illegal developers is still a major problem in the protected areas, e.g. Koh Samet, Phuket and Krabi. Encroachment has intensified in recent years. Legal action has been taken by the RFD. Unable to remove all the developers on Koh Samet, the RFD has proposed legalizing the remaining ones on short leases.

However, given past park mismanagement and the drive to develop ecotourism, legalization of illegal developers may not be a suitable measure as it may seen as encouraging further encroachment. More power has been vested in provincial and local areas regarding tourism development. In March 1998, the government established tourism promotion and development committees for provincial and local areas (tambon administrative organization). These facilitate development and management of coastal ecotourism, since *ad hoc* subcommittees on ecotourism can be established within this structure.

The new administrative structure replaces a previous liberal system with few or no controls. The tambon administrative councils now have greater authority to control the use of local natural resources. In the mid 1990s, Conservation International identified the Philippines as a country with tremendous ecotourism potential. It urged the government to develop ecotourism products. Clear and strong action was taken by the government with the passing of the National Ecotourism Act 1998. This Act sets out the institutional framework for a national ecotourism strategy, to be supported by a programme and a network of sites to be identified as National Integrated and Protected Areas (NIPAS) as well as other areas.

A national policy-making body, the National Ecotourism Development Council (NEDC), has been created to establish the national strategy and is supported by regional committees. The first national ecotourism congress was held in 1999 to finalize a national ecotourism master plan. In Philippines, the national ecotourism master plan is being finalized, the Department of Tourism (DOT) has identified four locations for ecotourism, three of which are islands. Bohol is marketed by the DOT as a prime ecotourism destination because of its diving sites and beaches. The DOT has also identified Coron Island (Palawan) and El Nido Marine Reserve (Palawan) as marine protected areas suitable for coastal ecotourism.

In 1998, several choice ecotourism spots were designated National Integrated and Protected Areas (NIPAs). These include Olango Island, with a wildlife sanctuary of about 1000 hectares. Palawan has been well-marketed by the ecotourism private sector and was recently identified in a study by the Japan International Cooperation Agency (JICA) as an area that will receive approximately $200 million in tourism development investment in the next decade. To some extent, Palawan's successful ecotourism image is the result of collective environmental awareness efforts. The province has been environmentally protected since 1992. The government (Palawan Council for Sustainable Development), city government (Puerto Princesa), NGOs and Palawan residents are involved in environmental protection. There is zoning of land and marine areas for tourism activities. Despite the higher awareness of environment, there are still some problems such as lack of enforcement, especially in the private sector.

Coastal ecotourism within a CRM (coastal resources management) framework is exemplified by two successful initiatives. Another CRM ecotourism project is located at Cambuhat, northwest Bohol. Here the project is based on Cambuhat's river, mangrove, estuary and lowland ecosystems, the community oyster farm along the river, and products made from local materials. The Philippines' potential for strong development of coastal ecotourism is linked to increasing environmental protection, reef conservation, alternative livelihood and marine protected areas. Pariwisata 21 (Tourism in the 21 Century) is the Indonesian government's vision and mission for tourism. This master plan, finalized in 1997, integrates the policies of 27 provinces.

Ecotourism is included, but there is some confusion. Although no national ecotourism strategy has been finalized, the Indonesian government issued new regulations in April 1994 dealing with the operation of nature tourism businesses in protected areas and requiring them to be implemented in accordance with the principle of conservation of biological natural resources and their ecosystems. In 1999, a new step was taken with respect to marine policy when Indonesia's coasts and seas came under a single Ministry of Marine Exploration and Fisheries. This has implications for coastal ecotourism.

As the political situation initially calmed down, the government wanted to rebuild the tourist industry by shifting the focus from land-based tourism to marine and ecologically based tourism (i.e. coastal ecotourism). The marine tourism policy was meant to attract investment in diving and cruising, especially in the eastern part of country, which has a large number of islands and has lagged behind the western part economically. However, political unrest has recently increased in eastern Indonesia. With the 1999 law on regional autonomy, there has been a rapid devolution of government. Substantial powers have been given to kabupaten/kota-madya (regency/municipality) governments, of which there are about 350. With political reforms and foreign aid, scuba diving operators and villagers are taking measures to protect coastal resources.

Villages have seized the opportunity for community involvement in resource management, as can be seen in reef protection efforts. Recent reef patrols in Komodo National Park, sponsored by scuba diving operators and The Nature Conservancy, were controversial as they divide the communities that welcome protection and those that resent intrusion by a foreign NGO. Such measures are more successful in the local communities around Bunaken National Park, which have charged $5 per diver, paid by the North Sulawesi Watersports Association. Malaysia was the first in the region to have a National Ecotourism Plan, completed in late 1995. This plan lists existing and potential ecotourism areas, focusing on 42 areas and highlighting ten areas including some coastal/riverine ones.

Malaysia adopted the IUCN definition of ecotourism. An action plan serves to implement, manage, strengthen and build the capacity of ecotourism areas. While functioning as a guideline for operators of (and participants in) ecotourism packages, the plan was set up to tap ecotourism's vast potential and is a tool for sustainable development of the tourism industry. Malaysia's ecotourism products are varied and well-known, e.g. Taman Negara,

Mount Kina-balu, the orangutan, and the caves and diving sites available on many islands and in Sabah.

Many small islands have faced similar infrastructure problems, e.g. with water and supplies. Islands in marine parks in peninsular Malaysia are not necessarily protected. The need for security of another kind was made evident when tourists on Sipidan Island in Sabah were recently kidnapped. Malaysian coastal villages are relatively well-off and developed. Thus, there is no community-based approach in coastal ecotourism similar to that of the Philippines or Indonesia. In recent years the homestay programme has been introduced and implemented in Johor, Kedah, Mela-ka, Pahang, Perak and Selangor. This programme is based on the concept of bread and breakfast. Tourists stay in fishing villages or on farms.

About 25,000 tourists have signed up. Potential for coastal ecotourism exists in Sabah and in peninsular Malaysia. Sarawak has little coastal ecotourism, although this state is in the second phase of an ecotourism plan up to 2005. Malaysia continues to develop and upgrade its coastal ecotourism through more systematic monitoring of the quality of island ecotourism and homestay packages. Apart from the private sector, much depends on local governments, island development authorities and island management boards guiding islands' coastal ecotourism. For example, island carrying capacity needs to be determined Viet Nam is a relatively newcomer to the tourist industry. As the state is both the regulator and a key operator, governmental conflicts of interest sometimes arise.

At the national level, the Viet Nam National Administration of Tourism (VNAT) and its Institute for Tourism Development Research (ITDR) are in charge of tourism. The state recently recognized ecotourism's importance. A National Ecotourism Strategy was developed in 1999. There are plans to develop tourism in the coastal area during the next ten years, with the coast from Quang Ninh Province to Ha Tinh Province having the greatest potential. Symptomatic of the problems and conflicts involved in overall tourism development, Viet Nam faces major problems with coastal ecotourism (e.g. environmental degradation, poor infrastructure, poor management, lack of investment). In the case of marine parks, problems include cross-management conflicts.

There are unclear or conflicting responsibilities for tourism within protected areas, as national parks are under the Forest Protection Department (FPD) while tourism development is the responsibility of the provinces and districts. Few protected areas currently have the capability or means to plan for, manage and develop ecotourism. There are conflicts between national park managers and provincial or district authorities concerning the priorities for, and development of, tourism within protected areas. There is a case for more international assistance (financial, technical, etc.) to demonstrate and promote the benefits of coastal ecotourism and conservation in Viet Nam.

Conditions are suitable for ecotourism pilot projects to demonstrate cross-sectoral collaboration (involving key stakeholders, e.g. the FPD, national park management, local communities). One focus is on Halong Bay, declared a UNESCO World Heritage site in 1994, where development of coastal ecotourism is not based solely on limestone islands but also includes the floating fishing population. Within the bay, coral reefs face the threats of illegal blast fishing, pollution from coal mining, and shipping to and from the harbour. Halong Bay could be the first site in the country to show positive links with coastal ecotourism and conservation. Australia's Nature and Ecotourism Accreditation Programme (NEAP) is the first scheme of its type in the world. It was designed to provide a mechanism by which the country's nature tourism and ecotourism sectors could continue to work towards the ideal of long-term environmental, socio-cultural and economic sustainability.

The programme is a voluntary, industry-based initiative developed in consultation with key stakeholder groups. It aims to provide those working at the sector's coalface - the operators - with a way to gain knowledge of best practice principles, apply techniques within their own operations that contribute towards sustainability, and embark upon a programme of continual improvement. NEAP was also developed to provide consumers and protected area managers with a way to recognize operators of genuine nature tourism and ecotourism products, thus conferring marketing and other operational benefits.

NEAP is now in its fifth year of operation, with over 300 accredited products. NEAP was conceived and developed as an industry driven and run programme. Development of an accreditation programme was identified in Australia's National Ecotourism Strategy as a key way to help ensure sustainability, raise industry standards, provide a means of industry self-regulation, and deliver marketing advantages to Australian ecotourism operators. Seed funding provided by Australia's Office of National Tourism for initial establishment of NEAP was augmented by substantial in-kind support from key organizations and individuals.

The programme is now owned by the Ecotourism Association of Australia (EAA). In administrative terms, it operates as a separate, self-funding non-profit entity. However, NEAP's viability in a wider sense (e.g. continued development and monitoring of standards) relies to a great extent on the commitment of a team of dedicated professionals, who give all or part of their time to the programme on a voluntary basis. From its inception, NEAP has been a collaborative and consultative effort.

The programme's initial and ongoing development has drawn on the collective expertise of individuals involved in fields as diverse as protected area management; guiding and guide training; environmental consulting; business accreditation; and tourism marketing. Another feature has been extensive communication and consultation with the programme's key constituents, operators and protected area managers, facilitated by pilot studies, workshops, newsletter articles and conference papers. The result is a programme that not only provides comprehensive criteria for assessing nature tourism and ecotourism products, but also seeks to create linkages with existing tourism business accreditation programmes and protected area licensing systems. An honorary Panel consisting of two EAA representatives, two tourism industry representatives and an independent Chair oversees the management of NEAP. The Panel usually meets monthly via teleconferencing to discuss accreditation applications and general management issues.

A central tenet of NEAP is the inclusion of a continuous improvement programme, which allows it to remain current with (if not to lead) the latest best practice principles and technologies, as well as to respond to the changing needs of the industry. NEAP was developed to apply to products (tours, attractions, accommodation) in two industry sectors: nature tourism and ecotourism. Nature tourism is ecologically sustainable tourism with a primary focus on experiencing natural areas.

Ecotourism is ecologically sustainable tourism, with a primary focus on experiencing natural areas that fosters environmental and cultural understanding, appreciation and conservation. Using these definitions as a basis, NEAP has developed a range of principles of eligibility for accreditation, each encompassing specific core and bonus assessment criteria against which products are assessed. As suggested by the definitions, ecotourism products must satisfy a wider range of assessment criteria than nature tourism, although products in both sectors must meet the same standard for natural area focus, environmental sustainability, responsible marketing and customer satisfaction. The key "filter" for distinguishing ecotourism products from nature tourism is interpretation.

Products must meet 100% of applicable core criteria to be eligible for nature tourism or ecotourism accreditation. A product meeting 100% of ecotourism core criteria as well as an additional 80% or more of bonus criteria (including further compulsory core criteria relating to interpretation) is eligible for advanced ecotourism accreditation. Provision is also made for discretionary bonus points, to be awarded for examples of innovative best practice. The application process for accreditation under the programme is based on self-assessment, augmented by a system of referee checks and audits.

While NEAP has received some criticism for implementing an application system based on self-assessment rather than independent audit, this has proved the most effective means of ensuring that the programme remains as cost-effective and non-threatening to operators as possible. Given that the vast majority of Australian ecotourism businesses are small if not micro in size, the expense associated with incorporating an on-site independent audit into the application process would simply put the programme out of their financial reach - thus negating the programme's aim of improving sustainability across the board. Additionally, the scope of the criteria means operators do not always have all the necessary management practices in place that would allow them to seek accreditation immediately after expressing interest in the programme.

For example, operators may focus heavily on the environmental management aspects of their businesses, to the detriment of other considerations such as providing interpretation of a suitable standard or engaging in consultation with traditional custodians. NEAP is also currently an industry partner, along with Tourism Tasmania and Tourism Council Tasmania, in a state-based pilot programme aimed at finding ways business and sector-specific accreditation can work together to the benefit of operators. Another significant development has been the recent launch of the EAA's EcoGuide Programme, designed as a complementary initiative to NEAP. The EcoGuide Programme is a certification scheme intended to provide nature tourism and ecotourism guides that meet specified competencies and standards with voluntary, industry-based "qualification".

NEAP has consistently generated a great deal of interest on the part of international researchers and tourism professionals. In November 2000, two members of the NEAP Panel were invited to attend a three-day workshop convened by the Institute for Policy Studies and the Ford Foundation on ecotourism and sustainable tourism certification/ accreditation. NEAP is also one of the few programmes that ascribes such fundamental importance to the integration of interpretation into ecotourism products.

However, it was also apparent that some aspects of the programme, particularly in the area of social justice (e.g. work-place relations, appropriateness of land acquisition) could be interpreted as inadequate when looked at outside the Australian legislative context. According to the World Tourism Organization (WTO), in 2000 world tourism grew by an estimated 7.4%. A record 698 million international trips were made in 2000 (WTO, 2001).

The number of domestic tourists is estimated to be probably as much as ten times the number of international tourists. Clearly tourism has a paramount economic role for countries around the world and, if planned and managed correctly, can significantly contribute to sustainable socio-economic development and environmental conservation. The appropriate interaction between biodiversity conservation planning and tourism planning and development has become a key concern for many institutions at the local, national and international levels.

The Biodiversity Planning Support Programme (BPSP) of UNEP/UNDP/GEF has a mandate to provide assistance to national biodiversity conservation planners as they develop and implement their national biodiversity strategies and action plans. Sustainable tourism has been highlighted recently as an area of major concern within the Convention on Biological Diversity (CBD). It was the focus of attention at the recent Conference of Parties in Nairobi (UNEP/CBD/COP/5/20). For the above reasons, BPSP is presently carrying out a study on integration of biodiversity into the tourism sector - with a specific focus on how best to incorporate "global best practice" into national biodiversity strategy and action plans.

Ecotourism in Costa Rica has experienced an interesting evolution over the last 20 years or so. Over the past five or six years the government authorities, with the strong collaboration of the tourism industry and a number of NGOs, have been endeavouring to consolidate the tourism process, fostering tourism activity with a strong nature component but with a multi-phased and varied character, diversifying the line of tourism products and services offered. The government now faces the challenge of integrating ecotourism into a diverse mosaic of tourist activities and attractions with the aim of offering a single extensive tourist product: "a peaceful, green, and clean country".

This is not an easy task, as there seems to be a dual policy of heavily marketing Costa Rica's natúral areas and ecotourism attractions, and at the same time trying to augment visitor numbers by means of huge beach resorts and urban hotels owned by transnational chains, cruise ships and prepaid air charter tours. From 1995 to 1998, tourism was the country's top dollar earner. Although still growing, in 1999 and 2000 it moved to second place due to the surge of high-technology industry, especially electronics. An important achievement of the Costa Rican government has been the division of the country into eleven "conservation areas", by means of which the National System of Conservation Areas (SINAC's) administration covers all the national territory in protected areas as well as in the rest of the territory, where biodiversity conservation is promoted and regulated. Apart from State-administered protected areas, Costa Rica has an important and very successful network of private reserves, established as non-profit entities.

Most of the associated reserves are involved in ecotourism activities. Despite the many bright points of ecotourism development in Costa Rica, there are still many shortcomings with respect to the harmonious interaction between tourism and conservation. These can be summarized in terms of three closely interrelated issues: inefficient coordination between responsible parties, serious negative environmental impacts of non-planned tourism, and a generalized lack of environmental awareness in society of the importance of sustainable tourism. The main challenge for Costa Rica is maintaining a high level of quality in its important ecotourism industry, while finding ways to provide more tangible benefits from this process for the national park system and preserving the country's unique biodiversity heritage. Tourism, which is the fourth largest generator of foreign exchange in South Africa, also ranks third in its contribution to the economy.

Although South Africa attracted just 0.9% of total world tourism arrivals internationally in 1998, tourism was the economic sector with the most significant growth in the country, having generated an income of US$ 8.9 billion. There were 5.9 million foreign visitors in 1999. The dominant forms of nature-based and adventure tourism include safari tourism, whale watching, white water rafting, hiking, bird watching, 4x4 trails, bush survival, deep-sea fishing, hunting and diving. There are also excellent opportunities for cultural tourism activities.

The most popular activity undertaken within the foreign visitor market is visiting game and nature reserves, followed by visits to historic sites. South Africa is one of the 17 "megadiversity" countries. It is one of the Earth's biologically wealthiest countries and probably has the highest level of plant endemism in the world. South Africa has 422 formally protected areas covering approximately 6% of the land surface area. There are also 160 privately owned reserves, apart from several thousand privately owned game farms that attract large numbers of ecotourists. Many privately owned game reserves (which are now basically ecotourism destinations) adjoin public protected areas, by which the area effectively protected is vastly increased.

There are a number of policy links between tourism development and biodiversity conservation and planning in South Africa. However, there is a perceived institutional gap in that there is no overall structure overseeing and coordinating biodiversity conservation and tourism planning in the nine provinces. Each of the provincial conservation authorities acts independently. These authorities do not answer to a central regulating body. In addition, successful conservation and tourism strategies are not efficiently transferred between agencies. Ecotourism has been playing a dual role in the new post-apartheid South Africa, serving to reintegrate the nation into the world economy and to help redress grievances and redistribute wealth to the country's poor.

Ecotourism is recognized as a tool for social change. A number of the community-based ecotourism developments sprouting up around South Africa are providing opportunities for sustainable development among local populations. It is important to remember that the apartheid era ended only a few years ago. A new South Africa is emerging, with great expectations but also considerable risks. The great challenge is to reduce the enormous socioeconomic gap between the white and black populations.

Ecotourism may play a key role in this endeavour, but that will require major efforts by all the parties involved as well as intensive training programmes. Tourism is the biggest contributor to Belize's economy. In 1999 it accounted for approximately 18% of GDP, 25% of total foreign exchange earnings, and one in four jobs.The trend during the past ten years has shown a steady increase in visitation. This small country, with its well preserved rain forests containing a wealth of biodiversity, its Mayan archaeological sites and living Mayan culture, and the second longest barrier reef in the world, has an enviable ecotourism resource base to present to the world.

Samoa's sustainable tourism objectives set the targets for the future of tourism in Samoa. They show how tourism's potential can be utilized, not only for economic ends but also to achieve environmental, social and cultural development. These objectives can be used as the basis for tourism action plans, to assist operators in considering the wider implications of their businesses and to serve as the benchmarks against which indicators can be used to evaluate tourism. With Samoa's sustainable tourism objectives in place, there was a clear need to develop sustainable tourism indicators to monitor performance. In the past, the tourism industry has relied on economic indicators to gauge its success. However, these only tell part of the story.

The number of tourist arrivals tells nothing about the impact of tourism in rural areas, and the amount of money tourists spend tells nothing about where the money goes. Sustainable tourism indicators focus on the linkages between tourism resources and the country's environment and culture, giving a more holistic picture of the sector's performance as well as the tools for anticipating adverse situations. The indicators should provide the impetus for action before valuable assets are irreversibly damaged. To be effective, Samoa's sustainable tourism indicators had to be carefully selected to suit the situation in Samoa, the expectations of tourism stakeholders, and the research capacity and resources of the SVB. The aim was to develop one or two indicators to monitor each sustainable tourism objective.

Issues in Leisure and Tourism

Leisure and tourism are fashion-led, and have seen a recent development boom. The nature of these sectors poses challenges for local planning authorities, and raises several key issues. Whilst the economic value of tourism is broadly acknowledged, planning policies may reflect a more ambivalent approach towards other forms of leisure which are often viewed neutrally or even negatively. Planning policies that follow from such attitudes may need to be re-evaluated to take account of new social trends and the growth of leisure in the overall economy.

As part of this, assuming that the development boom is likely to be sustained, it will be important to establish whether there are identifiable land use implications, and what these might be. Leisure and tourism developments will have economic development, community and environmental impacts, including those associated with travel and trip generation. It is not clear whether these are adequately understood and given due weight in the planning process.

3

Hospitality Management

'Hospitality is characterised by a core which addresses the management of food, beverage and/or accommodation in a service context'. The defining characteristic of any programme will be the study of the management and technical disciplines relevant to hospitality. It is expected that the learning and assessment experience of all students will be contextualised to the areas covered by this definition. Provision of hospitality education stems from a highly vocational focus.

Programmes in hospitality have evolved significantly beyond this vocational focus to combine technical, management and scientific disciplines as a coherent whole. Within hospitality, programmes in hotel and restaurant management, food studies, culinary arts and international hospitality management offer students some degree of specialisation.

The diversity of the hospitality industry has also led to the development of new areas for study such as licensed retail management and events management. It is expected that this diversity will be maintained so that institutions can respond to the constantly evolving needs of students and employers. Most programmes will approach the study of hospitality with an emphasis on management.

Hospitality degree programmes will, typically, involve the following components:

- the management of technical operations such as food and beverage and accommodation
- the management disciplines within the context of hospitality
- the hospitality industry and its global environment
- the hospitality consumer and the service encounter
- the opportunity to participate in a period of industrial placement.

Typical subject areas might include food and beverage production and service, facilities management, design and planning, food safety, quality assurance, food science and microbiology, operations management, human resources management, law, services marketing, consumer behaviour, financial management, organisational behaviour, strategic management, small business management, entrepreneurship, information technology. In addition students will normally be given the chance for specialist study which might include languages, licensed retail, tourism and leisure management.

The nature of leisure is taken to mean the full range of activities, processes and meanings associated with non-work time, although not exclusively so, recognizing that the boundaries between work and leisure are blurred. This would specifically include both rational recreation forms as well as forms of cultural consumption often connected with the popular and commercial sectors. While some aspects of the study of leisure will focus upon, or around, purpose-built facilities these are not the only resources or practices that may be associated with leisure programmes.

Thus, the term "leisure" refers to a broad range of cultural and recreational activities and experiences by which people through engagement in a variety of formal or informal modes of participation, seek to enhance the quality of their lives. The growth of degree programmes in leisure reflects the present organisation of work and the attendant implications for societies. Programmes have rapidly increased in number over the past fifteen years in response to structural changes in society, including the decline of manufacturing, the growth of the leisure industries and a parallel expansion in applied leisure research. The outcome has been diversity and a wide ranging number of programmes which cover a variety of areas including the public, private and voluntary organised sector of this fast growing industry.

Leisure has grown into a flourishing inter-disciplinary field of academic endeavour underpinned by a number of academic associations, internationally recognised journals and a substantive literature. Many programmes reflect this inter-disciplinary perspective and consequently leisure is studied for its inherent contribution to an understanding of contemporary society, as well as because this will contribute to the student's employability and career preparation.

While most programmes include some consideration of all of the areas of study below, different courses have different emphases. Many programmes have management in the title. Some of these focus particularly on business or organisational management. Others with management in the title are more concerned with the management of leisure resources through concepts of planning and policy. The honours graduate will satisfy the characteristics of one of the two principal approaches of "Studies" or "Management".

Leisure degree programmes will typically involve the study of one or more of the following:

— historical, philosophical, economic, political, sociological and psychological dimensions of leisure

— the structure, composition and management of the leisure industries

— the construction of the leisure experience in a range of managerial contexts comprising products, services and opportunities

— the disaggregation of leisure into concepts, activities, functions and meanings and

— the implications of these for personal and professional actions differential patterns of leisure consumption and use key directions and trends in the assembly of knowledge about leisure

Typical subject areas include, concepts of leisure, the leisure environment, women's studies, the sociology of leisure, the philosophy of leisure, sports studies, countryside recreation studies, arts and entertainment, recreation, leisure economics, leisure events, events management, leisure operations, leisure development, leisure policy, leisure planning, leisure resources management, leisure facilities management, leisure strategies and the management of leisure.

In programmes of study with sport in the title, sport refers to personal, social and cultural activity embraced within the participation, organisation, provision, and delivery of sporting activity, as defined by the Council of Europe: 'Sport means all forms of physical activity which, through casual or organised participation, aim at expressing or improving physical fitness and mental well-being, forming social relationships or obtaining results in competition at all levels'.

For the most part, the study of sport is centred on socially and culturally acknowledged forms of sporting activity, and on its performance (both in preparation and execution), provision, and social and cultural impact. Recently there has been increased interest in the relationship between physical activity and health.

Degree programmes in Sport have increased significantly over the past fifteen years in response to the growth in provision and employment in the leisure and service sector, and the interest and demand created by related school and post-school qualifications. The outcome has been innovative and wide-ranging sport-related programmes. Their currency and diversity is demonstrated by the orientation towards sport and exercise sciences, sports coaching, sport development and sport management.

Sport has emerged as an academic area with a developing body of knowledge. This is characterised by a balance of discipline-based knowledge and knowledge derived from the practice of sport. With programmes adopting a multi-disciplinary and/or inter-disciplinary approach, the study of sport has intrinsic intellectual value. At the same time programmes of study will enhance, to a varying extent, the students' employability and career preparation.

The breadth of coverage within sport is substantial and there are considerable differences of emphasis in content and approach to reflect, for example, science-based or management-based programmes of study. It is anticipated there will be a significant degree of flexibility and interpretation when institutions develop their programmes of study within this benchmark framework.

Sport degree programmes will typically involve the study of one or more of the following: human responses and adaptations to sport and exercise the performance of sport and exercise and its enhancement, monitoring and analysis historical, social, political, economic and cultural diffusion, distribution and impact of sport policy, planning, management and delivery of sporting opportunities.

The term tourism refers to the phenomena and relationships arising from the travel and stay of people away from their normal home environments for a variety of purposes. Programmes with tourism in the title typically have their origins in providing a vocational understanding relevant for potential employment in some or all of the components of what is loosely referred to as the tourism industry. This includes activities in the private sector such as tour operators, airlines and hotel companies, as well as public and not-for-profit bodies such as tourist boards.

Most programmes have broadened from their vocational origins to embrace wider issues relating to the nature, impacts and meanings of tourism, thereby furnishing an understanding of what is now a major world phenomenon. However, most programmes still lay emphasis on career and vocational objectives. Over the past fifteen years the number of programmes in tourism has proliferated. They have a wide range of titles. The most common are 'Tourism Management', 'Tourism', 'Leisure and Tourism Management' and 'Tourism Studies' but also included are other titles reflecting the focus of particular programmes such as 'Travel Agency Management', 'Sports Tourism', 'Rural Tourism', 'Sustainable Tourism'. Of the programmes with management in the title many focus particularly on business management. Others are more concerned with the management of scarce resources in the community through concepts of planning and public policy.

However, graduates of all programmes in Hospitality, Leisure, Sport or Tourism will be able to demonstrate: a critical understanding of the development of knowledge in their particular subject domain an understanding of the need for both a multi-disciplinary and inter-disciplinary approach to study, drawing, as appropriate, from service, research and professional contexts their understanding of the subject through both academic and professional reflective practice their research and problem-solving abilities by critically understanding methods of acquiring, interpreting and analysing information appropriate to their context of study an understanding and critical awareness of, the moral, ethical, environmental and legal issues which underpin best practice.

The typical graduates of programmes in Hospitality, Leisure, Sport or Tourism will have developed a range of intellectual skills including being able to:

— research and assess subject specific facts, theories, paradigms, principles and concepts
— critically assess and evaluate evidence
— critically interpret data and text
— describe and analyse information
— apply knowledge to the solution of familiar and unfamiliar problems develop a reasoned argument and challenge assumptions take responsibility for their own learning and continuing professional development.

Skills will be developed in various ways largely depending upon the subject domain within which the student is studying. The range of skills will normally include some or all of the following with graduates being able to: plan, design and execute practical activities using appropriate techniques and procedures undertake fieldwork with due regard for safety and risk assessment plan, design, execute and communicate a sustained piece of independent intellectual work using appropriate media recognise and respond to moral, ethical and safety issues which directly pertain to the subject domain including relevant legislation and professional codes of conduct.

A typical honours graduate in Hospitality will be able to:

— use technical and interpersonal skills and knowledge to propose and evaluate practical and theoretical solutions to complex problems in the core areas of hospitality:

— operate and manage human and technical resources apply theory to the solution of complex problems within the core areas of hospitality analyse and evaluate food, beverage and/or accommodation service systems, their implementation and operation.

— recognise and value the centrality of the hospitality consumer and meet and respond to their needs: understand and apply the theories and concepts underpinning consumer behaviour within the hospitality context analyse the needs and expectations of different hospitality consumers and develop appropriate responses analyse the quality of the service encounter and its impact on the hospitality consumer and the service provider.

— identify and respond appropriately to the diversity that prevails within the hospitality industry in relation to stakeholders such as: hospitality consumers, hospitality employees, hospitality organisations, government and external agencies.

The hospitality industry consists of a large number of different types of business, with each one having its own means of producing income. The main types of businesses in the category of hospitality are hotels, self-catering accommodation, guest houses, restaurants, pubs and bars and tourist resorts. Each style of establishment has one thing in common—they all add value to their business activity by providing a place for guests and giving service in exchange for a fee.

The difference between what it costs the hospitality establishment to provide the place and the service, and the fee received in return, is called profit. Bedrooms, bars, restaurants, room service, leisure facilities and valet service, etc. are called 'products' or 'outlets' by the industry. Each product or outlet is expected to contribute to the hotel's income, which is why they can also be referred to as 'profit-earning centres'. A hotel and other tourist accommodation receives most of its income from its main product, which is room hire or accommodation, representing around 45 per cent of its total revenue. This is why a hotel's occupancy rate (the number of customers occupying beds) is of continuing concern to the management of a property. Currently, annual average room occupancy varies between around 60 per cent and 70 per cent depending on geographic location. That means, on average throughout the year, between 60 per cent and 70 per cent of available rooms should be occupied.

Obviously, some months the percentage will be lower and other months it will be higher than the average. For those hotels which are dependent on the business traveller, fewer rooms will be occupied on weekends than on working days. One of the management's marketing jobs therefore is to fill the down periods with customers to maintain the desired occupancy percentage average. They do this by offering special-value packages, weekend rates and holiday package rates. Providing rooms for guests requires a considerable investment by the owners of a property in the building, its facilities and fittings. This money is recovered over a period of time by including a fixed amount (called capital recovery) into the room rate.

As well as providing a comfortable, often stylish property for guests to stay in, the hotel has to employ staff for cleaning, maintenance, reception, guest services and sales. In addition, it has to have people to manage and administrate. There are many sundry costs involved in the running of a hotel. These expenses, largely involving labour, are termed 'general overheads', and they too are incorporated as a percentage of the room rate. The amount which is charged for room rate, the end price to the guest, depends on three factors: (1) the perceived value to guests provided by the hotel's property and services; (2) the market demand for hotel facilities and services prevailing at the time; (3) the intensity of competition offered by other hotel operators. After room hire, the next highest income earner for hotels is food and beverage sales—that is, their restaurants, bars, coffee shops, room service and the food and beverage required for functions, conferences, etc.

Industry figures indicate that food sales account for around 34 per cent and beverages for 14 per cent of most UK hotel incomes. Minor operating departments, including telephone calls made by guests, provide a further 5 per cent of income. Rentals for shops owned by a property, such as a hairdresser, florist, newsagent, clothes shop, etc., contribute 1 per cent. These businesses are often independent operators who gain customers from the hotel's guests. The remaining 1 per cent of a hotel's income is contributed by services paid by guests for such things as laundry, valet, leisure facilities, health club, etc., depending on the type of operation. Apart from the establishments which provide accommodation only, nearly every other type of hospitality business makes money from food and beverage sales. They buy raw materials, such as food produce and beverages, and add value by using labour to turn them into some form of value added product or service for sale to customers.

As a general rule for food and beverage types of outlets, the cost of materials amounts to about a third of the sale price; the labour required to make and service the products amounts to another third; and the remaining third is gross profit. The gross profit has to allow for a percentage to cover either capital recovery or rent and the general overheads. What is left is net profit before tax. Owners and managers of establishments endeavour to minimise the running costs of materials, labour, overheads, interest paid on capital and rent so that they can maximise the amount of profit. This requires a careful balance between what the customers are prepared to pay and how much it costs to provide the products. The marketing function has to take this balance into consideration. Its purpose is to find customers and meet their demands by providing products and services which have sufficient value to attract them to buy at the right price. There are many factors to consider in marketing planning.

The principles involved are universal and can be adapted to almost any business or organisational activity. To continue with the analogy of marketing and a journey, there has to be a destination and a reason for going there. These are called marketing objectives. One has to prepare for the journey and find out as much as possible about what can be seen and enjoyed at the ultimate destination. It is wise to be prepared for any likely happening. This is market analysis. The means of getting there, the route to be taken and how the problems of travel can be overcome are called strategies. Strategies are designed to achieve objectives. Any establishment is totally in the hands of its people and their skills. Hiring the right staff is therefore vital.

A good manager does not 'control' people in the sense of using fear as a control mechanism, nor does a good manager use heavy authoritarian direction. Effective management is about giving direction by setting goals, allocating tasks and then facilitating, making it possible for the staff to do their work effectively and efficiently. This is management by measurement. It also uses negotiation with individuals when there is conflict. In a restaurant each persons work is particularly dependent upon someone else doing theirs. It is team work that makes an operation 'click'. If one person is causing a hitch in the procedures, not only will others in the chain be affected will the customer. Management's job is to make sure that each of the five systems is in place and happening the way it should. Management has to constantly observe and monitor each person's work and step in to help a person who is in trouble.

To achieve this there has to be a description of each person's function which can be measured against a norm, an average expectation of how and by when the activity should happen. The degree of competence required to perform a task has to be measurable. The Employee Performance Appraisal is one of several types of forms that can be completed by a supervisor for the purpose of assessing an employee in a general way. Far more precise is the form that can be used to assess a job function, which outlines a customer outcome and the performance criteria necessary to achieve it. The gradings are 'U' (unsatisfactory), 'S' (satisfactory) and 'E' (exceptional). Those who are 'unsatisfactory' need counselling or training. On some occasions, a person performing to an unsatisfactory level is unable to perform because of factors beyond his or her control.

For example, sometimes other people in the service team are obstructing the procedures, or it may be a piece of unreliable equipment. Another problem may be the procedure itself which is incapable of fulfilment in the time allocated. Measuring performance reveals problems. If a person proves to be unable to perform the task according to the performance criteria, other tasks will have to be allocated or the person dismissed. The customer outcome must be achieved. The purpose of 'control' in the sense of 'managing' is the development of a working culture, easing the interaction between people, smoothing the handling of procedures and maintaining the service momentum.

In the capacity of 'facilitator', whoever is responsible for supervising the service functions has to provide information and advice, training skills and staff development, and make changes when necessary to bring the marketing process into line with the marketing plan. In most service teams there are people who are natural catalysts around whom the service tasks flow more easily. They should be constantly acknowledged and rewarded. Unfortunately, there are also the odd 'rotten apples' who may be efficient enough at what they do but who are critical of management, find fault with others and are generally disagreeable.

Regrettably, people like that have to be removed because their presence has the opposite effect of the catalysts, causing friction and unfriendly feelings. Management or the directors, having approved the marketing plan, then have to keep up the required resources to fuel the plan's ultimate realisation. A shrug of the shoulders and an acceptance of unavoidable difficulties is seldom appreciated by disgruntled clients, quickly leading to a rapid downturn in sales and profit. Systems are in place in any well-run establishment for a reason other than keeping the customers; they are also essential to avoid unnecessary losses. Lax management can lead to staff dispensing free drinks or pilfering. Ignorance of the basic human motivations leads to staff discontent, which in turn leads to indifference, dissatisfaction and poor service, often with disastrous financial consequences.

Fear and coercion are the last resort motivators. A working culture and environment which provides people with esteem, pride and satisfaction will always prevail. However, wages, fringe benefits and good, safe, working conditions do not by themselves bring satisfaction which lasts. Motivation comes from the implementation of recognition and rewards commensurate with contribution, high organisational standards, good internal communications and the opportunity for self-control.

People will correct their own mistakes more quickly and effectively if they spot them first. Business consultants and hospitality industry specialists Horwath and Horwath are well aware of the large number of businesses which have failed over the recessionary years. In the past, investors were attracted to the hospitality industry by the notion that running a pub or a small hotel was romantic. In many cases, investors believed that little more than a convivial spirit was needed to ensure success.

In the 1990s Horwath and Horwath observe that survival depends upon well-balanced management expertise, traditional values of hospitality, value for money, high quality, investment in staff training and strategic marketing. A successful organisation requires management of the marketing plan as well as good marketing strategies. A number of establishments begin with the right ideas and lose their way because they become opportunistic instead of sticking to the original game plan and controlling the strategies that made them successful. Here is an example which is as old as the hospitality business.

Management does not really know what is happening or why, so it blames the customers for being fickle and resorts to advertising to 'get the customers back'. This does not work, so the restaurant goes into a slide and becomes just another restaurant struggling for survival. The point of the example is that management does not really know what is happening because it does not have the necessary checking and control procedures in place. A marketing plan has to be constantly monitored, otherwise it goes off track. The only difference between the marketing management of a large establishment and a small one is that the larger organisation has more people to attend to the various marketing functions.

Someone running the small place has to wear several hats or, in many cases, all the hats. This makes it harder on the small business operation because many skills are required. But that is not an excuse. On the other hand, with the larger operation, even though the load is shared the efforts have to be coordinated, placing a special responsibility on additional people to 'manage' the people who manage. In the nucleus of a business, three specialised skills are needed—financial management, marketing and product and production knowledge. A sympathetic managerial climate and sound, open communications are essential. This can be called 'the corporate culture'.

The structure chosen is directly related to who has the authority or power and therefore who allocates the responsibilities. In marketing, there are several primary functions to be performed: 1) Marketing planning (development and overview) New product development (future planning) 2) Direct sales representation (to corporate customers and travel agents, locally, nationally and internationally) 3) Advertising (direct with media or using an advertising agency) Sales promotions 4) Direct mail 5) Market research 6) Public relations and publicity 7) Customer services. Who performs them depends on the size of the operation, the structure and the systems decided by the owners.

Sometimes the structure and the systems evolve as the needs arise or growth occurs. In the case of a marketing organisation structure for a large property there are five main alternatives for a marketing management system. The managing director handles most of the marketing functions and requires only a sales force to make direct contact with existing and potential customers. A sales department with ancillary advertising and promotions. In this instance, the managing director appoints a sales manager to handle a sales staff and the advertising and sales promotions. The main planning functions are controlled by the managing director.

A marketing department separate from sales. This structure usually occurs when an operation grows in size and the managing director realises that specialised assistance is required for most of the marketing functions. A marketing manager is appointed to work with the sales manager. The managing director retains control of planning. In this case, marketing and sales are seen as separate and equal functions. A marketing department with sales as a subsidiary. Marketing in this variation of structure is perceived to be a holistic function, with sales being one of several functions. This is close to the modem concept of a marketing structure.

A marketing director is appointed with full responsibility for all marketing activities and may have several specialists for each of the various functions reporting to him or her. There are four ways of organising the marketing functions and, again, it depends on the size of the operation and from where it draws the majority of its business.

Functional departments—various marketing specialists reporting to a marketing manager. This simply means dividing the ten marketing functions into people or departments. If it is a large international hotel group, for example, the advertising manager plans for all markets and regions. This is centralised control.

Regional management—each region is self-sufficient and responsible for itself. In this case, for example, London would have a complete marketing structure and control all functions for the southeast of England. Edinburgh would have its own separate marketing structure. Sheffield and Leeds, being smaller markets, may share the functions, and so on. This is decentralised control

Product line management—a product manager is responsible for the marketing functions affecting each product. This approach would probably appeal to most middle line managers. It means, for example, that the food and beverage manager does his or her own marketing without direct interference. The person is given a target and a budget. The conference and banqueting managers, restaurant managers, etc., all work on the same basis. The overall marketing of the hotel as a corporate umbrella campaign may be vested in either the managing director, marketing director or sales manager.

Market management—separate marketing for customer groups. This approach divides the hotel's customers into groups, with a separate person responsible for the marketing functions affecting those groups. Thus the corporate market would be handled by one department, the holiday package market, another, the meetings, seminars, groups and function markets by another, and so on.

Some owners believe that marketing is just another function, and that it ranks equally in importance with financial, operational and human resource control. Others see marketing as being a 'selling' function, and give precedence to operations and finance. The attitudes of senior management, and therefore the management systems that they put into place in large hospitality establishments, affect both the structure of the marketing division and the roles of the managers of each function.

In many hotels, the product managers, such as the food and beverage manager, conference and banqueting manager and rooms manager, have equal status, and the marketing manager has to liaise with them. In a modem marketing structure, the marketing director/manager has control over the product managers and, in addition, has department heads who handle sales, advertising, market research, customer services, sales promotions and public relations. A sales director or sales manager would report to the managing director and may also be responsible for the whole marketing function in a sales-orientated organisation.

In a modem marketing structure, the sales manager would report to the marketing director. The person would be responsible for all the direct contact functions and would have a staff of sales representatives (also called account executives) and sales assistants. The department would be required to develop corporate customers, groups, seminars, functions and meetings, organise packages and contact travel agents and tour wholesalers. Operations manager has the task of looking after the customer from the moment he or she makes a booking. Often also called accommodation manager (mainly because in a hotel accommodation is the premium product), and may also be the administration manager.

The responsibility for the image of the hotel rests on this person's shoulders. Contact with the organisers of conferences, visiting celebrities, large parties, big accounts, politicians and government departments, all senior-level contact is part of this function. In addition, liaison with the media and a variety of publics is required to ensure favourable publicity whenever possible. Arranging for the development and placement of all forms of advertising in the media is advertising manager's responsibility. In addition, he or she must organise the creation of brochures and literature for the establishment.

An advertising agency is generally employed for creating campaigns, preparing the material and placing it in the media. Sales promotion manager has to create the promotional concepts and follow them through. The position is often included in the duties of the public relations manager and sometimes the advertising manager, as these two functions normally work together. This is specialist area, and one which is growing as establishments use direct mail techniques more and more to maintain contact with existing customers and endeavour to achieve further market penetration.

Maintaining a database of customers and potential customers is part of this function. Great skill is needed to gain the maximum results. Direct mail agencies are often employed. Frequently, this job is included in the duties of the advertising or sales promotion manager. Another area of specialisation for some places, used to back up the direct mail functions, sales promotions and advertised package offers, or to make direct contact with customers to sell particular products. The person in charge usually has a team of telesales people to control, advise and encourage.

Managers of accommodation, food and beverages, conferences and banquets, restaurants, entertainment and leisure divisions of a large property are also members of the marketing team, even though in most cases they will report to the general manager or an operations manager. A service strategy has to state precisely what will happen to and for the establishment's customers. It has to be consistent and measurable. The best way of achieving these objectives is to translate the strategies into competency-based criteria which detail every action involved in providing the service.

A service strategy is not a 'holy writ' directive. It is a guide to be followed as closely as possible, but should never be an inflexible system. The real skill of management is the creation of a service procedure which is a happy, interesting and even exciting outcome for the customers. That should always be the objective of a service strategy.

Good marketing planning should allow for contingencies, to cover 'what if?' situations. It is the marketing of the property overall which usually involves the long-term view, as well as considering immediate short-term progress—especially true of a large property which can take up to ten years before it returns a worthwhile profit for its investors. Product lines are considered to be medium-term and product items tend to be more short-term because they can be changed without affecting the customers' overall perceptions of the property. It is worth remembering that in business, as in war, failures have a common cause— growing too fast and entering additional territories with inadequate resources.

In a word, greed. It is advisable to secure the base of the business and then, with careful planning, expand or extend the operation. The outcome of planning is a master plan which guides and directs the operation through change. The purpose of a marketing plan is to apply discipline to the strategic process and avoid costly errors, but mostly to make sure that nothing is overlooked. Planning is a business process which encompasses an appraisal of what has been achieved in the recent past, a debate about how improvements can be made for the future and how they can be achieved.

There is a tendency in the hospitality industry to think that marketing planning is only for larger hotels and that writing a plan for a hotel with a very limited staff is a waste of time. However, because jobs are not as well defined in smaller properties it may be even more vital for the small property to commit its marketing plan to writing. The high failure rate among small businesses can be attributed directly to either inadequate finance or the inability of the operators to prepare a business plan. When an opportunity is presented by an altered circumstance in the operation's micro environment (internal factors), such as a failing product, or the macro environment (external factors), such as new legislation, the demise of a competitor, a market or product opportunity, the plan may have to be revised or a new plan drawn up to cope with the change.

In each case, the planning discipline should be followed for the reasons outlined earlier—to avoid costly mistakes. Planning discipline does not always follow the critical path in the same sequence. Nevertheless, it is essential that all steps are considered before approval by management. Similarly, the process of generating the plan—the planning discipline—need not follow the procedures used to write a report. The planning process may start with a market opportunity and lead to an examination of target markets and the development of strategies. In that case, the planner must work backwards and test the feasibility of the market opportunity and all the other factors along the critical path requiring analysis before finalisation and the preparation of a documented report. A marketing plan makes a set of recommendations. Upon approval, it becomes the final marketing plan or 'master plan'.

When completed, a written master marketing plan must incorporate all marketing activities, and all marketing activities must subscribe to a common corporate objective. It should be a living, working document which is referred to daily. In a way, having a working document is as basic as the old joke about the highly successful accountant who eventually became a multi-millionaire. His staff observed over the years that he had the habit of beginning every day furtively unlocking the top drawer of his desk and carefully scrutinising a piece of paper.

Everyone considered it to be the secret of his success. When the old accountant died, his ambitious assistant forced open the drawer to obtain the secret and make a fortune for himself. The document in the drawer which the greedy assistant read with shaking hands and disbelief simply said, 'Debts left, credits right'. Each product in the mix should be dealt with separately and have its own plan which can be either contained in the master document or be individually documented. This is because each product which is a profit-earning entity requires its own situation analysis, a marketing objective, target markets, a budget, strategies for the elements of the marketing mix and a detailed set of operational tactics.

In the case of a large hotel, there should be a master plan for the whole hotel and then separate plans for marketing the restaurants, bars, meetings and conferences, groups, tour wholesalers, and so on, for every line in the product mix. New products launched or introduced during the planning period get their own plan too. Advertising, sales promotions or selling plans are subsidiary plans which may follow the same format and fulfil the master plan. If there is a change of company policy or philosophy, the document has to be re-drawn to incorporate the change in strategic direction.

When an opportunity arises, or when change becomes necessary, the initial step is to review the company's mission statement, to orientate it with existing circumstances. Too often, management forgets what business it is really in. As marketing is the process of developing products and services to satisfy people's needs and wants and arranging for them to be sold at a profit, the question must be asked, Is the business doing this according to its original mission? For example, hospitality is concerned with people experiences, therefore hospitality marketing is mostly about understanding people.

Before proceeding, does management know enough about the current state of mind of its customers, potential customers, staff and the myriads of intermediaries and others who influence the purchase decision? The next significant question to be asked is, Would the change contemplated fit with the corporate objectives? If it does not, then a consultative process is necessary to abandon the project or re-align the corporate objectives. Business history is littered with examples of failures and near failures resulting from marketing moves which diverged from or exceeded the corporate brief, remembering that it is objectives which are the engine of achievement.

In most product failures, or new ventures which 'don't quite work out', more often than not it is the senior executive who has a bright idea and then arrogantly implements it. In such cases it is done without the proper planning procedures and probably against the advice of less timorous employees, the majority being hesitant to go against the wishes of their superior. In the planning process, package all the information and have a good, hard look at it. Market analysis is the beginning of the planning process. Its job is to gather all the information together and arrange it in a clear manner so that planning decisions can be made. There can never be enough appropriate information. Once all the information is assembled, it has to be analysed for problems and opportunities. A marketing document must take the reader from a state of ignorance through to awareness and understanding.

Even if the majority of readers are conversant with the subject and have a reasonable knowledge of its purpose and content, there will be others who will read it who will not have that advantage. But, more importantly, the document's purpose is also to present the rationale behind the conclusions and provide meaning to the recommendations. A large number of decisions are required in marketing planning. There is a very definite place for creative thinking in marketing. The person who is capable of 'lateral thinking', of grabbing a 'great idea' from the cosmos, can often run away with a wild success. More often than not, though, it is the tried and proven formulas in business which are most likely to bring success.

Some people claim that they go by 'gut' feeling. The gut feeling is, in reality, the individual mentally scanning a reference area of experience gained from the marketplace. In effect, they do their marketing planning in their head and do not write down or reveal the process. The person who 'shoots from the hip' without any proper planning is the one who places the organisation at risk. Then there are those in management who manage by inactivity, failing to recognise the imperatives for change and ultimately being forced to react rather than plan to act when the opportunities arise.

The best operator is the one who has a competent mixture of pragmatism and creativity and who plans carefully, justifying each step of the process. Positioning is a marketing strategy. Its purpose is to provide an organisation with an SCA by creating differences, advantages and benefits (DAB) which make people think about a place or a product in a certain way. Some people describe a place or property by saying it has 'a good reputation', which means in effect that it has earned a place in people's minds as a result of sound positioning. It also means that many recommend the place.

Positioning takes place in people's minds. Two places can look the same and offer the same facilities, but occupy totally different positions in the market. Positioning is what people think, know, feel or believe about a place. Hence the difference between a four- and five-star hotel can often be no more than a public perception, usually a strategic position decided by the management. In the case of many types of products, e.g. beverages and food, positioning is often the only difference between competing products. Taste tests with beers, wines, spirits and soft drinks suggest that the majority cannot discern any real differences in taste between brands. Some will stoutly defend that they can tell their favourite brand anywhere, only to be embarrassingly fooled by a blind tasting. Marketers who spend millions on brand promotion know exactly what they are doing: building a brand image which exists solely in people's minds.

Basics of the Hospitality Industry

The basics of the hospitality industry are the ways in which members of the industry transform the mundane needs of eating and sleeping into pleasurably heightened experiences. The images of escape, excitement, glamour, romance, conviviality and sometimes glitz are all part of the positioning process Information feeds position a property and indicate to prospective clients what type of place it is and what they can expect when they patronize it. Positioning attracts and also repels certain groups of customers.

An expensive property, for example, dissuades a large percentage of would-be patrons who simply cannot afford to stay there. A family-style restaurant will not appeal to a business luncheon group. An establishment cannot be all things to all people, which is why you must target the markets that have a natural affinity with each other. Positioning is such a powerful strategy when deployed properly that care must be taken with information feeds to ensure that the right message is being communicated. It is the sum total of the information feeds which establishes a position for an establishment. One information feed will not be sufficient to establish a marketable position. Support is required by other information feeds.

For instance, advertising and an impressive facade alone will not create a position that will attract customers for long. Ultimately, it is what happens to and for the customers which will achieve the strongest position. The key to successful positioning is to provide a recognisable, measurable difference or advantage which enables customers to make a choice in favour of one property. With leading hotels, for example, it is evident from every information feed they use that the place will be impressive and expensive, that every creature comfort will be catered for and every service requirement pandered to.

Customers buy the proposition in expectation of a good experience. In some markets there are many properties offering identical products; therefore it is one salient feature which will provide the main appeal. For each target market in the customer mix, the position adopted by the property must elicit a predetermined desired consumer response.Good marketers build images and they use facts to support the image. Therefore do not ever try to develop an image which cannot be sustained by facts.

Benefits arise from facts and support the facade of imagery. It is a fact, for instance, that Raffles Hotel in Singapore is one of the world's most famous establishments, and that it has a long history, mostly associated with the many famous people who have stayed there over the years. The benefit for the customer of this fact is the sense of romance and being part of a bygone era while enjoying the pleasures of its modernised facilities. Raffles retains much of the memorabilia of its colourful past to sustain the imagery which strongly positions the property in people's minds.

A property which promotes its facilities as being of 'world class standard' in so many words has to deliver a comparative level of excellence with the best in the world or else it will suffer rejection by its customers and a well-deserved reputation for being below standard. How you want a product or business to be perceived in the market's mind is a positioning strategy, and positioning strategies involve the use of information feeds to achieve the required objectives of positioning.

The decisions one has to make when selecting a strategic position for an establishment require information from market research about the market's knowledge of, and attitudes towards, the place. Successful marketers decide the position they want and fine-tune the market's perceptions to keep pace with altering market conditions, match competitive strategies and change or improve customer attitudes. To improve its position against some strong challenges thrown out by new and refurbished properties. Essential to a good positioning strategy is to achieve awareness through promotion. Imagery contributes to positioning. However, imagery is a created proposition which may be persuasive or inspiring, but images alone are not enough to motivate a customer to buy. Remember, positioning happens in people's minds and is dependent upon belief, thought, feeling and actual knowledge or experience. This is not new thinking.

Over 2000 years ago, the Greek philosopher, Aristotle, explained the three basics of persuasion: ethos (credibility), pathos (feeling or emotional appeal) and logos (logic and reasoning). He also said, 'Know your audience (target market) first.' Lewis identified three elements of true positioning: imagery, benefits, and difference. He said that it is relatively simple to create an image of some kind, although many hotels fail to do so, but images alone do not incline the consumer to buy. The element which does influence buying behaviour is the perceived benefits of the product or service. Positioning a product or service along benefit dimensions in an attempt to reflect consumers' attitudes forms the basis of an effective strategy.

Once the benefit dimensions have been defined, the marketer can isolate those target markets consisting of consumers who hold similar attitudes about a bundle of benefits as they relate to a particular hotel or hotel class. The third essential element of the positioning statement is that it differentiates the brand from the product class. In other words, it distinguishes the hotel from other hotels. To combine these elements, the positioning statement should be designed to create an image reflecting the perception of the property that management wishes its target market to hold and reflecting promises on which the property can deliver and make good.

Lewis states that consumers do not buy products or services, they buy expectations. Statements that both promise the consumer something and give him or her a reason to believe in the promise are the most persuasive because they let the consumer know what he or she can expect and why he or she should stay at a particular hotel. The various competitors for any market can be divided into the market leader, challengers, followers and market specialists, or niche marketers. The average customer does not care about these terms, but he or she is affected by their implications.

In hospitality marketing they matter a great deal to the properties involved in a particular market category, because they make a difference to how each property goes about marketing the service. The market leader is the property which has achieved the best top-of-mind rating by customers. It is the place that most people think of first in answer to questions like: 'Where should we stay? Where should we go for a great night out? Where's a good fast food place?' etc. Because market leaders are first to come to mind they are generally the places that get the biggest share of the available business in their market category.

The leaders' strategies have a broad appeal. They are probably positioned as being big, popular and extroverted. The market challengers are the ones who want to be where the leader is, so they are constantly chasing the same markets and trying to create strategies which will shift the leader's customers over to them. The market followers copy the leaders and challengers and offer a 'me too' alternative for customers. They follow at a distance, never promoting very hard, and are content to get the spillover from other strategies.

The market specialists and market nichers achieve a position by targeting specific groups of customers overlooked by the rest or not catered for by anyone directly. Theme and ethnic restaurants, vegetarians, art and cultural groups, music types—any strategy aimed at attracting one group by doing something special for that group is a market nicher. The positioning statement is a description of the position you want to occupy in people's minds. It involves the use of concepts expressed in adjectival terms which have emotive meanings to people with which they can associate.

For example, the Willard Inter-Continental, Washington may want to position itself as being 'an international hotel of traditional elegance at the centre of America's politics and history'. Yes, you could be dining in the same room with the President, governors and ambassadors from any country in the world. Hotels with less pretensions may simply want to be positioned as 'having the most comfortable rooms in town', or the pub that offers the 'widest range of ales in the region'. Positioning happens in people's minds. As most of us think in concepts, words are only the tools we verbalise in communication with others. Consequently, people may use different terms to describe the same feeling or belief. In advertising, terms are chosen to be evocative. The average person tends to use mundane terminology.

Hence someone may use the word 'solid' to describe a property because it is old. Or it could be described as 'experienced', meaning the same thing. The Savoy Hotel in London is a classic example of a grand old establishment which is positioned by promoting the appeal of solid experience, proven elegance and dignified service. Images change as organisations and facilities evolve, and so positioning changes, therefore strategies have to change. For example, a five-star hotel which was 'new' twenty years ago becomes 'old'. Old is OK if it means proven quality, reliable, traditional, experience, known excellence. It is not so good if it means tired, run-down and out-of-date. The 'old' hotel has to re-position itself or be down-graded to a four-star hotel. Maybe it chooses to take the lesser position but occupy the lower price end of the market and offer better value for money.

Perhaps it fights the challenger and, with an up-grade of its facilities, retains the leadership position. Advertising and various promotions do not change facts, but they are the communication means of conveying images and turning them into benefits. Each segment of the market has different reasons for purchase and seeks different benefits. For a property, a mixed image is as bad as a mixed metaphor. It should be clear to prospective purchasers exactly what is being offered by a property and in which form.

Promotion can achieve a new positioning change quickly, especially if the imagery is right and it captures what the positioning will mean to the customers in the way of a DAB. The Forte Posthouse brand positions itself to appeal to the business market: 'We're offering you a great deal for business'. A property should not attempt a positioning strategy which it is really incapable of fulfilling. The very nature of service makes it difficult for a customer to make a decision from the outside until the person has actually experienced it on the inside, especially as every property offers a conglomeration of products which appear to be much the same. It is argued that the excesses of advertising and brochure descriptions at least capture an enquiry. This argument is naive, though, because it is the referrals and the supporting evidence of many satisfied customers which eventually gives a place a reputation that fixes its position. A place that has won a reputation does not have to spend the same amount on promotion.

The successful operators promote differences which have advantages for the customer and support the promotion by having differences which the customer can experience. A price advantage is probably the most obvious DAB. That is believable because it is provable, but it is also the easiest for competitors to match. Nearness is believable and provable, like the Four Seasons Hotel, Tokyo, which states that it is within easy reach of both the Imperial Palace and the Shinjuku business district.

With a hotel, it is the room rate which sets the pricing levels for the rest of the hotel's products. Hence price is part of positioning. For example, one expects to pay more for a stay at a high-class, five-star hotel than at a budget lodge. Price helps to determine the customer mix and, conversely, whatever customer mix is targeted by an establishment will determine the price. Recent years have proved that the hospitality industry is a fiercely competitive one and sensitive to economic conditions; consequently the relationship between rates and occupancy has to be very finely tuned.

The purpose of a value-added pricing strategy is to make direct comparisons with competing properties difficult while making the offer appear to be worth more than is being charged. Price skimming is a strategy adopted by new properties with a well known brand name, a grand facade and a high-profile positioning. From the outset they charge a high price for their rooms and other products because they have a new, exciting, prestigious image which usually attracts a high-flying, 'nothing-but-the-best' style of customer, called in marketing the 'early adopter'. This strategy is maintained for as long as the property holds its position, and it is called 'skimming' because it is taking the cream of the market at the time.

However, when other, newer properties are built, and as the facilities become less of a novelty, prices are gradually reduced. Management usually has a policy on pricing which varies from being rigid to totally flexible. The objectives are usually survival, profit maximisation, market share, quality leadership and capital recovery. However, price changes can be forced upon a property by competition. A close competitor can 'steal' guests by offering better deals. Market conditions—an economic down-turn, for instance—can force every property into a price-cutting war.

The market and demand for accommodation will set the price ceiling and an establishment's costs will set the floor for prices. The price ceiling is the maximum price people are prepared to pay in a given market environment. The price floor is the lowest price a property can charge without losing money. Somewhere in between is where competing properties struggle for market share. Price is a value-for-money equation which potential guests have to deliberate over before making a decision. In some markets, setting a rate is almost a daily decision as rivals have the option to raise or lower rates with every enquiry.

In most city markets, there is, an over-supply of rooms for the majority of the year. Special events and seasonal demands are the only occasions when all rooms are filled. The marketing challenge therefore is to fill as many rooms as possible in the seasonal gaps of market demand. Price and perceived value becomes a significant strategy in this situation. On different days and at different times of the year, a room may be hired out to guests at rates which can vary considerably.

Similarly, the rate will vary to attract specific customer groups, such as tour wholesalers, large companies, conference organisers and frequent travellers. This is demand differential pricing. Holiday packages are products which the property markets as its own, such as a three-day stay at the property combined with sightseeing tours or a special interest package which takes in sporting or cultural events. These are products that can be advertised, promoted to corporate clients, sold direct to customers or marketed through other tourism-related companies. These are special, discounted room rates which are negotiated with tour wholesalers so that they can market their own holiday packages.

Wholesaling rates enable an airline, for instance, to market a product which entails a stay of so many nights at the property as part of a total number of benefits or events for the airline to package and offer as an attractive value-for-money holiday to their customers. Most large travel agents and transport companies package holidays in this way. From the establishment's point of view, the discount is offset by the volume of business it receives. Business people and conference organisers tend to plan their use of the property's facilities for working days.

Therefore most properties find that they have excess capacity over weekends. Weekend rates are discounted offers designed, to attract people to stay on over a weekend or to attract local people to indulge themselves. They can also be marketed in conjunction with transport operators to get the domestic market to have a 'short break' package enjoying the luxury of staying at the property. The business traveller is the most frequent user of hospitality and is therefore the target of nearly all properties. To attract their business, special incentive rates are generally negotiated.

The additional attraction is usually the use of special business services such as secretarial or 'person Friday' assistance, fax facilities, computers, photocopying, meeting rooms, video-conferencing and, in some cases, language translators.Large companies, or companies with a high usage rate of hospitality facilities, are targeted and offered a low rate for continued custom, and special deals are often included for the use of other hotel services. Another variant of this strategy is to enrol them in a special club which provides not only discounted prices for every facility at the property, but also discounts with participating stores, airlines, hire cars, theatre bookings and any other attraction the property can negotiate which is likely to appeal to the corporate customer.'The children stay free', is one type of offer which is a strategy that many properties employ to attract family customers. Another is an offer of a free child-minding or nanny service.

Special rooms arranged for the family to be together in a suite or adjoining rooms is another variation of the strategy. These types of products are frequently sold to use the excess capacity over weekends or for seasonal business periods. Professional, trade, business or social groups which hold conferences, training seminars, celebrations, special sporting or cultural events hunt for the best value they can get. Most properties 'bid' for this type of business and have a negotiable rate which has a floor value to the property (which means it recovers costs and retains a bare minimum of profit).

Most properties offer an all-inclusive price with meals and use of other facilities. Often the objective is to confuse the issue with add-ons so that price comparison with other properties becomes difficult. Some places negotiate with suppliers to help them with special prices to win the deal. A transport element and programme for accompanying persons in the offer is not uncommon. Some high-profile hotels do not like discounting because it may harm their prestige image. Instead, when they are in a competitive situation they upgrade favoured clients from, say, a normal room to the executive floor so that they can provide added benefits at no extra charge. Or they include business facilities for free.

They are, in effect, giving away some of their profits, but they are not seen to be discounting and are thereby preserving a claim that they do not have to reduce their prices to win business. Another form of discounting is a published 'no frills' rate involving basic accommodation. This is a last-resort pricing strategy for large properties, but a common strategy for properties struggling to be competitive in other ways. For budget accommodation the 'no frills' approach is central to the concept and its apparent success.

There are other variations on the foregoing strategies. All of them have the same intent, which is to win business at all costs, especially during difficult times or during off-season periods. Various customer mixes perceive different values for different benefits they receive. Many establishments have price levels for each segment (top rates for business people, low rates for families). This can result in a disparate customer blend which harms the image of the place. A 'get-what-you-can' price strategy therefore can lead to a loss of regular patronage. However, even the best hotels sometimes resort to a sell-up, sell-down pricing approach, sometimes called an 'open-door' strategy, as opposed to the 'closed-door' strategy reflecting a policy of price rigidity.

The 'foot-in-the-door' strategy is when an enquiring customer asks about rates. The potential guest is given a number of alternatives, ranging from the very low to the highest price. The client often will choose the middle price, not wanting to look cheap or too extravagant and seeking the best value. It is then, suggested to the client that for only another small amount of money he or she can get some added benefit, like a king-sized bed or a room overlooking some geographical feature. This is 'selling up'.

The 'face-in-the-door' strategy is the opposite. The price quoted is the highest. Often this will be accepted; if it is not, other alternatives are offered until a price is reached which is acceptable. This is 'selling down'. A market penetration pricing strategy is used when a hotel sets lower than usual prices because it wants to capture market share. This is a pricing strategy that will achieve much-needed cash flow at times. It would also make sense if the establishment wants to introduce a new product and needs to gain quick recognition and win some early sales. A price strategy will impact on other elements of the marketing mix, depending on the corporate goals and the marketing objectives.

Long-term discounting, for instance, must have an effect on product quality decisions. Management needs to have cost and profit predictions that will reflect the consequences of price strategy decisions. Whereas room rates set the overall position of an establishment, it can have different pricing strategies for each of its products. This approach can be used to put value back into a room rate which is perceived to be very high. Product-line pricing can be used to offer customers a choice of values. Hence, as well as an expensive, fine dining restaurant, it has a low-priced coffee shop. Or a cocktail lounge, a medium-priced lounge and a public bar. This way, everyone can find their own price level without feeling that they are being 'bled'.

The other strategy is to maintain a high value-for-money room rate and recover profits from its other products and services. Incentives can be offered, such as off-season rates, early booking discounts, preferred customer discounts, or special offers tied with a sales promotion. A hospitality establishment is no different from a retailer when it comes to making offers. Everyone likes a bargain, which is why sales promotions and premium offers usually attract additional customers, or bring regular customers into the establishment more often. Therefore the same types of strategies used by the large properties can be adapted by other hospitality businesses.

The principles do not vary, but some businesses are perceived in a certain way by their consumers and therefore sensitivity to market demand has to be recognised. For example, a restaurant which has the same prices for dinner, lunch and weekends is being a bit hopeful, and certainly inflexible. At different times of the day customers want different types of eating experiences. The luncheon period is normally patronised by business people who want a quick, light meal with a minimal amount of alcohol. A restaurateur could stipulate that his or her kind of place does not cater for the crowd, which is fine, but he or she could be missing out on business.

More importantly, he or she might be forgetting that the same luncheon customer is also a potential dinner, snack or even breakfast customer. During the dinner session, full prices apply because this is the time of greatest demand. Then he has a supper menu for late eaters or those who have come from their evening's entertainment. A varying level of prices and menus makes sense because it is maximising the use of the staff and the premises. The basis of effective advertising is to know in advance what the target markets are likely to think, feel, believe or know as a result of being exposed to the messages in the advertising. Thinking ahead, putting one self in the minds of the target market is part of the preparation of advertising. It is called formulating the consumer action proposition and means predetermining the reaction to the message and its presentation.

Creating an advertisement for mass media or other message delivery systems has to be driven by the communication objectives. In addition, the creative solution, which is the way that the message is presented, has to be encoded into words and pictures so that the markets it is aimed at get the message quickly and easily. The purpose of a creative approach is to use a message delivery system, such as a newspaper, to its best advantage by drawing attention to the message and making it easy to read and understand. Good creativity should considerably enhance the possibilities of readership. Creativity on its own though, will seldom save a poorly conceived or uninteresting message.

Any advertisement, for any medium, which obscures the message is a foolish waste of money. In print media, it is the opening headline that has the main job of conveying the words that spell out the key points of the proposition. At all times it must be assumed that the readers are largely disinterested in reading advertisements, so the headline is no place for subtlety. In many cases, retail travel agents are able to offer services to tourists superior to those available by direct purchase. The agents' success depends on their superior access to information and specialist knowledge of markets and conditions. This enables agents to offer a service of advice and guidance to the individual tourist. Agents are also able to act on behalf of the principal, be it hotel, airline, tour operator or shipping company, in a personalised manner.

The retail travel agent also offers a one-stop facility, allowing choice and enabling the customer to purchase the whole range of tourism products, thereby reducing the tourist's transactional search costs. The tour operator consolidates the transactions that an independent tourist would make separately, and sells a single package to the customer. This not only gives the customer the convenience of purchasing a single composite product in one transaction, it also enables economies to be obtained on the supply side. The tour operator is able to enter into long-term contracts for accommodation and transport.

Consequently, this permits high load factors for aircraft (ships and trains) and high occupancy rates for accommodation. Economies of scale and exercise of monopsony power can also reduce the operator's costs. This packaging enables mass marketing and standardisation to take place. Branding by the tour operators across destinations results in increased consumer loyalty to the operator. The operator can give explicit or implicit quality guarantees to the tourist and thus reduce the perceived risks of default, poor service and other transactional uncertainties.

Tour operators can market their products via brochures, providing an initial screening of the myriad tourist products potentially available. The marketing implications of transactions analysis can be derived by reversing the transactions flow and looking back over the transactions chain. It is a peculiarity of the tourism market that final service providers must aim their marketing at quite different targets, as illustrated by the different types of transactions chain. The direct purchase, self-assembly package implied by chain a requires final service providers to reach the individual tourist directly. In the other types of transactions chain, intermediaries occur and marketing needs to be directed at them.

These intermediaries may be tour operators and/or travel agencies. Similarly, tour operators must target marketing efforts at potential groups of tourists and travel agencies. The transport function is an important point in the exchange of rights in the tourism transaction chain. If this function is subcontracted to an independent operator this delicate and central function can go out of control: hence, the close integration of transport with other facilities in the integrated multinational. There are important cost implications also. Efficient utilisation of capacity is crucial in keeping costs down in transport as well as in accommodation.

Complete control of a fleet of aircraft or ships (one ship or aircraft for smaller companies) will impose severe cost penalties if these facilities are not fully utilised. Consequently, there is considerable instability arising from the necessity to balance control of transport with cost-efficient utilisation. The transport function is also important because it, uniquely, involves the transnational transfer of rights (and tourists). Its management, therefore, requires great skill and sensitivity. The theory has important implications for quality management in tourism. Control of the transactions flow enables the integrated multinational to monitor and control the quality of services. This is often difficult to achieve through external contracts, because of the intangible nature of services and the difficulties of exercising day-to-day control other than by direct line management. The analysis of transactions and transaction costs provides a ism framework for the unification of concepts and analysis in tourism research. It provides a core theory that allows the analysis of tourism demand through the transactions chain and the organisation of supply by its distinctive view of the forces driving organisational developments.

Strategies of Service

The people providing the service directly to the customer must have the support of everyone else. Albrecht and Zemke emphasise that the organisation exists to serve the needs of the people who are serving the customer. Management's primary function is to monitor and maintain the service standards. Management must make sure that nothing and no-one prevents the service product from happening.

In a service organisation, management's role is not merely giving instructions, it is to help those providing the service. If there are delays or upsets, what or who is causing them? Is it a procedural problem? Is there a weak link in the staff chain? Is more training needed? Perhaps the person is wrong for that job? Some consider the service culture to be reactive to customers rather than proactive. This is wrong. Customers recognise that the establishment has to make profit. They look for leadership from the establishment and want it to provide the magic that gives them a quality experience.

With a service strategy, you are involving the customers and the staff so that the strategic service mix works to everyone's satisfaction. It is a process of drawing together the expectations, needs and wants of the customer and the provider so that the customer gets value and the provider gets money. It sounds so simple, doesn't it? Then why does it not always happen? Part of the answer lies in the arrogance of a large percentage of human beings who are not really interested in other people's thinking. It is a 'We-know-what-is-best-for-you' attitude. Such types are rarely successful in the hospitality business. It results in a general preoccupation by management with putting products in place which they think are for the benefit of the customers, when often they are not what the customer wants or expects at all.

For example, a restaurant put on a special three-course meal for a very low price in anticipation of creating an influx of business, only to be disappointed because the customers did not come and those that did never came back. The restaurateur added more choices, but still failed to increase business. After two or three weeks of this he finally snapped at a table of uninterested customers. 'Well, what the hell do you want then?' They proceeded to tell him, and he finally realised that he had not been taking notice of what the customers wanted. He had not taken the trouble to review what the customers were consistently choosing from his normal menu. Nor had he ever bothered to talk to his customers about their preferences. The wants of the customer mix should always drive the service strategies.

Equally important, though, is to anticipate the customers' wants and occasionally provide something delightful that they did not expect. Michael Hurst experiments with various dishes and consults his customers before including the dishes on the menu. Effective service products achieve increased business by 'laddering'. This is drawing from the total market a number of people who are transformed from potential customers into advocates for the establishments. The objective of laddering is to identify suspects and target the best prospects (potential customers).

With the help of promotion a percentage of them will become customers. From this point the objective of service products is to provide customers with a quality experience that turns them into regular patrons of the establishment. Consequently, they will soon become firm advocates and go out and sell' the place to their friends and acquaintances. Most restaurants provide good food, reasonable service and charge average prices or prices which suit their customer mix. This is called a 'primary service'. Michael Hurst states that it is the small extras, the 'secondary services', which take an average customer experience and elevate it into something beyond his or her expectations. It may be the special brand of coffee, the bread and shortbread that have been made on the premises, the appetiser at the beginning of the meal which is not charged for.

Hurst claims quite rightly that there are many ways of doing things that are better and different which become the main factors in the customers' minds. The primary service product usually does its job of satisfying the customers without much comment. It is the extras that give the customers something to go away and talk about, giving the establishment the competitive edge. Service has to have measurable criteria. It has to have objectives and perform to a prescribed set of rules and standards. Its purpose is to define precisely what will happen to, or for, a customer by when and by whom. Measurement is achieved by deciding the required outcome of the service. The standard criteria are as follows: What is it you want the product to do to and for the customers? It is the answer to this question which determines the objective.

Forget the money objective. That is an overall corporate objective. This is a product objective, and it is its outcome, what actually happens and how that happening is accepted in the minds of the customers which counts. It may take several statements to sum up the outcome that the objective is set to achieve. Remember, for an objective to have meaning it must contain measurable criteria of achievement within a stipulated time frame. For example, a restaurant allocates staff numbers by customer numbers depending on the style of service of the establishment. So one waiter may be allocated to fifteen customers. Three chefs may be required to cook for 150 customers.

The service standard which is set requires each customer to be served with drinks within two minutes of sitting down, to have the first course on the table within five minutes of ordering, to have the second course on the table no later than twelve minutes, and so on. If it is not being achieved, management must find out why, isolate the difficulty and remedy it. 'Whatever it takes' is the rule that governs the provision of a service standard. The measuring criterion in this instance is keeping account of individual performances and comparing them with the average. Those who lag are trained, encouraged or helped until they come up to the standard required. Hospitality is team work, people working together to jointly achieve the objectives of an excellent guest experience.

A team leader is essential; a catalyst for the smooth functioning of the procedures required in delivering the product. Each person must know exactly what is expected of him or her and be constantly acknowledged as he or she performs. Achievement is a reward on its own, but nothing beats the rewards of money and extra privilege for a job that goes beyond the standard required. Not every action or function can be directly translated into money terms or measured by customer reaction. Much of what happens in a service product goes unseen by the customer.

As it is the culmination of little things that ultimately counts in the final assessment by the customer, the contributing functions need a points rating system ranging from poor up to excellent. It is surprising how standards are lifted and enthusiasm develops when staff are performing to known criteria. The desired outcome of a range of service strategies is the extent of the customers' consistent satisfaction. This can be measured in terms of increased sales made, and repeat business, which is the real measure of a product's success. There is another way, and that is to constantly research customer attitudes to find out if the number of complaints are reduced and whether the customers appreciate the various experiences being provided.

Guests, in the main, do not mind filling in brief questionnaires, particularly if a prize incentive is offered.Whereas the objective is to meet the satisfaction of the customer, money has to be made. At the end of a service period the money required from a product has to be added to make sure that it meets the corporate objectives. A non-profit product such as cleaning can be measured by a points rating system and judged by what it does not cost in terms of lost or disappointed customers. There is always an accountant adding up the costs of a product. That person has a job to do, which is to make Sure that more money does not go out than is coming in.

An accountant performs the function of being management's conscience. A product service has to be cost-efficient, with the customer satisfaction level being measured against the costs incurred and the profits made. A high-quality service orientation is such a powerful competitive weapon that it will soon come to be regarded as an essential part of business strategy, not a frill or a 'nice-to-have' feature. Organisations which cannot demonstrate a significant commitment to the needs of their customers will be left further and further behind. One of the principal laments of managers about implementing a service strategy is about the lack of cooperation and consistency of their staff. 'We tell them how to do it. We spend money on training. We try to motivate enthuse, but in the end we find the staff going back to their old habits and we give up in despair. What's the use? It's a nice idea, but it isn't realistic. People are people.' One has to feel sympathetic with this lament, which is about as consistent as the inconsistency of hospitality staff's ability to perform consistently.

The problem lies with management, and we will come to that in a moment. There is another management attitude which says: 'Our staff know what is expected of them. They don't always do what they should, but they know.' Experience shows that this is a false premise. The truth from research and a series of random interviews of staff reveals that in most cases they do not know what is expected of them. They may know the rules and they may know the procedures they have been taught, but in the majority of cases they think that what is expected is only to perform to those rules and procedures. This is an open invitation to rebel. It is human to buck the system, so as human beings occasionally they deliberately flout the rules and procedures just to prove that they are individuals in their own right and not a bunch of robots caught up in a system. After a while, flouting the rules becomes a habit and then they feel a bit guilty. As the guilt rises, so do the defence mechanisms, and then it is someone else's fault, not theirs.

Most service people think that they are doing their job for a remote, cold and uncaring manager, or a bunch of shareholders they will never meet and who have no interest in whether they live or die. Anyone who works in that sort of environment knows that as long as they do enough to not get fired they will get paid, and that is all that matters. That sort of knowledge takes precedence over any other knowledge because it is the truth. The answer therefore is to give them responsibility for their customers. When they realise that the people they serve could be theirs for a long time and that their real job is to keep them as their own customers it helps to change their attitude to the procedures. If, in addition, they are given a financial incentive for every customer they retain, and each time that customer spends money they get a little part of it for themselves and they get praised for their efforts, you have a person who is working for him or herself as well as for you.

If the right people are hired, they will know that the procedures are there to help them build their own customer base. Notice what happens when customers request to be served by a particular waiter that they like. It is a funny type of waiter who is not flattered, and naturally he or she responds with additional, personalised touches of service. Often a handsome tip is the reward. However, it is better if management supplies the reward so that there is a standard recognition for retaining a customer and providing outstanding service. This approach does two things. One, it personalises the service. The staff get to know the customers by name. Two, the customers get service because every person who walks in, phones in or writes in is worth money.

All of a sudden, the staff are scrambling to get to the customers first and claim them for their own! The ones who do not scramble are the ones you do not want. So, instead of management saying that staff are all the same, it becomes apparent that they are not all the same. If you want staff who give service you need to retain the scramblers and keep them motivated. Some managers may balk at this concept because they think that service people are mercenaries, merely hired for a job. In the case of waiters and commis chefs, they are often hired on a casual basis so that they can be laid on and off at will. And here is the real problem—management's attitude to staff.

Until that changes, and the staff are given individuality and respect by managers as being vital contributors to the joint prosperity of themselves and the property, the customers will be at the mercy of a high percentage of mostly unmotivated and uncaring staff. The staff are an integral part of the product being sold. Most motivational training is wasted. The staff see this type of training as an insult to their intelligence, and often it is. They think, 'Here we go again.' Most staff want to be nice to customers if they can and they think that they already provide 'service'.

Many of them want to do better, and often they know how it can be improved, but frequently they are restrained or demotivated by systems and uncooperative attitudes born from management which does not respect them as individuals. No-one asks them for their opinion. All too often there is little management supervision, only authoritarian direction. Systems and procedures are put into place without staff consultation or understanding of the problems that they often pose. Profit and expediency come first and the staff come second. Usually there is no means of measuring service or what the staff do except by casual observations.

As a consequence, most service training begins with the premise that it is the front line 'sales and customer service people' who need to have the right attitude. Wrong. Service is a marketing product which requires strategies that begin at the top, and it is management which has to respect, support and service the front-line people. Training should be conducted around the strategies and involve the people who will implement them, and that requires staff acceptance and commitment to the concept. A service strategy is required for each product in an establishment's 'product line'. Of course there should be an umbrella strategy for the whole establishment, but as each product is aimed at a segment of the customer mix, each one needs its own strategic plan.

With a product like accommodation, the service strategy begins with the initial hotel contact because being welcomed by name is the first service a customer notices. This is before he or she has had a chance to see a room, drink in a bar, anything. You can build a whole strategy very simply around a smiling, happy concierge by extending the rapport he or she establishes and spreading it throughout the organisation. It is so easy. It starts with calling the customer by name and remembering that name and the important details about that person's preferences. Some in the hospitality industry say that good service should go unnoticed. Exceptional service, that extra something in the way in which a place does things and gives it that competitive point of difference, is usually provided by the personalities of the people who provide it.

Service for the customer begins from the very first contact with the establishment. This initial contact may be with a travel agent. A property cannot directly control what a travel agent says or does, but it can indirectly control it by making sure that the travel agent is armed with information to pass on to the customer. That information has to be more than a description of the property, the number of rooms and the going rates. It must include the points of difference and the benefits, the reasons why the travel agent can recommend it to the enquiring customer. Proper briefing of the travel agent is not just a selling strategy, it is also a service to potential customers via an intermedialy. The handling of an enquiry by an establishment should also be perceived as a service to the customer. Let us take out the mercenary considerations of 'getting-what-you-can' for the room for a moment. Sure, that is part of the business of being in business, and most experienced travellers know that.

What most of them want is helpful information so that they make a decision, whether to stay at your place or another place. For a number of establishments this does not always work the way it should. A ring-around of hotels in London and Manchester once produced some interesting results. Despite the fact that the world was in a recession at the time, in most instances the answer to the simple enquiry about rates resulted in a single reply, 'so much a room'. No additional helpful information, and this from some of the best in the country. In one case the phone just rang without being answered. Those who responded properly to the enquiry handled the situation by first quoting the rack rate and then going on to mention some of the packages they had. Not one respondent added any reasons why the enquiring customer should consider their establishment ahead of the rest.

When this situation was related to some hotel managers the response was mostly a rejection that it had happened. They used an excuse such as: 'must have been busy', 'it was an off night, we all have them', 'probably struck the wrong person', 'I'm really surprised, our people are excellent as a rule.' No one seriously considered what could be done to improve the situation, nor did they admit that something should be done. The moment of truth for customers occurs when they arrive at a property. Most establishments are very good at making first impressions when guests arrive. Building appearance, decor, cleanliness, the door person, the reception by the concierge or receptionist and the booking in procedures are normally fine. This is where place's well-oiled machinery goes into operation.

There is usually evidence of good training at this point, and seldom does it go off the rails unless a reservation is lost. For a new customer there is the initial impact of the room—its decor, lighting, size, layout, cleanliness and tidiness, the bed, the smell, the music, TV, mini-bar, tea and coffee-making facilities, bathroom and toilet, linen fresh and crisp, etc. All of these items make their impression. The customer either feels at home at this stage or wants to run screaming from the building and catch the first taxi out of there. It is a very sensitive moment for the customer and the quality of the hotel is often judged on how that moment is handled. In a good place the service strategy is to explain how the room works: an induction course on where things are and how they work, such as switches and appliances, then information is given about the facilities and additional services which are available.

This is the opportunity for reassurance on the customer's decision. More than that, though, it is the time to establish rapport with the customer and prepare the way for 'selling' other services. Ideally, the person doing the induction should be the continuing contact for the guest during his or her stay so that advice, information and 'fix-it' situations can be readily handled by one person or another designated person when the original contact is off duty. This contrasts with most establishments which divide the hotel into a number of departments working as separate profit-earning outlets without anyone assisting the customer in his or her use or choice. The proximity of a hotel's restaurants to its accommodation should ensure that a very high percentage of guests use the facilities such as fine dining room, bistro, carvery or coffee shop. The problem is, such places are also competing with others in the streets nearby. So it is not enough just to be there.

Each hotel eatery has to offer a really exciting benefit to win a share of its own guests and add a number of customers from outside the hotel. Food is interesting and can be fun. Dining should be an important part of the total guest experience of an establishment. A strategy for this product requires close attention to first impressions, the guest's comfort, familiarity, welcoming staff, easy on the eye decor and style. It should build on tile ambience and quality experience provided by the rest of the hotel. Again, it is all the extra touches - hiring personality people especially that make the competitive difference for the customers. Details matter, such as having a baby high chair, cushions for the elderly, music which is used to create an ambience for the place, perhaps the smell of freshly ground coffee, newly baked bread and rolls and, most of all, the food quality—all add up to a place being a really great experience.

Getting the fundamentals of food and wine right and served well is basic to the business of a restaurant. It is not enough, however. There are many establishments which do the same. Doing the ordinary things in a better and different way is about style, and style combined with attention to every small need of the guest causes guest satisfaction. The bar facilities, for example. The bar does not have to the guest can have a drink. A service strategy can be developed around it so that it is the beginning of a dining experience, not just a place to wait for guests. For example, while the customers drink, the food order can be decided so that they go to the table as soon as the meal is ready.

Meanwhile, a skilled and personable bartender could be offering cocktails which enhance the anticipation and enjoyment of the food to come. The wine list can be a feature, offering distinctive wines of a specific country or region, wines of selected vintages, or special house wines of the month. Meals and presentation which exemplify the regional tastes can be a talking point for guests, with gourmet experiences that no-one else offers. Special theme nights and promotions lend interest and excitement to the eating occasions and provide reasons for guest participation.

The key concerns for restaurants will center around menu development, analysis of current offerings, packaging or presentation, brand decisions, design and decor, music, and layout. Decisions for hotels will include those for restaurants, plus decisions on rooms, meeting space, and services to be offered. Probably the most important decision a restaurant operator can make concerns the type of foods and beverages that will be offered. Almost everything else in the restaurant in one way or another is affected by the menu. Restaurants are focusing on varying types of self-service where the customer orders at the "customer counter," then either receives the order immediately or returns when his/her name or number is called.

A variation of the self-service style is for restaurant personnel to deliver the food to the customer, rather than requiring the customer to return to the counter. Casual and fine dining restaurants will almost exclusively use table service, where the customers' orders are taken at their table by a server, who then also delivers the orders. Many restaurants have adopted the food-runner system, where any server can deliver the table's order when it is ready. This increases the efficiency of the servers and helps assure that the food is promptly delivered.

French service, another type of table service, focuses on partial preparation of the food in the dining room and requires an additional number of personnel, such as a maitre d', captains, front waiters, back waiters, and bussers; its use is limited almost exclusively to fine dining establishments. Russian service consists of bringing the food to the dining room on an attractively arranged platter that is presented to the host and guests. Servers will then plate each customer's meal. The major product and service decisions for a hotel are made during its planning stages, when developers decide in which market to compete. This target market decision will dictate the basic design of the building and the layout and size of rooms, type and number of food-service facilities and restaurants, meeting space, ancillary services such as workout rooms and business services, and public areas. It will also indicate the level of service provided by personnel in each department.

For example, in the economy market, personnel at the front desk have one primary responsibility, to check guests in and out. In the midscale and luxury markets, front desk personnel, and concierges if available, will receive messages, help arrange itineraries, help solve problems with meeting rooms, make reservations at restaurants, recommend local entertainment venues, and, to varying degrees, act as the host of each guest during his/her stay. Subsequent decisions would be whether to offer such services as a concierge or late-night room service, a newspaper, quality toiletries, in-room service bar, or a continental breakfast.

Perhaps the fastest-growing service is the use of various forms of technology that either expedite the logistics of the guest's stay or increase his/her productivity. Various weekend, vacation, honey-moon, and business packages are marketed by combining available hotel services. Each hotel will have different opportunities for unique packages. The average customer is concerned with courteous, efficient service and good food or comfortably appointed rooms, at a good value. This can be accomplished in a hotel or restaurant with a simple design and decor as well as in one that is very expensively designed. For most businesses, money is the single most important and least expendable asset, so it is necessary to closely watch what is spent on design and decor.

To get the most mileage out of each dollar spent, imagination and ingenuity should be used to create a design that is compatible with the customer's demands and showcases the business's products and services. The key to renovation is to attempt to use existing features and limit extensive remodeling. It is not necessary to do something unusual with every surface, unless required by the concept or desired atmosphere. It is generally more economical and esthetically pleasing to concentrate on one or two areas or surfaces that could be developed into a focal point, then finishing the remainder of the room in an tasteful, subdued manner.

Track lighting can be used to emphasise the chosen focal point. Focal point could be a grouping of large or unique plants, a wall with various types of unusual art or artifacts, a mural, an unusual ceiling, an antique bar, or an exposed kitchen. A new hotel or restaurant can be designed with a philosophy similar to that of designing an existing facility. The difference is that there is more flexibility in creating the focal points. For hotels, the lobby offers the greatest challenge and benefit. Guests in the upper-midscale to luxury hotel market segments expect an eye-catching ambiance that differentiates the hotel from less expensive alternatives. There are a few properties with quite modest lobbies that were originally designed for the upper-midscale market, but because of higher guest expectations they have had to lower their rates nearer the level of midscale competitors.

Essentially, the lobby must match the concept. Hyatt Hotels have proved the importance of the lobby, through their use of atriums. Historically, lobbies were viewed as nonproductive space that should be minimised. They are now the focal point of many hotels. Many people will strongly equate the size of the building, referred to as building mass or curb appeal, with its overall image. For example, a restaurant in an in-line position in a strip shopping center will not have as much visible building mass as one located on the end of the strip center.

A hotel can increase its visible building mass by having its longest side facing the primary street from which people enter. Since customers in restaurants spend the majority of their time in a chair or booth, this piece of furniture should be of the top affordable quality and comfort. Couches, chairs, and tables in a hotel's lobby are equally important for a different reason. Lobby furniture and decor items, to a degree, set the tone for the hotel's image. Furniture in hotel rooms should be compatible with the hotel's image, be viewed as tasteful by targeted guests, and be functional, sturdy, and ideally one grade above that of the competition's. Unless the property's concept is centered around a particular theme or is attempting to target a well-defined customer base, care must be taken to minimise expenures.

Too often, money is spent on hotels and restaurants so that the designer can showcase his/her talent at the willing or sometimes unknowing expense of the owner. Sometimes the owner will want to spend a large sum of money to create a certain unique feeling or ambience. This is actually good for the industry because there is always a need for someone to stretch the limits of creativity to see what the customer will accept. One problem encountered more in restaurants than hotels is that overdone, gimmicky theme designs and decors can detract from the customer's experience.

Some customers may initially be impressed with the decor, but, in the majority of cases, this is not what will bring them back. Most hotel guests prefer tasteful, conservative decor, while most restaurant customers prefer comfortable but interesting surroundings. In the past, design and decor had to have a direct relationship to the business's concept. "American customers have now become more sophisticated-we no longer need to eat Italian food off a table with a red-and-white checkered tablecloth lit by a candle in a Chianti bottle". Design and decor must become more versatile and flexible to accommodate passing trends for food, design, decor, color, furniture, fixtures, and so forth. This approach can also limit expenses when renovation is required. Today's restaurant customers desire brighter, more casual, open dining rooms that allow them to see and be seen, to interact with others, and to be part of something fun and exciting.

Rather than making design or decor the main emphasis, many operators today make the activities taking place in the restaurant the attraction. For this reason, exposed kitchens and bakeries have become popular and quite effective for their entertainment value. Customers enjoy seeing the mechanics of an operating restaurant, especially appropriately attired cooks preparing their food. It gives them something to look at and something to talk about, increases their trust in the food's preparation, and relieves the monotony of staring at the same pictures on the wall, time after time.

Because of the ability of color to act as a mood changer, knowledgeable use of it is one of the most effective and inexpensive design tools. Blue, green, white, gray, and black tend to sedate and fatigue customers and employees. Yellow, brown, beige, red, gold, pink, and peach increase energy and promote activity. Decors that focus on bright and varied colors can make areas conducive to frivolity and excitement. Dark colors tend to moderate personalities and create a feeling of privacy and intimacy. A quality music system, proper musical selection, and appropriate volume can have a positive effect on the success of the business. Mistakes in these areas can be a major contributing factor in customer dissatisfaction.

The system, music selection, and volume should be geared to the hotel or restaurant's target customer, but be pleasing to the majority of customers. It is common to ask customers about their general experience, or how their room or food was; occasionally, someone should question customers about the music. It is important to consider the tastes of not only target customers but also secondary markets. Rarely will one type of music be the first choice for all customers, so sought. Since music influences the psychological and physiological well-being of customers, the selection and volume should have a positive effect on their state of mind and digestive system. Music for the mind and digestive system should be melodic, without loud bass (low-pitch) or treble (high-pitch) sounds, with no dramatic changes in volume or harsh beats, and should be as pleasant for the average customer who may not notice the music as for the customer who consciously listens.

Music can also be used to help cover up less desirable sounds of ventahoods, bussers, kitchen activities, and dishroom noise. For bars located in restaurants, the music system should have separate volume controls to allow proper balance between the bar and the dining areas. If there is a public-address system for paging customers, it should be tied into the music system so that it cuts off the music while a customer is being paged. Because of their ease of placement and unob-trusiveness, ceiling-mounted speakers are generally used for most hospitality businesses. These speakers should be omnidirectional, meaning that they will disperse the sound in all directions, rather than just straight down.

For proper sound coverage, ceiling-mounted speakers should be spaced at intervals of about twice the ceiling height, with a maximum distance between each of about 25 feet. The sound absorption qualities of all surfaces in the hotel or restaurant will influence the power of the amplifier, the type and quantity of speakers, tonal qualities, and the volume of the music. Softer surfaces, such as carpet and unfinished wood, absorb sound. Hard surfaces, such as metal, plastic laminates, and vinyl, reflect sound. There are three major categories of music for hotels and restaurants:

Background music: This is instrumental music, only slightly louder than the ambient sound in the room. The "ambient sound" is the average, constant sound in the room, including people talking, moving, and working; and air-conditioning and heating systems. Background music is generally used in hotel lobbies, public areas, and meeting rooms, and for upscale or formal dining rooms.

Foreground music. This is music with or without lyrics and loud enough to be easily heard over the ambient sound of the room without interrupting conversation. This could be easy-listening music at a higher volume, or mellow rock 'n' roll. Foreground music is used in most fast-food and casual dining restaurants.

Recreational music. Loud enough to dominate the atmosphere of a room, recreational music is generally reserved for bars and discotheques.

Midscale and luxury properties will also focus on functional needs but will generally not want to create the image that space was sacrificed to reduce costs. The type of food and beverages to be served and the service style are the most important elements to be considered in the layout and equipment needs of a restaurant. The best layout usually results from the cooperative efforts of the architect or designer, the general manager of the hotel or restaurant, the chef or kitchen manager, the head server, the owner, and consultant, if one is retained. Hotel and restaurant layouts should be based on the development of the work centers and work stations.Work centers is the smallest grouping of closely related tasks that are normally performed by one person.

The primary goal of a work center is to reduce the time and number of steps an employee or customer must take to complete recurring activities. A work center would include the concierge's desk, a front desk employee's station, a broiler cook's station, a salad bar, bar station, a wait station, and a desk in a guest room. Work sections are a group of related work centers where one type of activity occurs, such as the front desk, laundry room, preparation area or the cooking line in the kitchen, warewashing, the server's food pickup area, the bartender's work area, customer greeting and waiting areas, and dining room seating.

The primary purpose of this information is so that hotel or restaurant developers can work effectively with architects or designers to lay out the hotel or restaurant according to known facts rather than averages or estimates. Far too many hotels and restaurants are laid out and designed improperly by "professionals" (architects and designers) because of the hotelier's or restaurateur's trust or lack of knowledge.

Restaurant prices for most menu items will normally be relatively stable. Each six months or so, management will review the cost of each item sold, its current price, and various other internal and environmental concerns, then determine whether the price should be increased, left as is, or, in rare instances, lowered. When the price of an item with a high food cost fluctuates, a decision must be made whether to include the item on the menu at "market price," on a clip-on addition to the menu, on a blackboard, or simply announced by the server as a special.

One of the advantages, and often problems, of the hotel business is that prices are quite flexible. A room with a rack rate (the highest rate charged) of $100 could have a range of prices, beginning at a crew rate, Most prices for a hotel room would be negotiated between the buyer and seller. The hotel sales manager understands this going into negotiations, and if he/she has forgotten, the potential customer will certainly make the manager aware of it. Even front desk personnel and reservationists are learning more about negotiations. Each firm must attempt to charge a price that will help it achieve its long-term objectives—the most important of which is long-term profit. Marketers must also consider how price will influence the business's overall image, its ability to afford a certain type of facility, and its capacity to expand.

In the short term, more specific pricing objectives dealing with profit, survival, market share, sales maximisation, quality, and must be considered. In the past, this was generally the price point beyond which people would begin selecting alternative sources: in other words, a price that will yield the greatest profit, but not so high that customers would go elsewhere. Because of today's value oriented public, the chosen price is often not the highest acceptable price, but the one that maximises profits. A gross profit of 75 per cent matters little if sales and net profits are low. There are instances when this strategy will work, such as when competition is weak, but an overcharging strategy may unfortunately sacrifice long-term objectives for short-term profits. Competition will eventually enter the market, resulting in drastic reductions in sales and the business's image.

A business would be much better off with a lower gross profit, but hopefully higher sales and net profit. Several restaurant chains have recently adopted the approach of increasing their food cost percentage because of its positive impact on sales and net profit. In this case, customers realise that they get more for their money, so they return more often and tell their friends. All pricing is essentially based on negotiations between sellers and buyers.

In hotels, this is accomplished when a sales manager discusses price with a corporate travel planner and when reservationists or front desk personnel attempt to extract the highest reasonable rate from individual travelers. Because the majority of hotel rooms are sold through a reservation system, negotiations take place directly with individuals, or the representatives of individuals or groups. In restaurants, negotiations are more subtle. Rather than negotiate with individual customers, restaurants negotiate with their customers in the marketplace by establishing a certain position or image supportive of a certain price.

If the restaurant sets menu prices lower than what could be obtained, then the customer has gotten the better deal. If the restaurant can still make a satisfactory profit at the low price, then each party is happy. If the restaurant attempts to charge too much for its food or beverage, then the customer will refuse further negotiations until the price is reasonable. In setting prices, marketers must be aware of the price elasticity of their targeted customers-how sensitive customers are to changes in price. In economic terms, hospitality pricing has traditionally been relatively inelastic. This means that, as the price goes up or down within a moderate range, the level of demand (total sales) will change very little.

Like everything in marketing, things change, and the economics of the hospitality customer is no exception. Currently, because of intense competition, many sellers are offering discounted prices and specially priced packages of different sorts. As customers are getting used to looking for the best deal, demand is becoming more elastic, meaning that, as the price changes, total sales or demand will also change. Of course, other issues such as quality, consistency, and atmosphere will affect the degree of the target customers' elasticity.

Businesses, whether budget or upscale, with a reputation for quality will be able to limit the degree of price elasticity. Another means of exposing key elements in the customer's purchase decision is to determine how the customer perceives the value of the product or service. This theory says that customers will first calculate nonmonetary values of the product, such as the product itself, service, convenience, atmosphere, and image. They then calculate the price they are willing to pay for these values. This includes the monetary price, time, effort, energy costs consumed during the purchase or experience (e.g,, the time and effort necessary to get the family ready and drive to the restaurant and the cost of the gas), and the psychic cost (level of comfort and risk).

Based on the target customers' value assessment, the business then sets a price for the product or service. Setting a company's price based on what competitors are charging is referred to as competitor-based or going rate pricing. Because of the tendency for a hotel's customers to compare prices, and the fact that a hotel room costs the customer considerably more than a meal in a restaurant, hotels are generally forced to use competitor-based pricing to a greater extent than restaurants.

The primary problem with competitor-based pricing is that there may be a substantial difference in cost of sales and expenses between one competitor and another. The justification for it is that customers know what competitors are charging for similar accommodations and, therefore, will be wary of hotels charging a higher relative price. It is best to consider each of the three pricing approaches and the business's particular situation in determining prices. For example, if competition is intense, then competitor-based pricing will generally be the primary approach.

In the hospitality industry hotels and restaurants are considered to be retailers. The primary consideration for a retailer in regard to the marketing channel is its location, so this becomes the main issue to be addressed. In addition to its normal distribution channels, hospitality businesses will need to determine if there are alternative means of delivering the product/service to the customer or making it available to them. Most firms tend to stay with their primary or traditional marketing channels, such as individual business travelers, group, and leisure. Since this is where most of the competitors are, a less desirable channel may offer less resistance. These niches may represent great opportunities for growth for innovative sales managers.

Some hotels near hospitals sell between 20 per cent and 30 per cent of their rooms to insurance companies for out-of-town patients and their families. There is still a high percentage of the small business market that does not know of the benefits of having meetings away from their office. Many service organisations, colleges, and universities have not had sales managers call on them to offer special rates. Targeting major travel agencies is an option that has been used by many of the larger hotel chains, but not as much by smaller chains or independents.

International, national, and regional travel clubs offer another potential source of business. To improve the effectiveness of both marketing and operational aspects of the catering function, many hotels that were previously without a catering sales manager have added one. In some areas, customers are able to order food for delivery through the Internet. Some hotels are offering discounted rooms through the Internet. Many casual dining and even fine dining concepts have implemented delivery strategies. Competitors at all levels of the restaurant business are adding catering to their marketing channels.

The vertical marketing system refers to the way in which portions of the channels of distribution are related. For example, if all parts of the marketing system are owned by one company, it is called a corporate vertical marketing system. If there are signed agreements to supply products or services or help coordinate efforts, it is called a contractual vertical marketing system. If a dominant member of the marketing channel controls activities through its size and power, it is an administered vertical marketing system.

Place strategies may not be critical for an existing business if no changes in the marketing channel are contemplated. If the location was a problem, it should have been noted in the internal analysis section, then the firm should consider a strategy to reduce its detrimental effect on sales. One area of concern for the marketing channel is the hotel's reliance on marketing intermediaries, such as travel agents, tour operators, and reservation services. For an agreed fee based on a certain percentage of the amount of the booking, the marketing intermediary, generally a travel agency, will book an individual or group at participating hotels.

The booking can be made manually over the phone, or it could be placed through electronic booking services, such as Apollo and SABRE. These systems provide a variety of travel-related information and allow travel agents to book flights, hotel rooms, and ground transportation through a computerised database. Travel agents equipped with the appropriate software can provide individual travelers and corporate meeting planners with up-to-date information about hotels for their chosen destination, such as room availability, telephone numbers, fax numbers, recreation facilities, and rates.

No single decision will have a greater impact on the business's investment and success than its choice of a location. Its primary importance concerns the number of potential customers that can be attracted. Other significant factors include the available labor pool; a multitude of zoning requirements that could place limits on hours of operation, the serving of alcoholic beverages, or even whether a hotel or restaurant can be opened or built on the property; local health codes; construction costs; available parking; and various operating costs, such as monthly rent, taxes, insurance, maintenance, utility costs, and trash disposal.

Every city has a restaurant or two in terrible locations that are doing an exceptional amount of business. These restaurants should be viewed as exceptions, and any attempt to duplicate their location strategy should be approached with caution. The term location is used to describe the piece of land on which the building is located. A location survey will include all variables that make the location suitable or unsuitable for a particular use. Site refers to the place on that piece of land where the building will be or already is located.

Sometimes a particular location will be excellent, but the site has various problems, such as lack of visibility, parking, or access; or being too small, narrow, or too large. Though location research is becoming much more scientific, it is still a soft or social science impacted by human nature. Current geographic, demographic, psychographic, and behavioral attributes can be reasonably quantified, but constantly changing consumer trends, competition, economic conditions, and other environmental factors are difficult to discern with accuracy. Frequently, the statistics for a particular location will appear to be ideal, when operating results prove disappointing.

Unfortunately, there is no known method of assuring the success of a location decision. For the independent firm or small chain, the most suitable option is to complete a detailed location report to help gather necessary research. Large chains have the strategic advantage for location decisions of vast statistical data that enable them to compare the characteristics of a proposed location with similar, existing locations.

4

Policy Formulating

Leisure activities and community facilities are important aspects of everyday life. They are diverse in nature and have wide and varied land-use implications. In this respect it is important that residents and visitors alike can freely participate in formal and informal recreational activities including cultural events.

The land-use implications of sport and recreation can be significant. There is a growing awareness of the importance of sports and recreational facilities of all kinds in urban areas and increasing use of the countryside for those purposes. Increased leisure time, a greater awareness of the benefits of sport and recreation, early retirement and increased unemployment will have a profound effect on the demand for sporting and recreational facilities during the Plan period.

Participation in sport and recreation can help improve the individual's health and sense of well being; promotion of sporting excellence can help further civic and national pride and has a valuable social and economic role. NorhEast

Linconshire adopted a local plan for leisure tourism .The Council is mindful that sporting opportunities should, whenever possible, be made available for everyone including the elderly and those with disabilities for whom access to facilities is especially important. Amenity Open Space can either be in private or public ownership and its allocation does not imply that there is public access to the land.

Areas of Amenity Open Space in private ownership have been allocated by virtue of their sporting/recreational function and/or the important role they play in terms of enhancing visual and residential amenities. Súch areas may include open spaces in villages which form an integral part of the settlement's intrinsic character. It is important that areas of amenity space are accessible to all sections of the community, particularly those without access to cars. The Council as the main provider of amenity space will seek to improve the accessibility of such areas to people with mobility handicaps such as the elderly, infirm, blind or partially sighted people, wheelchair users and other forms of physical impedance such as parents with young children.

Informal open space is used for a variety of leisure pursuits, such as walking, dog-exercising, picnicking, enjoying the natural environment and as casual play space for use by children. It does not include land used for outdoor playing space purposes such as playing pitches, greens, courts, athletics tracks, putting greens, training areas and children's equipped play areas.

Within North East Lincolnshire, the majority of informal space is concentrated in areas like Weelsby Woods, The Freshney Parkway, Cleethorpes Country Park, Coombe Briggs Meadow, Homestead Park, Immingham and Bradley and Dixon Woods. The recreational and amenity value of this space to the population of the Plan Area in particular as casual playspace for use by children is recognised and this Plan will seek to protect such areas from inappropriate forms of development and encourage the provisions of additional open spaces where possible.

The Council also recognises the visual importance of informal amenity areas in addition to their obvious recreational role, particularly in the main urban areas and settlements. Such open spaces are vitally important components of the Plan Area and play a crucial environmental role by enhancing visual and residential amenities and by acting as wildlife corridors or areas. Outdoor playing space is comprised of playing pitches, greens, courts, athletics tracks, putting greens and training areas in both public and private sector and children's equipped play areas.

The only recognised National Standard for outdoor playing spaces the National Playing Fields Association (NFPA) '6' acre standard which was established in 1989. A survey of the Plan area entitled 'Facility Provision in North East Lincolnshire' was carried out during early 1997 by the Council's Leisure Services Department and a Post Graduate Researcher at Sheffield Hallam University. This identified 293.9 hectares of Outdoor Playing Space which suggests a surplus of 2.9 hectares occurs. This standard covers broad areas and does not take into account local deficiencies or surpluses of certain types of open space. However it is still considered to be the starting point for the Local Authority in determining open space standards.

North East Lincolnshire is reasonably well catered for when the broad NPFA standard is considered. In general, North East Lincolnshire's open spaces are compliant with the standard's size and distance to travel criteria. However, local deficiencies have been discovered in relation to Local Amenity Open Space, Small Open Spaces and Local Recreational Areas/Parks which should be located within a distance of 200-400 metres. In particular, older terrace areas of the Grimsby/Cleethorpes conurbation are deficient in informal open spaces at a neighbourhood level. These areas, typified by high density terraced housing are lacking the open space opportunities less densely developed areas on the periphery of the urban area offer.

Often within these areas 'Brownfield sites' come forward for redevelopment purposes. Such developments will be expected to take into account local deficiencies in open space, based upon the adopted standards. Settlements outside the urban areas have also been found to be deficient in terms of open space provision. However, the extent of open space provision has to be considered with regard to the settlement's population and its proximity to other settlements or major urban areas. New residential developments increase pressure on existing open spaces which are often inaccessible to them. To counter this, it is important that the Plan Area's outdoor playing space provision is retained and enhanced wherever opportunities arise.

Developers of major housing schemes or other substantial developments in areas of recognised deficiency will, therefore, be expected to provide, or contribute towards, amenity open space including where appropriate informal and outdoor playing space. The Council will monitor the provision of such open space in association with development proposals. In terms of football pitch provision North East Lincolnshire has 76 adult pitches available through both the public and private sectors for leisure use. Although there is no nationally accepted standard for playing pitch provision, the Sports Council through its 'Playing Pitch Strategy' suggests a standard of 1 pitch per 1840 people which relates to a requirement of 87 pitches - a shortfall of 11.

At the local level, a much more focused neighbourhood assessment needs to be undertaken. Through consultation with the Council's Leisure Services Department information has been gathered on the distribution, latent demand and quality of existing pitches within the Plan area and from this it is evident that existing playing pitches can effectively cope with the current demands placed on them by the Adult/ Junior Leagues. However, problems in supply/demand occur principally during the winter months when pitches are unplayable due to water logging and icy conditions. This leads to backlogging of fixtures and an increased pressure to overuse existing pitches often at the expense of pitch quality. Continued improved preventative maintenance is therefore required to minimise cancellations and backlogging.

It has been estimated that up to 10 additional pitches are required to allow some of the more extensively used pitches (at Sidney Park, Hardy's Recreation Ground, Sussex Recreation ground, Homestead Park and Duke of York Gardens) to be returned to passive recreational pursuits or rested. This would allow pitches to be rested on a rotating basis so that essential maintenance such as relaying can be carried out. There is also scope for 4 additional pitches to be provided at Bradley Pitches, but such work would require additional changing facilities and improved car parking arrangements.

Localised deficiencies of pitch provision occurs within the main Grimsby/Cleethorpes urban area resulting in players having inadequate access to local teams/facilities.

Such areas include the Willows, Wybers Wood, Scartho, Littlecoates, East Marsh, Cleethorpes Central and Hainton. In general there are no publicly accessible pitches to the north west of the main urban conurbation. The Council will therefore seek to re-address this imbalance by securing by negotiation suitable sporting facilities in areas of recognised deficiency.

In certain instances it may be advantageous for an existing playing field to be upgraded in terms of pitch quality and associated facilities enabling an intensification of use. This would, however, require an assessment in relation to the accessibility of the playing field to the development site. There are approximately 90 Junior pitches under the control of the Education authority or private sector. These pitches are in general relatively poor in quality and are extensively used by both the Junior Football League and by the schools, with little scope of use by the Adult League due to size restrictions and pitch maintenance implications.

North East Lincolnshire is well catered for with regard to non-football related pitch sports. Once again pitch quality is a major factor in maximising the use of existing facilities. One recognised deficiency identified by national standards relates to the provision of Rugby Union and League pitches. However, there appears to be no latent demand for additional Rugby facilities within North East Lincolnshire.

Rural communities are often isolated and do not have direct access to leisure facilities located within the urban areas. Frequently, they rely on school facilities to provide land for ball games or pitches. There has been a need identified in the larger communities for Community Halls including adequate storage facilities which could be utilised for a variety of sporting and recreational activities such as badminton, target bowls and 3-a-side soccer. In terms of outside playing space 'multi use games areas' with associated floodlighting which can be used for Netball, Basketball, and 5-a-side soccer have been identified as cost-effective means of providing a wide range of facilities.

In addition outside grass sport areas which are designed to accommodate ½ soccer pitches and changing facilities as well as artificial cricket squares and bowling greens, offer a wide range of formal sporting opportunities. All of the above have been identified as being deficient to some extent in the rural communities. This is recognised by the Plan, and the Council will seek to re-address this by seeking developer's contributions or through separate grant aided funding.

Allotments make a valuable contribution to meeting the community and leisure needs of the Plan Area and because of their green nature can help to reduce the impact of the surrounding built up area. Additionally, they make a worthwhile contribution to local food production and help to protect against over development.

The urban area of Grimsby has eight statutory allotment sites providing 1839 plots owned and controlled by the Council. There is a further total of 9.47 hectares of allotments located within the urban area of Cleethorpes and the defined settlements of Humberston, Immingham, Laceby, New Waltham, Stallingborough and Waltham.

As part of the Millennium Park Scheme on the former Macaulay Lane Tip Site, part of the allotment site adjacent to the former tip is likely to be lost with the remaining allotments consolidated on the northern part of the site. It is important that Amenity Open Space is readily accessible to all members of the public. Within areas of recognised deficiencies of open space or areas subject to major residential development the Council will explore the possibility of securing additional amenity open space with public access, serving the immediate needs of local inhabitants. Such areas have been identified on the Proposals Map as proposed Amenity Open Space.

Further sites may be required during the Plan period as a result of quantitative and qualitative deficiencies being identified through the Local Plan monitoring process and the Council's Sports and Leisure Strategies. The Council will secure Proposed Amenity Open Space areas by entering into planning agreements to provide or improve recreation and sports facility provision or in some cases it may be appropriate for the Council to purchase the land concerned.

A strip of land off Cromwell Road is reserved as Amenity Open Space to provide a future pedestrian access link to the Millennium Park Site at Macaulay Lane which is being promoted as a mixed-development site including open space/parkland. A site has been allocated at Peaks Lane, Grimsby as a Proposed Employment Site and as part of the development of this site, an opportunity exists for the developer to lay out amenity open space on adjoining land to complement the surrounding countryside and assist in meeting the Plan Area's need for more Amenity Open Space. The release of such land will be secured, if necessary, through planning obligations between the developer of the Proposed Employment Site and the Council.

The Council is seeking to improve the existing Roval Drive recreation area in Immingham with access required across the western end of Coombe Briggs Meadow, to the proposed housing site to the north. There has been considerable recent growth in housing in New Waltham, emphasising the need for more community facilities, particularly public open space. In particular there is a shortfall of both formal and informal open space to the south of Station Road which acts as a barrier to the facilities at Greenlands some distance to the north. The two areas of proposed amenity open space situated off Enfield Avenue, to the north and south of the existing school playing field, provide opportunities to address the current shortfall.

Development of the adjacent housing site should incorporate appropriate pedestrian and cycle links; including to existing development, which promotes the area's accessibility. The land to the south of the identified proposed amenity open space, land known as Humberston Grange, is recognised as being of local landscape and wildlife interest. The Council will seek to maintain this area's local landscape character.

Assembly and leisure, sports and recreation facilities can vary greatly in size and purpose. They can be facilities for the local community to enjoy or multi-million pound investments such as cinemas that serve a large catchment area. Indoor recreational facilities are an important aspect with regard to satisfying the leisure needs of the local community. North East Lincolnshire is currently served by several indoor facilities which cover a wide range of leisure facilities.

The Grimsby/Cleethorpes and Immingham urban areas offer a high level of provision and accessibility to sports halls as reflected in Humberside County Council's 'Five Year Strategy for Sport and Recreation in Humberside' where it is noted that 65-75% of total demand is located within 5 miles of an existing centre. Any immediate requirement for new provision in those areas are small scale and localised. The Council's existing Leisure Centres are located at Cromwell Road, Grimsby, Immingham and at the

Kingsway, Cleethorpes. These centres offer a wide range of traditional indoor recreational facilities serving the needs of the plan Area. An additional facility is the Grimsby Auditorium located adjacent to Grimsby Leisure Centre, Cromwell Road, a multipurpose performance venue accommodating up to 1600 people offering an extremely high quality lighting and acoustic arena together with a flexible seating arrangement.

Other facilities include Immingham and Scartho Road Swimming Pools and a variety of other private indoor sports clubs. These services are currently well utilised but it is foreseen that due to ever changing leisure trends, that a number of new facilities or the revamping of existing centres may be required. Such facilities should be accessible to the population they serve and make the best use of recreational land available. The use of derelict disused or reclaimed land or buildings will be particularly encouraged.

North East Lincolnshire has a number of outdoor recreational facilities including the King George V Stadium, Grant Thorold Park, Peoples Park, Weelsby Woods, Bradley Woods, Dixon Woods, Duke of York Gardens, Cleethorpes Country Park, Sydney Park, Homestead Park, Pilgrim Park, Coombe Briggs Meadow, as well as other areas of amenity open space. There is a recognised demand for all weather pitches which enable active sport participation throughout the year regardless of weather and light conditions. The Council recognises the strategic importance of such facilities and will promote the active use of them.

The Borough also provides a number of venues for the staging of professional and semi-professional sporting events. The King George V Stadium hosts athletic events; the Cleethorpes Cricket Club ground on Chichester Road is occasionally used for one day county cricket and Blundell

Park is the home of Grimsby Town Association Football Club. In recent years Grimsby Town have been investigating the possibility of re-locating their stadium.

The development of a full size synthetic grass pitch on Clee Fields has partly met the immediate demand for such a facility in the Grimsby and Cleethorpes urban area. The effective use of this facility as substitute for scarce grass playing pitches depends on the Football/Hockey Associations taking advantage of its multi-use and intensive use capabilities. There is however, demand for an additional full sized multi-use games area (MUGA) within Cleethorpes to accommodate adult mid week competitive leagues.

At present, the Plan Area is served by 6, 18 hole golf courses and 2 nine hole courses, these being:- Immingham Golf Club; Cleethorpes Golf Club; Grimsby Golf Club; Manor Golf Course; Humberston Golf Club; Waltham Windmill Golf Club; Humberston Country Club; Bourne Leisure Golf Course and Willow Park Golf Club, Grimsby. All are privately run and offer varying degrees of non-membership accessibility. The Plan Area has recently witnessed a massive investment in golf courses with 4 of the courses being developed within the last 3-4 years.

Golf courses can open up the countryside for recreation, but they can also have a significant impact. Golf courses principally serve urban areas and therefore should be sited as close to them as possible thus reducing the need to travel by car and avoiding widescale recreational uses into the open countryside. Many golf course proposals are accompanied by developments such as hotels, holiday accommodation, additional built sports facilities or leisure complexes and conference centres.

Certain types of sporting or leisure activities can have particular planning implications by means of noise generation. Such activities include:- motorcross, speedway, microlites, powerboats, pistol/rifle shooting on outdoor ranges and clay pigeon shooting and outdoor sport facilities and event areas due to the increased use of PA systems and spectator noise. It is important that local conditions and circumstances are taken into account when determining proposals which are essentially for a 'noisy sport'. Local amenities, both of residents and of the area generally will be of paramount importance.

Unless it can be proven that a proposal site located within or adjacent to the built environment will not harm the environment or general amenities of the area it is felt that such activities would be more suitably located away from the urban areas. Newer leisure activities, such as war games (paint ball) can cause disturbance and danger as well as noise problems. Grimsby Town Association Football Club has been investigating the feasibility of relocating to a new stadium for over the last six years.

The current ground at Blundell Park has served the football club for over a hundred years and has been modernised in an incremental way. However, some of the stands date from the original development of the ground. With the requirement for football stadia to be all seating the capacity for spectators is limited to just over 8,000 at Blundell Park. This is a considerable limitation for a league football club where money through the turnstiles is a primary source of income. Furthermore, the quality of facilities available to spectators is also below standard on account of the ageing infrastructure.

Blundell Park is confined to its current site area by surrounding residential areas. This confinement presents a number of basic problems. Firstly, any reconstruction of the ground would have to take place within a space defined some one hundred years ago as the prospects of outward expansion are unfeasible. Secondly, a significant expansion of the capacity of the stadium will impact upon the surrounding houses both in physical and amenity terms. In physical terms it is likely that the stands would overshadow existing properties.

In amenity terms the increase capacity would mean much larger crowds, increased noise, inconvenience and an acute lack of parking which is at present a severe problem as only on road parking is available. It is also recognised that the location of the existing ground limits any opportunities the Football Club may have for promoting other business ventures; corporate hospitality, conferencing facilities and other commercial uses for the stadium. Such business ventures are also an important part of financing the operation of a football club.

Many people get pleasure from using the countryside and urban footpaths, bridleways and greenlanes. It is important that public access to the countryside is maintained whilst ensuring that the character of the countryside and interests of the farmers are unharmed. This can be best achieved by means of the extensive rights of way network already existing in the Plan Area and by the Council actively promoting, directing, protecting and creating, where appropriate, existing and new routeways. It is also important that routeways, where practical, are accessible to people with mobility handicaps.

Recreational links from the urban areas/defined settlements to the open countryside are of particular importance as they act as recreational gateways facilitating public access to the wider countryside areas beyond. Such routes, however, by their proximity to higher areas of population density are relatively highly trafficked and can suffer from problems such as overuse and vandalism. Due to the importance of the rights of way network as a recreational resource its quality and quantity should not be reduced.

In relation to security and animal husbandry it is often desirable to have stablehands living on or adjacent to equestrian sites. However, the uncontrolled development of residential uses in the open countryside is contrary to other Plan policies. Equestrian proposals involving new residential uses in the open countryside will, therefore, only be considered acceptable where a submitted business plan clearly demonstrates that the proposal is economically viable and that it is essential to the daily running of the business that it includes a residential use. In order that the long term viability of the business can be adequately assessed, residential uses will be restricted by the imposition of temporary planning permissions over a fixed period, normally for five years.

Tourism is one of the country's fastest growing employment sectors. It covers a wide range of diverse but related activities and facilities to cater for the needs of both day and longer term visitors, such as:-accommodation, catering, transport, tourist attractions and information provision. Tourism makes a major contribution to the national economy and to the prosperity of many cities, towns and rural areas, and its continuing growth generates a range of economic activity and new job opportunities.

There is also an overlap with sport, recreation and retailing which meets the needs of tourists as well as local people. Other related activities include business centres, sales events, music festivals and professional and academic meetings which combine tourism with their specific purposes. Within the Plan Area the tourist industry is centred upon the resort of Cleethorpes which has a long established association with tourism. Tourist attractions elsewhere include the National Fishing Heritage Centre located within the Maritime Quarter of the Alexandra Dock, Grimsby Auditorium, Waltham Windmill and the Lincolnshire Wolds AONB.

The vast majority of tourist and visitor attractions are associated with the summer season and are geographically centred on the resort, although recently there have been significant changes in tourism trends. It is important to acknowledge the growth in countryside pursuits, interest in the country's heritage and a lengthening of the tourism season. Increasingly, the natural beauty of the areas of landscape importance are establishing themselves as visitor attractions in their own right, as are attractions such as Waltham Windmill and the Immingham Museum.

The majority of tourism developments are small scale in nature and can be successfully accommodated in line with the tourism policy. However, in exceptional cases, opportunities may arise for large scale or innovative projects which exploit new market trends which could include hotel complexes, exhibition centres, theme parks or major new visitor attractions operating all year round.

Amusement centres are now a familiar scene in many of Britain's holiday resorts. Whilst these are generally acceptable in resort areas they can be damaging to retail areas and can severely harm the amenities of local residents in mixed commercial/residential areas, especially at night. Therefore, the development of these uses within the resort of Cleethorpes will be encouraged to locate primarily on the North Promenade which is considered to be particularly appropriate as it is a relatively self contained area where such uses can be maximised.

Along Alexandra Road, Cleethorpes, there is increasing pressure for changes from retail to resort uses. In this location there is a definite mix of resort related functions and other activities. There is, therefore, scope for allowing additional amusement centres provided that no single use becomes dominant. Often by their nature amusement centres are used as meeting points by youths/teenagers. Such uses are best located in Town Centre locations where their associated side-effects such as noise, disturbance, litter and congestion can be absorbed.

However, within certain Town Centre locations the proliferation of non-shopping uses such as amusement centres can lead to a breakdown in traditional shopping frontages. It is considered essential in terms of securing the long-term commercial interests of the Town Centre that existing Primary Shopping Frontages are retained. An over-concentration of amusement centres would fragment the shopping scene and would inevitably be detrimental to its overall viability and vitality.

Another important factor in assessing amusement centres is the pedestrian conflict that can occur immediately outside the premises. Pedestrian flow in terms of free movement and across/egress can be affected by youths/teenagers gathering outside of such establishments. In order to minimise possible pedestrian conflicts the footpath must be of an adequate width to cater for pedestrian/centre users.

Social Issues in Accommodation Sector

Hotels use significant amounts of energy for daily operations and recreational activities. In many facilities, energy costs are the second-highest operational costs after payroll. This high demand for energy is often due to the use of energy-intensive technology to provide modern comforts and conveniences, such as air conditioning, to large numbers of guests. The vast majority of hotels and resorts meet their energy needs by purchasing energy produced through the burning of fossil fuels (coal, oil and natural gas), which contribute to local air pollution and global climate change.

The extraction, refining and transport of fossil fuels can also cause environmental damage. Improvements in housekeeping and efficiency measures and use of renewable energy can decrease dependency on energy produced through fossil fuels.

Investments in more efficient energy use and improved housekeeping practices can lead to significant reductions in operating costs and energy bills, with relatively short payback periods. The average 300-room hotel spends an estimated $1.2 million per year on energy. Using renewable energy can reduce local air pollution, maintain destination quality and enhance the guest experience.

Energy efficiency and conservation practices can enhance reputation among guests and others who are concerned about reducing global energy consumption and the effects of climate change.

Management of Wateruse

In many areas of the world, demand for water exceeds supply and is seriously straining available water resources. Some of the most water-stressed areas in the world, such as the Mediterranean, are also home to some of the largest international tourism destinations. Guest demand for water usually far exceeds that of local residents. In addition to the water required for each hotel room and general hotel management activities such as kitchens and laundry, features such as swimming pools, lawns and golf courses can add significantly to total usage.

Excessive water use can degrade or destroy local water resources, threatening the availability of water for local needs. Problems may be made worse in areas where high tourist season corresponds with periods of low rainfall.

Hotels can produce significant quantities of wastewater, both graywater, which mainly comes from washing machines, sinks, showers, baths and roof runoff, and blackwater, which comes from kitchen dishwashing and toilets. In a number of destinations, little or none of this waste is treated, and pollutants such as fecal coliform bacteria and chemicals are discharged directly into the environment.

Poor sewage treatment can lead to pollution of ground and surface water, and degradation of marine resources, such as coral reefs. Among people, inadequate treatment of human waste can cause infection, gastro-intestinal disease, leptospirosis and cholera. In some coastal areas, beaches have been closed to the public because of high levels of chemical and organic pollution.

The Accor Thalassa Institute of Essaouira in Morocco has installed its own wastewater treatment. Additionally, at the IBIS Meknés, wastewater is recycled to irrigate the green areas, thus limiting the use of freshwater. Grecotel worked with local authorities in Greece to install a wastewater treatment plant that treats water from both the hotel and local communities, thereby helping to preserve local water quality.

The Le Sport resort in St. Lucia treats wastewater in three interconnecting lagoons that filter wastewater with aquatic plants and mesh. The filtered water is then disinfected further with ultra-violet rays and used for irrigation on the resort's grounds. In its first year of operations, the new treatment method saved about 3.8 million liters of water and thousands of dollars. Disney World, in Florida, USA, recycles 15.2 million liters of wastewater a day for irrigation of landscaping and golf courses. The company found this method was not only environmentally responsible, but cost-effective, as using municipally treated water would have been much more expensive.

At Great Keppel Island Resort, in Australia, organic wastes are shredded, composted for several weeks and then fed to the worms at the resort's worm farm. The worms produce a rich product that is used in the resort's gardens instead of fertilizer. This system reduces waste and eliminates the costs of removing trash from the island. The recycling program at the Banff Springs Hotel, in Canada, has cut waste by more than 85 percent. Since 1998, the Novotel NorthBeach in Australia has recycled, on average per week, 5000 kg of glass, 500 kg of cardboard, 700 kg of paper, 100 kg of plastic and 1500 kg of organic waste which is sent to farmers.

Storage and Disposal of Chemicals

Excessive or improper use, storage and disposal of chemicals and other hazardous wastes in daily operations can result in pollution and contamination of local environmental resources. Use of pesticides, fertilizers and herbicides for gardening and to control insects can lead to toxic runoff into streams, coastal waters and groundwater. Chemicals used for cleaning guest rooms or in recreational facilities such as swimming pools can contaminate local soil and water supplies and may pose a potential hazard to human health. Leakage of CFCs and HCFCs from refrigerators, air conditioners and other cooling equipment, as well as chemicals used for dry cleaning, in aerosols, fire extinguishers and foams, contribute to the depletion of the ozone layer.

Effective management of chemicals and hazardous wastes can reduce water treatment costs and the quantity and cost of chemicals purchased by the hotel. Proper use, storage and disposal of chemicals and hazardous wastes can ensure compliance with government regulations and reduce potential fines or clean-up costs.

Biodiversity and Nature Observation

Tourism development can have significant environmental impacts on both inland and coastal areas. Beyond simply reducing negative impacts, hotels can also seek opportunities to benefit biodiversity and nature conservation by contributing to improving the state of the environment at a local, regional or national level. Such action can be particularly important in countries where capacity and resources for environmental conservation are limited.

In many places, the natural environment is the basis of a holiday. Contributions to conservation can help to preserve natural tourism resources. Support for conservation can minimize the risks of future environmental problems and preserve destination quality. Promoting responsible ways to enjoy the environmental resources in a destination will improve the guest experience.

Tourism development can have significant impacts on local communities. Environmental damage from development may degrade or restrict access to resources, such as farmland, water or forests, upon which local people depend. In some cases, people may be displaced by hotels or other guest infrastructure. Local people who initially welcomed tourism as a source of employment, wealth, resources and infrastructure may find that development fails to provide them with the benefits they envisioned.

Although hotels do generate jobs in many service and support sectors, these jobs often do not go to the local people who are most impacted by tourism development, particularly those who lack skills or start-up capital. Much of the revenue from tourism may never make it to local communities because of foreign ownership of hotels or use of imported goods. Finally, insensitivity to local cultures, traditions and practices on the part of guests or hotel staff may lead to conflict and anti-tourist feelings among local communities.

The tourism industry provides employment for 230 million people - about ten percent of the world's formal labor force. There is a growing movement to ensure that tourism develops ethically and respects human rights. The 1948 United Nations Universal Declaration of Human Rights states that all human beings have certain basic universal human rights. These rights include the right to life, liberty and security of person, freedom from torture and slavery, protection under the law, freedom of thought, religion and travel, and the right to work, form trade unions and have an adequate standard of living and well-being.

The U.N. Declaration calls upon "every individual and every organ of society" to promote and respect human rights; as parts of society, hotels and other tourism businesses all have a role to play in achieving this goal. Most of the focus on human rights in the tourism industry has revolved around labor laws and poor working conditions (such as long hours, low pay, lack of job stability and limited career prospects), as well as the use of child labor or forced labor, child sexual exploitation and gender issues. Also included are non-discrimination issues, poverty issues, environmental and indigenous issues, including land rights, protection of human dignity and freedom of association and the rights to collective bargaining.

Canadian Pacific Hotels and Resorts have developed the Green Partnership Guide for employees, which includes company-wide goals on waste management, energy use, product purchasing and water conservation. Ramada International Hotels & Resorts has offered cash incentives to employees who come up with the best environmental ideas, presented awards to individual staff members, departments and hotels, and recognized staff members' ideas in the company newsletter. Each year, Grecotel, the largest hotel chain in Greece, hires a third party to analyze its performance against preset targets and ensure that targets are being met.

Development Strategy for Leisure Tourism

Tourism and Leisure will most likely mean different things to different readers. Because many of the sub-sectors are inadequately described by SIC (standard industrial classification) codes we have adopted scaling factors, which estimate the proportion of employment within a SIC that is appropriate to the sub-sector.

Of a total workforce of just under 2.6 million in the West Midlands, just under 305,000 are employed by the wider tourism and leisure cluster (not including the estimate for volunteers). This means that the tourism and leisure cluster accounts for 12% of all employment in the region making the sector one of the most significant sources of employment. Core employment totals just under 251,000, in turn representing 10% of regional employment.

There are considerable differences in the qualifications held by employees in the tourism and cultural sectors. With the exception of hospitality and the related areas of retail and transport, most sectors have a higher proportion of graduates than the national average and a lower proportion with no qualifications. Arts and entertainment has very high roportions of its workforce with degree or higher degree qualifications. This presents major issues with regard to workforce development with everything from basic skills to higher-level very specialised training being required. Partners are keen to learn why some sub-sectors manage to attract higher qualified staff than others.

The picture will chance significantly by 2008, when much higher numbers of people will need and hold higher qualifications, and fewer will have no qualifications. Currently, 12% of the workforce have no qualifications. This will decline to 31,606 by 2008 and account for no more than 9% of the workforce at that time.

The tourism and leisure cluster has a significant requirement for upskilling. Sector Skills Councils in development across the domains of tourism and leisure (including hospitality, travel, tourism, events, sport, active leisure, arts, entertainment and cultural heritage) agree that there are both common skills that are useful for any employee working within or moving jobs between the industries within the cluster, but also specific skills needs that vary depending upon the type of job, its level and its specialist field of expertise.

The 7 common generic (transferable) skills needs prioritised across the tourism and cultural domain are seen nationally as being:

(1) Communication skills

(2) Customer care

(3) Management / leadership

(4) ICT and new technology

(5) Basic skills

(6) Ability to follow instructions

(7) Ability to show initiative

The DfES Skills Dialogue for the Tourism and Cultural Industries provides an evidence-based assessment of skills needs across the domains of six (then) National Training Organisations - Hospitality Training Foundation (HtF), Travel, Tourism and Events NTO (TTENTO), Sport and Recreation National Training Organisation (SPRITO), Metier (the NTO for arts and entertainment), Cultural Heritage NTO (CHNTO) and Information Services NTO (ISNTO).

The recently formed Regional Tourism and Leisure Skills Group completed two skills workshops in 2003 that arrived at the following conclusions: "Despite the diversity of occupations and skills employed within the cluster, there are common issues faced by those diverse businesses. These are best summarised as being a deficit in attitudinal and basic skills amongst entry level applicants both young and old, a shortage of skills at craft level, a lack of leadership and management skills at first line owner manager and strategic levels, a need for more responsiveness by providers of education and training and poor communications between industry and training suppliers."

The workshops allowed delegates to describe what type of skills and labour shortages they felt the cluster most commonly experiences. These are summarised in the next table. A further skills and employment matrix was produced during the workshops, which considered the existence of skills issues across 23 areas from customer service skills and management development through to language training and career progression. These issues were considered for three domains (1) sport (2) museums / libraries and (3) tourism. Almost every domain for almost every skills area was thought to be an issue.

Therefore, there is a real need to help determine priorities for action through this study, otherwise resources simply will not spread far enough to meet all identified challenges. The Regional Tourism Strategy consultation paper for the West Midlands acknowledges that business tourism is a big business in the region. The West Midlands is the second most popular region for meetings in the UK (after London), and the Birmingham City region is in the top league of business tourism cities in Europe. It is expected that business tourism will grow. As such, it is important for us to consider the skills needed by people servicing business tourists. Business tourism encompasses:

—Organisers and delegates to conference

—Exhibitors at and visitors to trade fairs and exhibitions

—Incentive travel award winners

—Corporate hospitality

—Individual business travellers

Over the last 10 years there has been a 53% growth in all business trips, and the conference and incentive travel segments are predicted to grow faster than any other tourism sector to the year 2010. Business tourism visitors demand very high levels of service and those bringing events to Britain need a degree of expertise and dedication, which are specific to the business tourism sector.

Business tourism is year-round, peaking in spring and autumn, but still with high levels of activity in the winter months, thus sustaining permanent, full-time jobs. It is estimated that the sector employs around 530,000 people both directly and indirectly (nationally), and that for every £30,000 of additional business tourism revenue to Britain another job is created.

Having said that, respondents from the sport and leisure subsectors appear to focus more upon the need for job-specific skills, whilst those in the hospitality, travel and tourism subsectors focus on attitudinal issues as much as job-specific or technical skills. There is, as you would expect, a correlation between skills needed and type of occupation. Some of the gaps can only be filled by very localised or sub-sectoral initiatives, whilst broadly speaking, the cluster at large appears to demand a much greater ability in respect of servicing visitors or customers, making better use of IT, improving the abilities of owner managers, managers and supervisors and team-working.

There is also a real issue with the employability skills of new (especially younger applicants). This indicates the need for a range of pre-service initiatives to be improved so that applicants are more work-ready and committed to the idea of employment than currently appears to be the case. Further consultation with partners suggest it is possible that some of the occupations affected by skills gaps listed are also in the category of 'hard to fill' vacancies. There is also evidence that certain sectors have difficulty recruiting ethnic groups to vacancies.

Recent survey work by LOCUM Destination with accommodation providers and attractions in the region suggests that some occupations are particularly hard to recruit. The following table highlights the proportion of businesses saying they had difficulty recruiting paid staff: Further analysis revealed that the most acute recruitment difficulty for serviced accommodation providers was in fact for chefs followed by other kitchen staff and housekeeping staff. For non-serviced accommodation businesses, housekeeping staff appear to be most difficult to recruit followed by management staff.

There are no established tourism and leisure specific networks for HE/FE/private providers in the region. There was a general feeling that networks that brought together providers (particularly practitioners) would be useful. Collaborations are taking place in different ways, but the group seemed interested to know more about the FE / HE / provider Network model that has been established successfully in the North West. This idea has been further developed over the course of the study, and it seems that providers would be willing to develop such a network as long as it:

— Adds value to the service and activities already provided;

— Builds on existing local, sub-regional and regional networks that providers already belong to - though none of these are dedicated to meeting the needs of the tourism and leisure cluster specifically;

— It is inclusive;

— It is adequately resourced;

— Has the opportunity to have a continuous dialogue with employers and the regional Cluster Opportunities Group (COG);

— Promotes best practice and sharing of ideas. Impact would like to see the development of a regional bid by these providers, perhaps to AWM, with a 5-year plan to meeting the needs of the tourism and leisure cluster. It will require resource for development, website presence, course design and delivery and evaluation. Impact's guidance would be to form the Network around the following guidance and ideas:

Individual Higher Education tourism and leisure providers within the West Midlands have been proactive in establishing relationships with industry. They view the development of links as key in ensuring that the courses and other services offered are appropriate to industry needs. There are a number of ways in which these relationships have already been developed.

Despite the establishment of relationships with industry there still appears to be a lack of awareness from industry on how HEIs can contribute to leisure and tourism in the region. A key issue is the lack of understanding by many in industry of the qualities of tourism and leisure graduates and the contribution they can make to businesses. There is not only a requirement to encourage the recruitment of graduates, but also ensuring that they are used to their full potential once employed. Another issue is the lack of awareness of the courses that HEIs offer. Many provide a range of education and training opportunities from short courses, work based learning opportunities to the more traditional degree and post-graduate courses. These are often delivered in very flexible ways to meet the needs of industry.

There is a great deal of expertise and enthusiasm within West Midland HE tourism and leisure providers, which needs to be harnessed. Whilst it is important that HEIs develop relationships with industry on an individual basis according to the needs of employers and institutions, it is also important that West Midlands HEIs develop a more coordinated approach to their overall relationship with the West Midlands tourism and leisure industry. This will ensure that the range of leisure and tourism services that HEIs provide meet the region's needs in relation to skill development, course provision, research and consultancy.

HEIs recognise this and networks are beginning to be established in order to facilitate collaboration on a range of projects to address skill needs. An objective of the establishment of the post by the West Midlands Higher Education Association (WMHEA) of cluster innovation manager is to facilitate this coordination to enable maximisation of the complementary tourism and leisure related expertise that exists within HEIs.

There are 174 providers of work-based learning in the tourism and leisure cluster in the West Midlands. Of these 174 providers, 158 run programmes in the core sectors and 112 providers run programmes in related sectors. There were 10,208 people in the West Midlands in subjects covering the core tourism and leisure sector. There were also 7,717 people in work-based learning in related but relevant or related sectors.

The number of people in work-based learning in subjects related to core sectors account for 15% of all enrolments whilst related subjects account for a further 11% of enrolments. The total number of people in work-based learning in tourism and leisure related subjects is well above the proportion of people in tourism and leisure in the West Midlands' workforce.

5

Leisure Tourism in India

Leisure is currently one of the most exciting sectors in India. Though developing fast since last two years, the industry is still at an early stage of development. But with the increasing entry of some of the more established Indian entrepreneurs and corporate houses, the industry could be worth Rs 50,000 million (£735 million) per annum within the next 2 - 3 years. The sector is already worth Rs 10,000 million (£147 million) per annum.

Industry experts agree that the sector has great potential. Leisure consultants are experiencing a boom in demand for their services. Cultural attitudes within India are changing. The increasing incidence of Cable TV is exposing the population to a wider range of leisure pursuits. And the idea of an annual family holiday/ pilgrimage to the home village is being overtaken by more frequent weekend visits to leisure facilities within and around the cities.

The current size of the consumer market for the leisure and amusement sector is estimated at 25 - 30 million. This reflects a middle upper class with a monthly disposable income in excess of Rs 5,000 (£75). But with a population of 1 billion, 30% of which is under 20, and economic growth set to continue at 6% per annum, the number of consumers can only increase.

The sector is developing throughout India but the major projects are planned in the metropolitan cities, their suburbs and other major cities in Western and Northern India. The major cities in Southern states like Hyderabad, Bangalore, Mysore, Cochin, Thiruvananthapuram are also showing increased activity. However, projects in Eastern India are limited to Calcutta in West Bengal and Bhubaneshwar in the state of Orissa. Interest in the leisure business is not limited to the entrepreneurs. Consultants are beginning to focus on business prospects in the leisure industry.

The few leading amusement parks in India, such as Essel World and Water Kingdom, are of a very high quality with equally high standards of maintenance and safety. They are also well attended and profitable businesses which demonstrate that it can be done. Smaller attractions around the country however suffer from the absence of patent requirements and safety regulations.

Many 'rides' are either USA imports or inferior copies manufactured in India. Safety is a serious issue at amusement parks and there is currently no legislation to ensure that attractions are regularly maintained or checked for safety. The Indian Association of Amusement Park Industries (IAAPI) are pressing for the introduction of proper safety regulations and there may be a role for UK consultants with expertise in this area in future.

Amusement Park: Industry sources estimate the current size of the amusement park market as Rs 4,000 million (£60 million) per annum. This is estimated to grow to Rs 13,500 million (£200 million) by end 2003. The face of the industry is changing with a boom in single site operations. There are already 100-odd big and small parks scattered across the country.

Family Entertainment Centres (FEC): A typical FEC comprises a mix of bowling lanes, billiards and snooker tables, go-karts, video, laser and virtual reality games, mechanised rides, juke boxes, big-screen projected TV, multiplexes, Net-browsing terminals, shopping mall and food and beverages outlets. A number of corporate groups are investing large sums in FECs. There are currently 200 FECs in India.

Similarly the FEC sector will grow very rapidly. The number is expected to double in the next three years with investment increasing from Rs3,000 million (£45 million) to Rs20,000 million (£295 million). One such promoter has already obtained support from the UK based Commonwealth Development Corporation.

Retailing: Experience over the last five years confirms that Indian consumers react favourably to international concepts of convenience shopping and customer service. The retail sector is evolving into an exciting and competitive market place. In recent years international brands like McDonalds, Swarovski, Lacoste, Domino's, Wimpy's, Pizza Hut, Pepsi and Benetton have entered the Indian market.

Multiplex Cinemas: The cinema/ movie hall sector is expanding rapidly. More than 100 new multiplexes / shopping malls projects are to be ready by 2003. UP, Maharashtra, Gujarat and Punjab have already declared investment friendly multiplex policy.

Amusement Complexes: Consumer demand for greater sophistication will result in operators looking abroad for consultancy and advice in design and operation of amusement/ water parks. Two major Indian amusement parks have previously engaged UK consulting expertise.

The Indian amusement attraction manufacturing industry is also growing, aided by high import duty of 57% approximately under HS code 95.04 on foreign equipment. But the current range of Indian products is small compared to the US and Europe. There are good opportunitiesFor overseas manufacturers to establish JVs and technology transfer alliances with Indian manufacturers.

The Tourism sector is a poor performer, constrained by lack of infrastructure and little Government or private sector investment. It has until very recently been considered an elitist activity rather than a means for social inclusion and economic growth. Central Government is preparing to remedy this by making funds available for the States to prepare strategic plans. Some opportunity exists for UK consultants.

The tourism economy including support services such as hotel and travel totals Rs 905 billion (£13.15 billion), accounting for 5 - 6% of India's GDP, vis-à-vis the world average of 10%. Direct employment from the tourism sector is estimated at 15.5 million (6% of India's work force) and the indirect employment at over 42 million.

Compared to a 2.54 million inbound tourists in 2001, the figures dropped to 2.38 million in 2002. However, the period between January to October 2003 has witnessed a marked improvement compared to the same period last year and inbound tourism has improved by more than 15%. In fact, during Jan - Oct 2003 India has received 2.11 million tourists. The figure for 2003 is projected to 2.7 million. The tourism receipts stood at US$ 3.04 billion in 2001, the figure was US$ 3.02 billion in 2002. However, tourism receipts have seen a 17.4% rise in January - September 2003 compared to the same period last year.

State government's have also become proactive and are taking progressive steps to develop tourism infrastructure. Uttarnachal, Rajasthan, Kerala, Uttar Pradesh, Tamil Nadu, Andhra Pradesh are amongst such states. Karnataka was among the first states in the country to introduce progressive tourism policy in 1992. The government has announced updated Karnataka Tourism Policy 2002-07 that focuses on private sector participation in development of tourism in the State. Similarly the State government of Tamil Nadu proposes to increase the state's share of tourist flowing into country from present 4 to 9 percent to 10 to 12 percent during the year.

According to World Travel & Tourism Council the travel and tourism demand in India amounts to Rs 1,200 billion (£17.4 billion) and by 2010 this will reach Rs6,200 billion (£90 billion). It will grow at an annual rate of 8.3%.

A number of constraining factors have resulted in this diminished performance, principal among them, a lack of infrastructure and capacity to handle any increased tourist flow. Other examples are transportation services and systems and hotel capacity. For instance, the number of quality hotel rooms is limited to approx. 68,000 (1 to 5 star deluxe). The metro cities accounting for more than 35% of this supply.

Heritage and Conservation: The Archaeological Survey of India (ASI) established in 1861 functions as an attached office of the Department of Culture and the Department of Tourism. Its major activities are maintenance, conservation and preservation of centrally - protected monuments/ sites.

At present the ASI has declared 3600 monuments of national importance in the country, which include 16 world heritage monuments/ sites.

Like any other country the museums in India are considered to be repositories of country's cultural heritage. The Museums are acquiring, conserving and preserving historical, technical and other materials against decay. The Central government of India and the State governments are reported to be drawing up long-term plans to conserve cultural heritage in all forms.

Heritage Hotels: A new classification of heritage hotels has been introduced to cover functioning hotels in palaces, castles, ports and large residencies built prior to 1950. So far 62 properties have been classified in the heritage hotel category providing a capacity of 2000 rooms.

Competition: The US has already recognised the potential of the leisure/ amusement sector. The Commercial service of the US Embassy in Delhi and the American Amusement Machinery Association (AAMA) organised "India Amusement Expo" (featuring coin – operated family amusement machines and games) annually from 1996 to 1998 in Delhi. Similarly they have regularly organised a delegation of Indian businessmen to visit Asian Amusement Expo, the premier Asia Pacific leisure event in Singapore. They also regularly organise a delegation of Indian businessmen to visit the IAAPA show (International Association of Amusement Parks & Attractions) in Dallas, Texas. A large delegation of Indian businessmen is likely to participate in this year's IAAPA Annual Convention & Trade Show at Florida, USA in November 2004. This show is considered to be the largest amusement industry exhibition in the world. Apart from US the competition is from Korean and Japanese suppliers.

Trade Association: In early 1999 a group of 30 entrepreneurs from all over India gathered to form the Indian Association of Amusement Parks and Industries (IAAPI). Prior to the Association, each player had been working alone, resulting in high government taxation and prior regulation. The association is making efforts to address issues like entertainment tax, insurance, safety, training, exhibitions etc.

Exhibitions: The Indian amusement trade association - The Indian Association of Amusement Parks & Industries (IAAPI) organised its first trade show on amusement, entertainment and leisure in February 2001 in Mumbai. from 2 - 4 February 2001 in Mumbai. Apart from direct participation, more than a dozen British companies participated through a catalogue display organised by BDHC Mumbai.

The IAAPI organised its second annual show at the World Trade Centre Mumbai in March 2002. In all 50 companies participated of which 15 were from overseas. The Trade Partners UK,(now known as UK Trade & Investment) - British Deputy High Commission stand saw participation from 13 UK companies through catalogues, showing a wide range of products and services including kids playground equipment and rides, leisure, theme and amusement park consultants, ticketing solutions and circuses.

Recreation, leisure goods and services is an under-developed, under-exploited sector with huge potential. Sector is likely to grow by 300% per year over next 2-3 years, to be worth Â£735 million. A 9-member scoping mission of cultural heritage and tourism industry experts from the UK visited Delhi, Bhopal, Kolkata and Mumbai in January 2003. The purpose of this mission was to identify potential opportunities for UK cultural heritage & tourism industry to work in India, demonstrate expertise available from UK and recommend future support for the UK.

The possibilities for leisure activities in India are enormous. All you have to do is make up your mind and select your own destination. Tuck yourself away in pleasant seclusion of the numerous hill stations, whether in the Himalayas or the Nilgiris, the Western and Eastern Ghats or among any of the other hills and mountains. Or, just glide along the backwaters of Kerala—the mirror-still lagoons, the palm—fringed canals—on country crafts or luxury cruisers.

Or perhaps you would prefer to take a fishing rod and go angling, perhaps for your own supper. Alternatively, head for any of the many beaches which compel you to share their expanse and sense of ease. Plus, you can take a break at one of the many excellent golf courses all over the country. Well, the options are all here, if you have the inclination.

Beaches

With over 7000 kms of coastline, India has a number of beaches of different kinds—some sandy, others rocky, some dotted with palm trees, or scattered with shells, or backed by a rock-face with caves containing ancient art-work.

So, whether you're looking for a hint of adventure, or for a touch of romance, or only for a lazy and lovely holiday swimming in the open sea, there is sure to be a beach which suits your mood perfectly.

The names that immediately spring to mind are Goa and Kovalam — although Chorwad and Ahmedpur Mandvi in Gujarat, and those of Lakshadweep and Andaman and Nicobar Islands are also well developed and yet not crowded.

Goa, of course, is famous for a number of beaches. Calangute rose to fame in the '60s and '70s as a hang-out for hippies, a hot-house of drugs and nude sunbathers. For a more remote, pleasant and peaceful beach, there is Baga, only a couple of kilometers away. Other beaches in and around Goa are Anjuna, Chapora, Colva and Sirigao. In Lakshadweep, Kadmat, Kalpeni and Minicoy are islands surrounded by lagoons. These are restricted areas, but Bangaram and 3 small islands near it are open to foreigners. These are all uninhabited, but huts have been constructed in the native style to provide accommodation to visitors.

Further south are the beaches of Tamil Nadu, Pondicherry and Kerala. Marina Beach in Chennai, and Mamallapuram Beach close to Chennai, are the major beaches in Tamil Nadu. Although not a beach resort, Kanyakumari, which forms the southern tip of the country, looks out over the Indian Ocean, the Arabian Sea and the Bay of Bengal. It affords the rare spectacle of watching the sun set on the horizon at the same time as the moon rises on the other side. But some of these beaches are not recommended for swimming.

In Kerala, Kovalam is famous for it's beauty, and also offers opportunities for swimming, surfing and water skiing. Calicut is another picturesque resort on the Arabian Sea in the west.

Other water-fronts

For people looking for a beautiful site for a restful holiday, beaches are only one of the 'water-side' options. India has numerous rivers and lakes which also have delightful and pleasing resorts. There are lakes in hill resorts like Nainital, and Ooty etc. and there are beautiful water-falls like the Jog Falls in Karnataka, and the two waterfalls at Sivasamudarum, a short distance from Mysore.

The network of backwater canals crisscrossing Kerala and its enormous number of rivers running down to the sea, its lagoons and beaches formed by these waterways, make Kerala a beautifully green destination. Alleppey, in Kerala, is famous for its water carnivals and boat races.

Hill resorts

The Himalayas running across the northern and North-eastern states have innumerable hill stations, valleys, and snow-capped peaks which are ideal for a quiet get-aways. Mussoorie, Nainital, Dehradun, Shimla, Kullu, Manali are famous and popular, but there are some which, being not so well known, are less frequented. The North-east has a number of beautiful places but it is always advisable to check the status in terms of special permission required for these areas before planning a visit.

A relaxing holiday in Darjeeling in West Bengal can be combined with the fascination of life at a tea plantation here. The Western Ghats in central and south India offer a large number of picturesque destinations. The Nandi Hills near Bangalore; Chamundi, a peaceful little resort near Mysore; Kodaikanal, Yercaud, and the famous hill resort of Ootacamund, or Ooty, in Tamil Nadu, are only some of them.

The western coast in Maharashtra has Lonavala, Khandala, Matheran, Panchgani and Bhandara. Backwaters india's various leisure options include the backwaters of keral,exquisite hill stations,excellent golf courses and secluded beaches,himalayas,hill resorts,chinese fishing nets,trout fishing,golf,fishing villages

Life in Kerala largely centres around water and much of its mystical beauty lies in its quiet, shaded and deep backwaters. Cruise along these, through fishing villages, dense tropical forests, overhanging coconut trees, discovering as you go along, secrets of a little-explored world.

There is a Kerala where whole lives depend on these backwaters and as you sail along them, you see small tiled houses just on the edge of the water, men working at their boats and children playing among the coconut groves. Along the way you see boats carrying families, or loaded with coir or a newspaperman on his early morning rounds. In the distance you see Chinese fishing nets silhouetted against the blue and the orange of the sky.

And, in the months of August and September, after the monsoons, these backwaters come alive to the excitement of the snake boat races. Kerala Tourism's comfortable cruisers with good arrangements for parties and small conferences, well stocked kitchens and modern conference facilities can make idyllic settings for you.

Golf

In India you can play golf almost anywhere and courses are often set against dramatic backgrounds. In the hills and in the high Himalayas, in metropolitan cities and in small towns, by lakes and forests, or surrounded by tea estates, out in the desert and in old British cantonments. You can stroll off the course to share a cup of piping hot tea at a nearby 'dhaba', tee off from the highest 18-hole course in the world, watch a peacock dance on the green or play on a course that is enriched by old monuments and beautiful buildings. In India, playing golf will enable you to experience the country in a unique manner.

Well, tourism has been identified as an important avenue for employment and income generation, foreign exchange earnings and at the same time having a multiplier effect on the economy. The expenditure of the tourist circulates at all the three levels of the economy: i) National ii) regional, and iii) Local. This means that if the tourist expenditure circulates locally and the leakages are low, a significant improvement can be made in the income and living standards of the people of the region or locality. However, a developed region can often divert the benefits towards itself at the cost of the underdeveloped neighbouring regions. Such situations have been experienced in both international as well as domestic tourism.

Further, intense competition can be there within a country between different regions, destinations or leisure spots and among the various suppliers of services. As tourism becomes established as an economic activity, marketing strategies concentrate on increasing the volume of tourists. This, at times, creates a host of unforeseen consequences. Thus, it is necessary that the objectives of tourism development in relation to a region, city or (a rural area) leisure spot be clearly stated.

In fact, the developmental role of marketing has to be kept in mind while marketing regions, cities or leisure spots(a rural area). This developmental role is to be further strengthened by socially responsible marketing. The destination marketing in the international markets includes a variety of aspect say from information gathering to planning, image building, etc.

(Nevertheless) when it comes to cities and leisure spots/ heritage sites - particularly in the rural areas, marketing becomes a major problem. This is because the local bodies are either not aware about the developmental role of tourism or are constrained by their own politics or lack of funds. In India we find different destinations in different stages of what is termed as the product life cycle. For example, a region like Goa, a city like Shimla or a leisure spot like the Badkal Lake have reached a maturity level. They no more require promotion and have similarly exhausted their carrying capacity.

Their problem on the contrary is of retaining their image, checking the decline and doing away with the negative impacts of tourism. In marketing jargon what they require is internal marketing, product improvement, checking the decline, proper maintenance, etc. On the contrary look at a region like Kumaun which is struggling hard to promote its attractions in different cities (other than Nainital) and rural areas and develop its tourism products. If proper questions are not posed and answered, the planners and developers blindly imitate outside concepts and models of development without taking into consideration the local needs, customs, attitudes and constraints. In such a situation the destination may not take off at all or the entire developmental investment may go waste.

For investors also, promotion of rural tourism investment could bring in higher returns on comparatively low investments. India, traditionally, is a long haul destination and provision of rural tourist destinations in its basket of destinations will go a long way in showcasing and marketing India in a better perspective. Further, tourism can also be sold as post-convention destination not only for the conventions held in India but also for neighbouring countries.

Alternative Medicines

Total Health has been a matter of prime concern for all.

Improper life style and faulty diety patterns adversely affect the bio-rythemic cycle causing an imbalance in the psycho-physiolocaly conditions yielding a disturbance in mind-body relationship. Added to this, with the advancent of technology on the one hand, man is bestowed with boons in the form of luxuries and has engaged himself in a materialistic thrive on the other, resulting in illness which no one desires.

Besides this ecological imbalances, addictions, side effects of drugs and self medication have created an adverse impact on the required fitness of an individual which is so essential for routine created an adverse impact on the required fitness of an individual which is so essential for routin activities and all around progress.

WHO has identified more than 300 alternative therapies like Accupressure/ Accupuncture, Aromatheraphy, Reiki - Pranic healing, Folklore medicine etc. which are popular in different part of the World.

Today even in countries like USA, Canada, Germany etc alternative health science therapies are gaining ground. Together with modern system of medicine alternative health sciences / therapies offer cheaper and easily adaptable solutions to various ailments for positive health.

Angling

Angling and trout fishing is a delight in the States of Jammu & Kashmir, Himachal Pradesh and Uttar Pradesh. The innumerable fresh water streams and lakes provide the ideal setting for this exciting sport.

The river Jia Bhoroli, Kapili and Manas are the ideal places for angling. Jia Bhoroli and Manas are famous for its Golden Mahseer. An annual Angling competetion is regularly held at Jia Bhoroli where a good number of anglers both from out side the state as well as abroad participate every year. Angling is so popular and enthusiastic sport that there is an organised body by the name 'Assam Bhoroli Anglers Association' which organises this sport in the month of November every year, in collaboration with the State Forest Department

Ayurveda

Ayurveda is a science of life. It deals with the way of Healthy life by incorporating elements of anatomy, physiology, pathology, symptomology and cure of diseases.

Health is defined as the state of body when balanced doshas, balanced Digestion and metabolism, proportionate tissues(Dhatu), balanced function of all systems, cheerful disposition of senses, mind and spirit is achieved.

In Ayurveda, a person may be treated as a whole with customized approach looking into his constitution, age, sex, habitat, capacity and other relevant factors for the betterment of health / cure of disease.

Presently practiced Ayurveda is effective in all type of diseases except in some of the acute conditions where emergency treatment and surgery is mandatory.

Panchkarma a part of Ayurveda, is very effective for elimination of waste products from the body, rejuvenation and rehabilitation of chronic patients.

Properly prepared ayurvedic medicines and processes are eco - friendly and usually give no adverse effects if taken in right manner. Ayurveda first focuses on the health of the patient and then on the specific cure of the disease so as to expedite recovery in holistic manner.

Kerala: Backwaters

It's an intricate network of innumerable lagoons, lakes, canals, estuaries and the deltas of forty-four rivers that drain into the Arabian Sea. Over 900 km of this labyrinthine waterworld is navigable. The largest backwater stretch in Kerala is the Vembanad lake which flows through three districts and opens out into the sea at the Kochi port.

The Ashtamudi Lake (literally, having eight arms), which covers a major portion of Kollam district in the south, is the second largest and is considered the gateway to the backwaters.

The Ketturvallom

Showcasing a unique heritage The kettuvalloms (houseboats) of Kerala are giant country crafts, measuring up to 80 feet in length. It took great skill and meticulousness to construct these giants by tying huge planks of jack wood together, without the use of a single nail.

Today, these goods carriers have been adapted to make the most exciting tourism product in India, the luxurious furnished houseboat. A kettuvallom usually has one or two bath attached bedrooms, an open lounge, deck, kitchenette and a crew comprising oarsmen, a cook and guide.

The dynamic and growth oriented Govt. of Gujarat is determined to develop Tourism as a key industry to make it an important contributor to the state's economic and social growth and to offer a right blend of Business and Pleasure. This will be achieved by active participation of private, national and international corporate bodies to bring in their expertise and investment with supportive Govt. policies and facilitation.

The current Indian tourism contribution to GDP is 1.8% and it is targeted to reach 6% in the next decade. If this can be re-targeted to reach 10% an additional 1.2 crore jobs can be created. A majority of the 2 crore NRIs, are Gujaratis who are prosperous as professionals and traders. This untapped resource can be motivated to become prospective tourists and investors in this sector and the GDP level can be improved considerably.

Gujarat is gifted with a vast mix of tourism potential to satisfy the fancies of widest range of tourists. The tourism policy gives a special thrust to the event based tourism wherein the government's active support, encouragement will be made available. To promote tourism and showcase Gujarat, special events and international fairs shall be arranged.

The kite flying festival on Makar Sankranti day in the month of January is a riot of colours with colouful kites soaring the skies of Gujarat in varied shapes and sizes, Gujarat government gives this festival a high priority and invites people from all over the world to participate. A kite museum has been set up in Ahmedabad where kites from various parts of the world are displayed. This event promotes universal brotherhood and friendship where young and old irrespective of caste, creed or religion participate and enjoy.

Come Navratri nine nights of fun frolic and fiesta wherein young girls and boys in their most colorful traditional attire dance to the rhythms of drums and dandiyas.

This is a festival dedicated to the Mother Goddess celebrated by Gujaratis all over the world. There are other important festivals like Janmashtami, Holi Dwarka festival and Somnath festival etc., Traditional tribal fairs and festivals are a rare and rich heritage of Gujarat. The colourful Tarnetar fair, the Chitra Vichitra fair, the Holi fair at ChotaUdepur, the Vautha Cattle fair where donkeys in thousands are bought and sold, the desert fair of Kutch are Vibrant and pulsating. There is song and dance everywhere.

The vast potential of 1600 Kms coastline in Gujarat offers excellent potential for tourism development. The policy proposes to identify 9 different beaches in Gujarat and work out detailed action plan for the development of these beaches to attract tourists. Water sports of all varieties will be encouraged at these beaches and a clean environment, Good safe eco-friendly accommodation with five star facilities and security arrangements will be other important aspects required along these beaches. Private participation and adequate planned investment will make these projects viable propositions and can attract international tourists.

Health Tourism

Gujarat with its high-tech medical facilities and highly qualified medical professionals is fast becoming an important player in Health Tourism. Competitive rates and timely medical attention and five star facilities at polytreatment group hospitals have been regular attractions for NRIs from across the globe.

Health tourism shall also be encouraged with special emphasis on Naturopathy, Yoga and other indigenous therapies. The Policy proposes to create what is called Viswa Gram (Global Village) by erecting Structures and Models of Different Countries on the banks of rivers and along the Long Network of Narmada Canal at various places. NRIs and other visitors coming from various countries can stay at these places and feel at home. Facilities of international standards with the presence of Gujarati Culture, Cuisine and crafts will be provided. Special Shopping Arcades will display the best in arts and crafts of Gujarat. Private enterprise can reap rich rewards in this sector.

Wild life tourism

Gujarat is the only home of the Asiatic Lion .The wild life tourism of Gujarat also has attractions like the only wild Ass sanctuary at Little Rann of Kutch, Black Bucks of Velavdar, leopards, sloth bear, Indian Bustard and other animals. Birds across the seas regularly visit to nest in Gujarat at Nalsarovar and Kutch. The important species that visit are the Siberian Crane, Flamingoes, Pelicans and Falcons. The Policy envisages an improvement in the tourist traffic of wild life enthusiasts and ornithologists by providing adequate infrastructure and accommodation which is suitable at various forests and deserts.

The desert safaris of Kutch are a tourist attraction already and further improvements are to be promoted and implemented. A rich civilization once existed on the banks of river Indus called the Indus Valley Civilization. Recent excavations at Dholavira in Kutch and Lothal near Ahmedabad, showcase the rich socio-cultural heritage of our ancestors. The tourism policy proposes to develop these sites as tourist destinations. Special package tours can be arranged by private tourist operators with adequate and active support from the government to promote this circuit.

Historical Monuments

Emperor's Ashoka's rock edicts, several Buddhist cave temples and Queen Ranakdevi's Mahal at Junagadh and the exquisite forts and palaces at Champaner are some of the finest examples. Ancient historical monuments have a pride of place in the tourist circuit and the policy wants to promote a Buddhist circuit exclusively to attract the Buddhist tourists from south-east Asian countries.

Reverberating Rhythms of Hills

Gujarat's hills though not very high, offer the best vistas, with rich flora and fauna, swift flowing streams and waterfalls. The Saputara hills, Girnar Hills, Wilson Hills are some of the finest. Rock climbing, mountaineering at these hills can take you closer to the sky to feel the cool clouds. Hang gliding and Para-jumping are to be promoted in these areas as tourist attractions.

The spiritually inclined Gujaratis have always worshipped their Gods and Goddessess with regular pilgrimages, offerings and oblations. The religious fervour and piety can be found in the temples at Dwarka dedicated to Lord Krishna, The Somnath Temple with one of the 12 Jyotirlings, the Ambaji Temple and the Pavagadh temple dedicated to Mother Goddess Ambaji are finest examples of Hindu religion. The Jains have their own pilgrim centers with exquisite architecture and sculpture.

The numerous temples at Palitana and the Hutheesinh temple in Ahmedabad are fine examples of Jain architecture. The Policy aims to preserve and maintain these places of worship and develop religious tourism as a major promotional campaign. Special events on festive occasions are to be organized at Dwarka and Somnath to attract tourists.

Circuit Tourism

A focused approach along the guidelines of Govt. of India

has been adopted to develop and promote tourist circuits. Kutch circuit, Saurashtra circuit, North Gujarat circuit, Central Gujarat circuit, and South Gujarat circuit have been chosen as the important circuits and all promotional and infrastructural facilities will be developed to boost tourist traffic. the Sun Temple at Modhera. The seven storied step well at Rani Ni Vav, the toran at vadnagar and several others which express the cultural tradition that existed centuries ago and the monuments are comparable to the best anywhere in the World and are symbolic of our rich heritage.

Special events like the annual dance festival at Modhera are massive attractions and the government gives priority to such events to promote the rich cultural heritage and tourism..Infrastructure Development Infrastructure is the backbone of any development activity that is proposed to be taken up. Providing infrastructure of international standards is going to be the key for ultimate success of Tourism Policy of the State. It is therefore necessary to critically analyze facilities like road networks, rail networks, airports and information corridors, vis-a-vis their linkage with the tourist places and take all necessary steps for upgrading these facilities in a definite time frame.

Such an approach would be very essential for the overall tourism development of the State. Attraction of private investment for the development of infrastructure will be very necessary and given the strong presence of Gujarati community world over. This Policy strongly addresses to the creation of conducive environment for attracting investment on all tourism related activities in the State.

Government shall act as facilitator, coordinator and promoter and enable development of tourism in the state. The physical facility creation of land bank scheme, earmarking certain land on the beaches, tourist places, wayside locations and State/National Highways for the tourism projects both in the rural and urban areas.

The Government shall allot the land on long-term lease basis or by way of outright sale for the tourism projects and the lease rent or sale price of the land shall be fixed in a manner to make the project viable and at the same time protecting the interest of the Government. For the purpose of investment in tourism sector, depending on the size of the project and its importance to the State's development, concessions shall be provided either on the lease and its tenure or on the rate to be charged for Government land and on stamp duty and registration fee on land transaction for the Tourism Projects.

Government shall equate all tourism related activities with that of Industry, accordingly, the structure for electricity tariff, electricity duty, non-agriculture land charges and local taxes shall be worked out. The policy proposes to ensure that for the development of Tourism in the state, different taxes like Luxury Tax, Entertainment Tax and Sales Tax are rationalized and simplified in a manner that Tourism projects are encouraged.

The Policy envisages privatization of as many projects as possible. The fiscal reforms mentioned above are primarily to attract investments on tourism related projects from the private sector. The Policy would also ensure that the projects that are conceived under the Tourism Policy should be so structured so as to ensure maximum participation by the private sector. A special emphasis would be given for investments from the NRI sector.

The Policy would also take steps for privatization of the existing assets of Tourism Corporation of Gujarat Limited in a time-bound manner. Considering Tourism as a thrust area, action plan shall be worked out for the development and promotion of the tourist locations by the district administration.

The government shall consider such institutions as priority tourism projects and provide land at subsidized rates to the private sector setting up such institutes and ensure fast track clearance. Such institutes will have to be established and run according to national standards and shall be encouraged to tie up with national and international institutes to provide world class training.

Courses shall be worked out for creating a pool of private tourist guides who could assist the tourists visiting various tourist places in the State. In the present day of digital communication, a new concept of digital tourist guides shall be encouraged and developed to enable tourists to get the benefit of complete knowledge of the places that they visit, through the multi-lingual digital tourist guides.

Students of Gujarat shall be encouraged to develop an interest for e-mail communication with the students and other persons abroad and interact with them about Gujarat and its varied socio-cultural aspects to motivate them to visit Gujarat. To attract students for these activities of attracting tourists in state, scheme of 'E mail Fan Club of Gujarat' will have to be worked out.

Tourism policy 2003-2010 identifies all round development of projects to bring out all facets of tourism potential in Gujarat. With positive, growth oriented and supportive philosophy of the policy makers, this offers a gold mine of profitable and long term investment and business opportunities for national and international corporate bodies and private enterprises.

Hospitality Industry will get a boost by setting up hotels, tent cities, Viswa grams, village hotels, and heritage hotels. The allied industries will also develop along side like shopping arcades, boutiques, theme restaurants, beauty parlours etc. The beach resorts and winter sports will be developed at 9 chosen beaches which will have clean environment with lawns and other plantations, safety measures and plenty of sea food. Water sports like surfing, yachting and scuba diving are to be developed in and around these resorts. It will also promote other allied industries and special shopping centers.

Special entertainment zones are to be developed for fun leisure and health. rides, water parks, children's parks, future clubs and theme restaurants, health spas are proposed to be developed. Cost effective, star pilgrim hotels and dormitories with A/C facilities and at close proximity to the pilgrim centers are to be built. Good restaurants with tasty food and shops that store religious and other items can be developed around these centers.

The River banks and canal banks are to be developed as tourist spots with motels, improvised shelters with fast food joints, theme restaurants and shopping centers. Boating and yachting will be added attractions. Innovative Private investment and expertise will be encouraged and supported. The continuous traveler and the discreet tourist require fuel for his vehicle, food for his palate and rest rooms to get fresh. Kiosks, tent camps and other amenities are envisaged to be set up in 20 places (5 in each zone)with active participation and investment from private enterprises.

The Dinosaurs lived in Gujarat millions of years ago and their traces are found at several places in the form of fossils. The tourism policy gives a boost to develop dinosaur fossil parks at Balasinor and Kutch.

Viswa Gram (Global Village) is a concept to create villages with dwellings to replicate the international houses where tourist will feel at home. The theme restaurants and the shopping arches will have a universal appeal and the people belonging to diverse cultures will have a peep into Gujarat's culture, cuisine and crafts.

The pride of Gujarat, the Royal Orient Express will soon get a boost when the meter gauge tracks on which it runs will be converted to broad gauge. As the Royal Orient Express picks up the speed, it will carry more tourists in search of rest, recreation and regal splendour.

Leisure, Tourism and Environment

Leisure, Tourism and Environment: experiences and environment provides a broad-based overview of leisure and tourism experiences within a spatial, natural and social environment. Experiences are the main source of tourist attractions and shape the themes that define the attractions. Many experience based themes can serve the attraction: cultural heritage, thrills and adventure, sand sun sea, romanticism, activities, meeting people, play and so on and so forth. The choice of certain themes has sometimes a political background when the attraction is designed to symbolise political identities. Not all tourists experience the same. Their associative feelings about tourist places can vary according to different personal or social backgrounds as well as different tourist roles.

The places where tourism finds its destination are more or less specifically created or preserved. For cultural tourism the experience of the past is a special focus of interest and tourism is an important legitimation for preserving of reconstructing cultural heritage. But, the past is no longer.

Much of the tourist attraction is linked to the imagination of the visitors.

Imagination, so to speak, redefines and shapes the environment. Accordingly the imagination is oriented to either simple pleasure, temporarily being away from everyday stress, sincere interest in special places, undergoing a more or less shocking experience or a lasting dedication to the 'other' places. The meaning of the environment varies according to these different 'modes of experience'.

Experiences take place in the brains of people. Much attention will be paid to mental processes and the way we get access to the symbolic representations in the brain. The knowledge on this subject is linked to psychology, philosophy of consciousness and neurobiology .

An important domain of leisure and tourist experience is the natural environment. Human beings have always been part of nature. The preferences of nature experience and the evaluation of natural situation are connected by several scientists to the evolution of human beings. Not only positive experiences stem from nature, but also fear and anxiety. The value of nature for tourist attraction is mainly defined so far by the ecological qualities.

Many experiences are socially constructed. Different narrative mechanisms work in the formation of mental representations: stories, photo images, movies and mass media. More and more, experiences become key issues in the assembling and selling of products. That is why nowadays we tend to speak of 'the experience' society'. Experiences, as the are produced and sold, are targeted to different social groups and their corresponding behaviour and preferences (lifestyles).

These lifestyles are created within the context of social class, social interaction processes, commodification and communication. Lifestyles also come into being by deliberate socialisation and education. There is a realm of leisure activities, which is not always clearly visible to the public world, but enormously important: the world of leisure groups, clubs, associations and voluntary organisations. People share experiences and imaginations. Therefore, they get together in more or less organised associations within which they produce and reproduce the experiences that arouse their enthusiasm. In many cases, these world of enthusiasms involve such dedication of the participants that we can call this type of leisure: serious leisure, which implies a strong commitment to the activities.

Tourism: A Growing Industry

Tourism is a high growth industry globally. Though currently only 3.5 per cent of the world's population travels internationally, by 2020, this figure is expected to double. In India, as well, economic growth and infrastructure development are expected to increase tourist arrivals: the World Tourism Organisation projects a 7.5 per cent annual increase in the number of tourist arrivals in India till 2001. There are many other reasons why tourism should be a major growth engine for Andhra Pradesh's economy.

The tourism industry generates large-scale employment. The labour to capital ratio for the tourism sector is one of the highest: each million-rupee investment creates jobs for 48 people compared to 45 in agriculture and 13 in manufacturing. In addition, the tourism sector has a high employment multiplier: in India, direct employment due to tourism is 8.5 million while total employment, including indirect employment, is 20 million. Tourism is also a large foreign exchange earner: the industry is the third largest foreign exchange earner in the country after jewellery and ready-made garments.

Most importantly, tourism helps generate higher incomes: the growth of tourism creates a variety of jobs in areas like transportation, hospitality services, and retailing, jobs with much higher salaries than the current per capita income of Andhra Pradesh. The growth of tourism will also help to combat poverty in the State by boosting demand for goods produced by its large number of artisans and for a host of small-scale services, such as car hire, cafes, tour guide services, and so on.

By 2020, Andhra Pradesh will be a leading tourism destination in India offering a variety of experiences to its visitors. The State will offer all the high quality amenities making for a pleasurable stay and will enjoy a stellar reputation with visitors. Over 2.5 million international tourists and around 70 million domestic tourists will visit Andhra Pradesh annually. Andhra Pradesh will achieve this ambitious vision by capitalising on its wide spectrum of tourism locations ranging from historical and religious sites to natural attractions like beaches. The State has tremendous unexploited potential.

Properly developed, this can help the State attract a large share of foreign and domestic tourists. To capture the tourism opportunities available, Andhra Pradesh will position itself as a destination state-cum-transit hub. Develop several high quality tourist destinations to attract more visitors to Andhra Pradesh and induce longer stays.

Create a tourist friendly state in which people are enthusiastic about and wel-coming to tourists. Provide the infrastructure required to make tourism in Andhra Pradesh a con-venient and enjoyable experience. Promote Andhra Pradesh both in India and internationally as an attractive tour-ist destination.

With its ancient history and scenic locations, Andhra Pradesh offers numerous and distinctive opportunities for attracting domestic and international tourists. The State has remarkable historical sites such as Golconda Fort, Charminar and the Nizam's palace in Hyderabad. It also has celebrated religious sites like Tirupati, Nagarjuna Konda and Amaravathi. Andhra Pradesh also has a vast coastline with its share of scenic beaches like those near Srikakulam and Visakhapatnam. And in Hyderabad, Andhra Pradesh has an increasingly popular business destination.

Tourism is well established in Andhra Pradesh. The State already accounts for 24 per cent of domestic tourist arrivals in India (inter versus intrastate). In 1996, domestic tourist arrivals in Andhra Pradesh amounted to 33.4 million and have grown at an annual rate of 10 per cent since 1990. The most popular destination was Tirupati, which cornered a 50 per cent share of these arrivals. In 1996, over 60,000 foreign tourists visited Andhra Pradesh, constituting growth of 8 per cent a year since 1990. However, the State accounts for only 3 per cent of India's foreign tourists. The most popular destination for foreign tourists was Hyderabad followed by Puttaparthi.

But Andhra Pradesh could do much more with its tourism destinations. Existing tourist attractions are largely underdeveloped. For example, in Tirupati, the aver-age tourist stay is only 2.5 nights and the average expenditure on accommodation is only Rs.146 per tourist. In a survey of 1400 visitors, nearly 75 per cent indicated that they would stay longer if there was more for them to see or do. The State could also develop several new destinations for Buddhist pilgrims at Kondapur, An Outstanding Tourist Destination Ghantasala, Jagayyapeta, Chandavaram and Saligramam, or for beach lovers on the coastline and at other historical sites. The lack of appropriate development and publicity has limited the scope of these locations.

Andhra Pradesh is not unique among Indian states in terms of missing out on opportunities. In fact, India, in general, is far behind Asian countries in its development of tourism. This is where the opportunity lies: in such a situation, Andhra Pradesh can emerge a winner by making the pre-emptive strike.

The State has three opportunities to position itself as a tourism destination: become a stand-alone destination; be a transit hub, working as a gateway to India along the lines of Singapore or Dubai; or be part of a wider tourist circuit, linked to destinations in neighbouring states. Andhra Pradesh will pursue all three. Andhra Pradesh is well positioned to become a stand-alone destination, given its variety of locations ranging from historical and religious sites to beaches. However, it does not have a distinctive value proposition, such as Rajasthan with its historical heritage. Its central location in India makes Hyderabad well suited to be a transit hub. However, to successfully achieve the status of another Singapore or Dubai, it will first have to build the infrastructure and linkages required to other Indian and international cities. The State will concurrently pursue both options, developing strategies to position itself as a destination state-cum-transit hub. This will allow the State to cater to both types of tourists.

Andhra Pradesh will also pursue the third option: becoming part of a wider tourist circuit. This will allow it to tap into a wider pool of tourists. For instance, the State can attract Japanese tourists by linking its Buddhist sites to Gaya and Dharamsala to become part of the 'Buddhist circuit'. The State Government has already done much to develop existing popular destinations like Hyderabad, Tirupati, Visakhapatnam and Nagarjuna Sagar-these have been awarded the status of Special Tourism Areas.

Master plans have already An Outstanding Tourist Destination been developed for Hyderabad and Tirupati. They will also be prepared for other Special Tourism Areas to ensure integrated development and identify avenues for private investment. To create a more comprehensive set of high profile destinations that fully exploit the State's tourism potential, Andhra Pradesh will identify, nominate or even create additional tourist areas. Destinations of the following categories will be developed:

— Buddhist religious sites in addition to Nagarjuna Konda to attract Japanese and other Buddhism devotees.

— Two or three beach resorts on the northeastern coastline close to Srikakulam and Visakhapatnam.

— Business destinations such as Visakhapatnam and, perhaps, one or two other cities (these could also be possible gateways to other forms of tourist activities, such as beaches).

Developing all these areas as tourist destinations will require a variety of initiatives. Many of these initiatives are best undertaken by the private sector. For example, the metropolitan areas which attract business people and other relatively wealthier travellers should have well-organised entertainment and shopping facilities. The 'underground' market in Atlanta, USA, a major tourist attraction, is a case in point.

Singapore's Sentosa Island resort that combines several leisure activities is another example. Similarly, the beach locations in Andhra Pradesh would include not only hotels but also shopping cum entertainment villages on the lines of those in Phuket, Thailand or Cancun, Mexico. Overall, a significant amount of private investment will be required in the key destinations to build hotels, retail outlets, transportation services, leisure centres like mini golf courses, bowling alleys, entertainment parks, theatres, health spas, etc.

These facilities are already mushrooming in other major tourism and metropolitan areas in India. Andhra Pradesh cannot afford to be left behind. But it just might be if the many existing barriers to private investment in setting up such facilities are not removed. To list some of them: land acquisition prices are too high, often exceeding the norm of 10-15 per cent of project cost. Strict Floor Area Ratio (FAR) and Floor Space Index (FSI) regulations prevent industry from quickly recouping land costs. Red tape leads to an average project clearance time of three years, too long by any standards. Concessions promised in the tourism policy of 1994, such as industrial water rates, have not been delivered.

Andhra Pradesh will need to rapidly change its policies and procedures to overcome these drawbacks. It can learn from successful government-business partnerships An Outstanding Tourist Destination in other countries like Australia and Canada that have yielded tremendous results in increasing the number of tourists and their average spending. Andhra Pradesh will create the first such effective partnership in India.

To become a tourist friendly state, Andhra Pradesh will need to ensure that tourists feel welcome in the State and that its people feel enthusiastic about tourism. This calls for action on many fronts. First, the State must offer the basic amenities a tourist requires (and takes for granted in developed and many developing countries). In addition to quality hotels, local transportation, taxi services, entertainment and shopping centres mentioned in the last section, tourists want access to clean public toilets, freely available telecommunication services, tourist information centres, conveniently located banks and currency exchange centres, among other services. Second, a tourist-friendly location should have an abundance of skilled service enterprises and people providing the services listed before. Third, tourist locations should be clean and well maintained. Finally, a tourist-friendly attitude must be developed; tourists should always meet with polite and helpful treatment.

Accordingly, the Government will act to create the environment and services required. It will encourage the creation of small businesses in the Special Tourism Areas to serve tourists. These will include STD booths, Internet access centres, fast food joints, etc. The State will also develop and launch an awareness campaign to help create an environment favourable to tourism. Finally, the Government will encourage the creation of appropriate vocational training institutions to provide State residents with the skills to serve the tourism industry.

To promote tourism in Andhra Pradesh, large investments in infrastructure will be essential. Accordingly, specific initiatives, such as expanding trunk infrastructure and improving arterial roads in tourist locations, will be undertaken. Expanding its trunk infrastructure in the form of highways, airports, ports, power, telecommunications, etc., will give Andhra Pradesh the basis to develop the transportation links to its tourist locations.

For example, a flourishing international airport at Hyderabad will itself provide a major fillip to business tourism. Improving arterial roads in tourist locations will have to be given high priority. Some obvious examples are the Madras-Tirupati road link and the development of a high quality roadway to Nagarjuna Sagar. Location specific requirements, such as a ropeway in Tirupati or cable cars in Nagarjuna Sagar, will also need to be developed. In addition, these tourist spots will need uninterrupted power and water supply.

The Andhra Pradesh Government will aggressively promote tourism. Currently, the State spends only Rs.1 crore a year on tourism; in contrast, Rajasthan spends Rs.9 crore. Furthermore, the State Government undertakes most promotion activities without taking the help of the Central Government or other agencies. The Government of India tourism offices in India and abroad do not carry or distribute enough promotional material on Andhra Pradesh.

Recognising the need to do much more to promote the State to tourists, the Government will effect a major change in its approach. As a first step, the different tourist segments will be analysed and tailor-made promotions will be developed for each of them. These promotions will target mainly tourists with adequate spending power. The State will use best practices in other countries to develop powerful promotions. For instance, the State could emulate Canada's approach: involving the private sector in promotional efforts.

In Canada, the private sector was actively involved in planning and executing the promotional campaigns (not merely funding). This gave them a sense of ownership and increased their commitment. The Government will consider setting up a joint government-business promotion board and allowing this board to hire professional advertising agencies and public relations companies to promote Andhra Pradesh. In addition, it will encourage the more productive use of Government of India tourism promotion offices.

Tourism represents an attractive opportunity for the people of Andhra Pradesh to reaffirm their pride in themselves and their State. By achieving Tourism Vision 2020, the State can gain its rightful place as one of the best leisure spots in India.

In 2003, the Indian rupee appreciated 15 per cent against the dollar. Considering that the dollar is the currency that is used by most international travellers when they book seats and hotel rooms in India, travelling to this country actually became more expensive during the year. Yet in dollar terms, there was a 23 per cent increase in international travel related foreign exchange earnings during 2003.

In Asia, where there are vast national and regional differences, many less-experienced travellers put Indiay in the same basket following the bombings in Bali and outside the Marriott, Jakarta. The inflow into Asia was also impacted by the SARS virus, which severely cramped the appetite for travel to the region. The year 2003 was marked by the Thai Government announcing tourism revenue of US$ 1.7 billion and Australia registering a 20 per cent dip in tourist arrivals in the first half.

India, though, presented a refreshingly different picture. There was a 16 per cent increase in the inflow of foreign tourists compared to 2002. And, thanks to the peace dividend with Pakistan, the growth momentum has continued with a 17 per cent month-on-month increase in Jan. 2004. How has India's tourist sector managed to offset these downside factors? Part of the explanation can be attributed to India's emergence as a value destination. For example, the Conde Nast Traveller in its Readers Awards selected India as one of the top 10 preferred destinations for the discerning (as opposed to backpack) traveller.

Evidently, a growing number of foreign travellers presumably those with deeper pockets, are putting India on their travel maps despite having to spend more dollars for the same number of rupees. However, India hasn't lost its appeal as a value-for-money destination. In another survey conducted in 134 countries, the Lonely Planet Travel Guide billed India as one of the top five destinations for the independent traveller. Nevertheless, both rankings indicate India's growing popularity among foreign tourists - a trend that is likely to grow, with the Department of Civil Aviation's decision to kickstart the inbound charter travel business.

In January 2004, the Civil Aviation Ministry announced landing rights for charter flights at any of 18 airports in the country. Customs and immigration facilities will be provided at short notice, at airports where such facilities did not exist. Indian passport holders have also been allowed to travel in incoming charter flights - a right earlier reserved only for foreigners. The government has also removed all restrictions on the frequency and size of aircraft for charters. From now therefore, private domestic carriers too can use their fleet to have chartered flights going abroad on a regular basis.

At another level, the Asian American Hotel Owners Association (AAHOA) has committed to promote India as a tourist destination in the US through its network of 22,000 member hotels. Strategic tie-ups with such associations could be a significant factor in the years to come, since over 40 per cent of American hotels are owned and operated by People of Indian Origin (PIO).

For instance, the emergence of India as a hub for cheap medical treatment—close to 100,000 patients visited India in 2003 to get themselves treated at Indian hospitals. Similarly, with health spas sprouting all over the country, an equally significant number of tourists are coming to India for a health kick. Sure, India still has some way to go before reaching the level of countries like Thailand and Australia. But the country has finally managed to etch a place for itself on the world tourism map.

6

Trends in Leisure and Tourism

Economic and Social Trends in Leisure Tourism

Economic, demographic and social trends shape our consumption of leisure and tourism. Whilst there were some radical changes in leisure development during the 1990s eg the development of leisure parks and eating out places, tourism has tended to develop broadly along established lines, although short-break holidays and urban tourism in former industrial cities a new phenomenon that emerged in the 1980s have consolidated and expanded.

Disposable income and consumer expenditure have increased by 2.5% pa in real terms over the last 25 years and are likely to continue to rise at a similar rate, supporting increased consumer confidence and steady growth for leisure markets in the long-term. Demographic changes are affecting the demand for different leisure products and thereby reinforcing the unpredictable nature of the leisure sector. The main change is the ageing of the population as a whole.

The sex structure of the population is also shifting. The age up to which males outnumber females is projected to increase from age 47 in 1994 to age 61 in 2021. The number of children aged under 16 is projected to fall by nearly 9% by 2021 but there are significant short-term shifts, both up and down, within the crucial younger age groups (up to age 24) that could have significant effects on the market for individual leisure products.

Along with demographic change and increasing leisure choice resulting from increased income, a number of profound changes within the structure of society have, over the last 25 years, impacted.on our consumption of leisure. There is a significant change underway in the number and structure of households. Household numbers continue to increase as the size of households decreases, due to higher levels of divorce, increased life expectancy, a reduced birth rate, more single parent families etc.

Over the last twenty-five years, the number of women entering the labour market has increased. In 1971, 10 million women were employed in the UK while by 1997 this figure had risen to 12.7 million and it is forecast to rise to 13.1 million by 2001. Consequently, the disposable income of women has also increased, which in turn has opened up a new market for special interest female activities notably health and fitness.

Over the same period, there have been other changes in society which have improved opportunities for women and reduced gender discrimination in both work and leisure contexts. However, some surveys reveal that gender remains an important determinant in terms of access to, and choice of, leisure opportunities:

— Women's access to leisure, in general, has increased but many women still have less leisure time due to work and family commitments, participate less in most leisure activities and draw on a narrower range of leisure options than men. They spend most of their leisure time in and around home and family;

— Actual physical danger or fear of sexual harassment also restricts women's choice of leisure activities and leisure spaces. Fear for safety is predicted to remain a growing social trend.

There are conflicting views on the issue of time availability for both sexes. The working hours of those in low status jobs have reduced, but for many of those in employment, work pressures are actually reducing leisure time. Even for many not in employment, there is a perception that time is limited. The time-money paradox suggests that free time is available in inverse proportion to income levels. In the light of such constraints on leisure time, there is an increasing need for time-value as well as value for money in leisure and tourism development.

Accessibility of Leisure and Tourism Travel

The presumption that leisure travel is the fastest growing purpose of travel needs to be qualified in the light of recent statistics. Leisure miles per person per year have gone up but less than the overall figure for all journeys. Leisure spending is generally divided into leisure goods spending and leisure services spending. The former comprises primarily in-home spending on electrical retail goods such as TVs, videos, stereos etc, whereas the latter includes out-of-home leisure spending on cinemas, bowling, gambling, eating and drinking in restaurants and pubs etc, entertainment and other out-of-home leisure activities.

The growth rate of leisure spending varies depending on exactly what definition of leisure spending is adopted. There are significant variations between sectors and individual activities of overall leisure spending, eg: spending on in-home leisure remains about one third of out-of-home leisure spending but is projected to grow at a faster rate based, in part, on technology and the digital revolution.

In-home leisure spending has experienced much higher growth rates than out-of-home leisure services spending and leisure (goods) spending has significantly increased its share of total consumer expenditure. These individual markets have the potential for extraordinary rates of growth and decline as has been evidenced in the past, more so than in non-leisure industries. For example, the cinema and health/fitness market is currently projected to continue to grow, ten-pin bowling has arguably reached saturation in recent years while bingo has experienced difficulties in recent years. Individual segments of the pubs/bars/ restaurant sector can perform quite differently.

In UK, Business Strategies Ltd (BSL) produces forecasts for different aspects of the economy including consumer expenditure and components of consumer expenditure. Leisure services includes catering (meals outside the home), recreational and cultural services, betting and education. Leisure services expenditure as defined by BSL has shown growth of 2.5% pa in real terms over the last 25 years, the same growth rate as for total consumer expenditure and disposable incomes. BSL forecasts that leisure services expenditure will achieve a growth rate of 3.2% pa over the ten years from 1998 to 2008.

Since overall tourism activity in the UK is driven by both domestic and overseas visitors, and by leisure and business travel, it is the outcome of the interplay of many different factors. Domestic leisure tourism responds to the same forces as those driving overall leisure consumption, most notably changes in disposable income. Overall, tourism trips have grown significantly in recent years but there are important variations:

— short-break holidays have grown steadily while domestic long holidays (4+ nights) have declined or remained static. Many traditional coastal resorts have been particularly affected by this trend;

— all leisure day visits increased by 10% between 1994 and 1996 and a further 3.5% between 1996 and 1998;

— overseas visitors to the UK have grown rapidly in recent years; and obusiness travel has increased in line with recent economic growth.

In contrast to the main industrial and commercial property sectors, the leisure and tourism property sector encompasses public sector, non-profit making activities and a rapidly growing private, profit-oriented sector. Therefore, the sector comprises several segments:

— full commercial or business properties eg hotels, cinemas, tenpin bowling, nightclubs, bingo halls, pubs/bars and restaurants;

— quasi-commercial properties, provided sometimes in the public and sometimes in the private sector, eg swimming pools, health and fitness centres, attractions, museums and theatres. These facilities may operate on a partial cost recovery basis; and

— non-commercial leisure properties such as municipal parks.

These segments do not stay static. Over time, and with increasing affluence, some property types, which were associated with public sector provision, have become more commercial eg some museums, heritage attractions and leisure centres. Perhaps the key feature of commercial leisure is that it undergoes continuous change, which a more affluent public both stimulates and is constantly responding to.

Some leisure operators and the property they occupy have more recently adapted to deal with changing fashions. It could be argued that cinema, bingo, bowling, hotels and caravans have existed for a considerable time, but what has changed is the manner in which the product is packaged and delivered to an increasingly selective audience. All commercial property sectors, retail, office or industrial, to a greater or lesser.extent are responsive to market demands and quick to change, although arguably not to the same degree as the leisure property sector.

One of the key property market changes in the 1990s was the concept of grouping together leisure facilities into a leisure park or centre. Other advantages of leisure parks identified by the private sector in the survey in order of priority are:

— a choice of things to do;

— encouragement of repeat visits;

— a safe and well managed environment;

— synergy between leisure uses;

— investor confidence; and

— synergy with retail uses.

Leisure parks are now seen by the property industry as a long-term change creating economies of scale for developers with benefits to consumers, operators and investors. "The leisure industry is providing something which the consumer didnt know they liked until they saw it."

A multiplex cinema is usually the key ingredient for any leisure park or commercial leisure centre and there are few such developments without one. It acts as an anchor for the site and creates the footfall that attracts other complementary uses, such as restaurants, to the same location. Tied up with the growth of the multiplex is the dominance of a few multiplex operators.

Major, multi-facility leisure developments appear to be based on faith in the continuing supply-led growth in the cinema market, which has been phenomenal over the last 15 years. It is also extremely unusual to find a leisure park/ centre that does not have some kind of food offer.

In UK, the leisure park concept has only emerged in the 1990s, but already it is changing with new and larger concepts materialising incorporating retail and a wider range of leisure uses eg SnoWorld Sports Village in Milton Keynes. Typically, these schemes are more than twice the size of a large leisure park, incorporating an indoor ski centre, health and fitness club, other sports facilities, multiplex cinema, 10 pin bowling, family entertainment centre, night-club, restaurants and lifestyle retailing. They also differ from leisure parks in having all uses in one, large, multi-level building rather than in separate leisure buildings. Other major leisure schemes include the Printworks and the Great Northern site in Manchester city centre along with Star City, Five Ways and Broadway Plaza around Birmingham.

The growth of larger scale out-of-centre leisure developments very often in locations that are relatively inaccessible by public transport - combined with the decline of some uses in town centres have made some types of leisure activity less accessible to those wholly or partly reliant on forms of transport other than the car. These large leisure schemes are notable for the inclusion of a substantial retail element. A natural cross-fertilisation of leisure and retail is considered to exist, so that people using leisure facilities buy something in the adjacent shops and vice versa.

Visitors to leisure attractions have become increasingly used to buying theme-related merchandise as part of the leisure experience. Similarly, retailers have looked to leisure as part of shopping centres to encourage a longer visit and thereby spend more. One manifestation of this is the number of restaurants and cafes or food courts in shopping centres. Another example is at the Trocadero in the West End, where mainstream retailers such as HMV, Whittards, Sock Shop and Accessorize benefit from the high pedestrian flows by trading alongside major leisure attractions such as Funland, the UGC multiplex and speciality operations such as Planet Hollywood. The same logic applies to the Metro Centre at Gateshead, one of the largest shopping centres in the UK, which has a large leisure centre forming part of the scheme.

There are also a number of locations in the UK where leisure operators have taken space next to retail parks (and factory outlet centres). Both share a number of common requirements; good location, access, visibility and car parking. It is said to provide the owner with a wider tenant mix, reduce reliance on durable goods retailers and it may introduce a higher rental level per unit of floorspace. A retail park with a leisure element, arguably, has greater drawing power from a wider area, simulating to a greater extent the wider range of consumption activities that exist in a town centre.

The inclusion of leisure in the design of retail complexes has proved to be a growth area in property development schemes. The different forms of tourism attractions and visitor accommodation make up a fragmented segment of the leisure property market both in terms of product type and investor. Tourisms growth means that pressure for development is widespread. In land-use terms, the main source of development pressure is for new accommodation.

Over the last two decades, there has been considerable growth in the number of new hotels being developed in the UK. There is a well-established need for more, better quality hotel stock in most segments of the market in the UK and particularly in London. Elsewhere, although new full-service hotels will be developed eg traditional four star, the main area of growth is in budget hotels. Over the last 10-15 years, new supply has been dominated by this sector. These developments started in the UK in 1985 with the first Little Chef Travel Lodge.

Budget hotels are purpose-built, low-cost, high quality facilities normally sited adjacent to, and serviced by, a restaurant/bar and situated in positions with good access to the primary road network and commercial areas. They range in size from 40-120 bedrooms. They do not have leisure facilities but some brands do feature small meeting rooms. The concept was developed in response to a need for inexpensive B&B accommodation, particularly for business travellers.

New caravan site development in recent years has been limited around the UK. "In many parts of the country, the caravan park industry is mature and the need for brand new parks perhaps limited". Planning constraints have also restricted new development on the favoured coastal sites. There has been an explosion in the growth of attractions overall; 47% of all attractions have been opened over the last 20 years although most are small-scale, often involving the opening to the public of heritage buildings or natural features in inaccessible locations.

The number of large-scale new attraction developments is small; with the exception of the Dome, the last new major theme park developments were in the 1980s. The newest of Englands top twenty charging attractions is Legoland, opened in the early 1990s on the site of the Windsor Safari Park. There is a number of new lottery-funded attractions coming on stream in the next two years eg: the Eden Project in Cornwall, the Lowry Centre in Salford but it is unlikely that many more will be developed.

Public funds for new attractions are now more restricted and there is a real concern about the viability of many new attractions. Priority is now being given by most public agencies to enhancing existing attractions rather than creating new ones. The growth of the commercial leisure sector suggests that a strong case exists for institutional investment in this sector. Yet, until recently this has not occurred and even now is not widespread.

The main factors which have deterred investors until recently were:

— the relatively small (but growing) number of leisure operators who were multiples (ie low risk tenants);

— the lack of a large market with comparable market evidence of leasing arrangements, rent levels and yields;.

— a valuation technique dependent on the capitalisation of the profits of specific businesses, rather than the capitalisation of market rents;

— the perceived high investment risk in an industry prone to changing fashions;

— the need for large, purpose-built buildings for many new leisure concepts and increasingly high fit-out costs; and othe perception that leisure property needs intensive, high quality hands-on management.

The emergence of leisure parks, the significant increase in capital values due to higher rents and greater investment demand have all improved leisure development viability and helped to stimulate a development boom in the late 1990s. New development activity in the entertainment sector increased by over 100% between 1995 and 1998 but has since fallen back slightly.

Many commentators consider that there has been a dichotomy in the approach of Government towards leisure uses. This has its origins in previous centuries and is based on the different views held about the relative merits of different types of leisure activity. In the past, the public sector has provided or subsidised many sports facilities, cultural and artistic venues including museums, galleries and heritage attractions. In addition, the state has developed and maintained land for formal and informal recreation. Policies have been designed to offer protection to such uses with legislation such as the Theatre Trust Act 1976, or to promote additional provision. These uses have been considered intrinsically beneficial to individuals and society because of the benefits that they are considered to offer to individual health, cultural or social well-being, civic pride or social cohesion.

The importance of tourism to the national and local economies has long been recognised by Government. The English Tourist Board was set up in 1969, and its successor, the English Tourism Council, receives public funding from the Department of Culture, Media and Sport to support the tourism industry. In the past, there has been substantial grant aid for hotels and attractions. In contrast, the approach of Government to many other leisure uses in the past has been neutral or negative. Legislation relating to gambling or the sale of alcohol has traditionally sought to control or even discourage such uses, with alcohol consumption and gambling circumscribed by licence and subject to taxation.

Policies have generally been aimed at the perceived need to protect society and the environment from the adverse effects of such uses. Policies relating to popular cultural uses such as the music hall, its successor the cinema and professional football have traditionally been neutral. Such uses, arguably, were considered to have less intrinsic social or cultural benefit than the arts or were considered to be capable of surviving without subsidy or other assistance. Thus, the majority of Arts Council funding has traditionally been given to the fine or high arts, with massive funding to the four major national companies.

Planning policies and decisions have tended to follow this dichotomy of approach with those uses considered to have intrinsic health, social or cultural benefits being subject to policies designed to promote or protect such uses. Very often these uses are publicly provided on the basis of target standards of provision. Thus policies have sought to create or protect open space, leisure centres and swimming pools and to protect theatres from changes of use.

In UK, national and local planning policies for tourism uses have reflected the economic importance of tourism and have been aimed at encouraging tourism development, although this has been balanced with the need to protect the natural and built heritage that attracts tourism. Planning policies relating to many commercial leisure uses have, in contrast, tended to be neutral or negative in approach. Thus development plans have not contained policies to promote or protect cinemas, snooker halls, amusement centres, bingo halls, pubs and clubs. Instead, policies have tended to be designed to discourage such uses or to control the external effects of these uses.

This sharp differentiation in the attitudes of policy makers and decision-makers towards different types of leisure use has begun to be eroded in recent years with a more positive approach adopted towards uses such as restaurants, pubs and cinemas. Increasing attention has been paid to the social, cultural and economic value of many of the uses found in town centres. In the 1990s, national planning policies, including PPG6, have mentioned the positive benefits of such uses and some development plans contain positive policies for developing the evening economy. For example, the cultural and social value of cinemas, as well as their economic value, has been reflected in policy.

The value of uses that were often subject only to negative policies, such as pubs and restaurants, has been reflected in changing policy at all administrative levels along with recent relaxation of licensing laws. Leisure and tourism have become major catalysts in economic development and regeneration and many local authorities have sought to encourage such projects on the basis of:

- job creation;
- image development; and
- infrastructure support for local business.

Such considerations have often raised significant planning consequences. The recent adoption of the principles of sustainable development in planning policies and decisions has had a significant influence on leisure development. In particular, the control of trip generation and encouragement of accessibility by all means of transport have major planning implications for leisure and tourism.

The environmental impacts of leisure and tourism development remain a dominating issue in policy terms, generally considered under the following headings:

— *impact upon the built environment*: The beneficial re-use of redundant buildings for leisure and tourism has been seen to contribute to the vitality and viability of town centres and bring life to rural areas. Historic buildings can be preserved and given new uses and the areas in which they are located benefit. At a more general level, leisure and tourism can make a positive contribution to the vitality and viability of town centres. In extreme cases, this can lead to amenity problems and social impact;

— *impact upon the natural environment*: Visual intrusion is a key aspect to development in the countryside along with the impacts upon air, water, flora and fauna, soil erosion etc; and ocongestion and pollution. Congestion and pollution is largely to do with vehicular transport but it is also to do with pedestrian congestion; the weight of numbers at specific destinations and the nuisance effects of noise, smell, litter and crime/vandalism. Visitors can interact with a local community in both a positive and negative manner. They can help to support local communities and services; in some cases, the social value of pubs to rural communities has been recognised in appeal decisions. In other cases, visitors can alter the character of an area, the nature of local shops and disrupt the local community.

Leisure time Mobility

World Commission on Environment and Development defines the aim of sustainable development to be "to satisfy present needs without endangering the capacity of future Sustainable development is often divided to following areas: generations to satisfy their own needs". Sustainable development is often divided to following areas: ecological (environmental) sustainability, economic sustainability, social sustainability and cultural sustainability. Permanent sustainable society is hardly possible to achieve without achieving sustainability in all of these areas.

Leisure time activities and leisure time mobility have important impact to all areas of sustainability in society and their trends should be evaluated in a holistic way using all areas of sustainability. Leisure time is one important factor of human contentment and well-being together with family, friends and work . Leisure time balances work life and offers social relationships. Even though leisure time is expected to be relaxing and peaceful, it is also often expected to offer new, even extreme experiences.

Clearly, leisure time is an important factor to consider in a socially sustainable society. One important aspect of socially sustainable society is participation, which has an emphasized role in leisure time. Long term trends in developed countries have been rising income and rising consumption per capita. Leisure time activities, travelling, and all leisure related services and good production have an important and increasing economical role.

Molitor estimates that "leisure will begin to dominate jobs and economic activity in the USA around 2015, when 'free time' will occupy over half of total individual lifetime activity". The share of consumption directed to leisure time activities, recreation, traffic, and travelling has grown through out the last century. In 1997 the share was 28 % in Finland 1 . It is quite clear that all business, consumption, transportation and travelling connected to leisure should not be forgotten when economic sustainability of society is considered.

Leisure time mobility is responsible for significant share of trips made in passenger traffic. In many countries work trips are not any more the biggest trip group or as fixed by the time of day or week as they used to be. Leisure time travelling is naturally also responsible for significant share of environmental impacts of passenger traffic. Also some share of environmental impacts of industrial and service production and goods transportation can be regarded to be caused by leisure time activities, services and consumption of commodities.

There are some characteristics of leisure time mobility affecting the future demand for travel. Leisure time travelling is responsible for between 40 % and 50 % of all mileage travelled in most western economies. In Finland leisure time trips cover about 40 % of trips travelled, 65 % of mileage travelled and 40 % of time travelled. If some part of shopping trips is considered to be voluntary "time killing", the share of leisure time trips is even greater.

Finnish 6 - 17 year-old population makes 1.6 leisure trips daily on the average daily, while over 65 year-old population makes less than 1 leisure trip. If trips are divided on the basis of the trip purpose to obligatory trips (work, school and work related) and to somewhat voluntary trips (shopping, personal business and leisure time), the amount of voluntary trips is almost the same in all age groups, except for over 65 year-old women. Some part of shopping and personal business may be in some age groups more leisure time activity than necessity.

According to Hjortol and Sagberg trip rate decreases quite slowly and evenly between the ages of 50 and 84. Vilhelmson divided trips to work trips and other trips. In his study the amount of other daily trips did not start to decrease more rapidly until in the age groups of over 75 year-old. On the basis of these studies it can be concluded that even though the amount of daily leisure trips decreases with age, the age group of 60 to 75 or even 80 is still mobile and makes quite many leisure time trips.

Although the amount of so called voluntary trips is quite stable in different age groups, their mileage includes strong variations. Mainly two age groups, under 18-years old and over 65 year-old population,.differs from the average. The main reason for this difference is a smaller access to car compared to other age groups. Required age for driving licence in Finland is 18 years. In the year 1995 in Finland 80-90 % of population between 20 and 66 years of age had a driving licence. However, the share was a little over 40 % in the age group of 67 - 79 years and only 12 % in age group of 80 years.

The share of elderly people with driving licence will increase rapidly during the next decades. It is also quite probable that the access to car in retired age groups will increase notably during next decades, although not as fast as the driving licence ownership rate. It is important to notice that in the age groups between 18 and 65 years the leisure trips correspond for about half of the mileage, and even 70-80 % in the age group of over 65 years. When the share of elderly people owning a driving licence and maybe also car is increasing during next decades, it is quite probable to expect an increase in the mileage because of the available leisure time among elderly population.

In medium-long trips leisure is as important trip purpose as work and school. Over 70 % of over 120 km long trips are made for leisure purposes. Car is the dominating travel mode in medium-long and long trips. Approximately 85 % of 100-150 km long trips is made by private motorised transport, mostly by private car. Share is smaller in long trips, but still over 60 % of trips over 200 km are done with private motorised transport.

In Finland 60 % of distance travelled for leisure purposes is done by private car. The share of bus, taxi and train together is 14 %, and walking and cycling together 6 %. The share of group "other modes" is one fifth of length travelled and it includes mostly trips made by airplane and ferry. Even though car is clearly the dominant mode of travel in leisure trips, it is important to notice that the average number of occupants of car is bigger during leisure time trips (2.2 persons/car) than during other trips. It is lowest during work trips, 1.2 persons/car.

Mobility has grown notably in Western Europe during last decades. The growth has concentrated in air travel and car travel. Between years 1965-1989 the passenger kilometres travelled by air and car grew 700 % and 287 %, respectively. This is a sharp contrast to the growth figures of train and bus, which for the same period were 33-38 %.

EC has estimated the external cost of travel to be 87 euros/1000 passenger kilometres for car, 48 euros/1000 pass km for air, 38 euros/1000 pass km for bus and 20 euros/1000 pass km for rail. The estimates do not include congestion costs. The two modes of travel, air and car, with most rapid growth are also the modes to cause most external costs. It is quite obvious that this trend can not be considered ecologically sustainable, even if development in technology would soften its consequences in the future.

On the other hand, when sustainability is considered from the social and economical point of view, travelling by car and by air has many benefits. The most obvious one is speed, which is a highly valued quality. Car also allows individual and flexible travelling, which is particularly important in leisure travelling. EU policy has focused to change the modal split towards public transport modes, but results of the policy have been limited.

Car ownership rate in European countries is already at high level and the growth in car ownership rate and in the size of automobile stock will in certain point stop. The breakpoint is still some way ahead, because the automobile stock grows still by approximately 3 million cars every year in EU area. However, with the increasing demand for air traffic due to both holiday and business purposes, no significant break in the long-term trend is eminent. The limiting factor of air traffic is mainly the capacity of airspace and airports.

Western Europe is not the only region where air travel has grown rapidly. The worldwide mileage of air travel was 1189 billion passenger kilometres in the year 1983 and already 2628 billion in the year 1998. Between those years the growth has been biggest in Asia and Pacific area and North America. At the same time the growth in Europe was approximately 80 %. The growth is assumed to continue.

In an attitude survey carried out in the Finnish city of Kajaani and Tampere Region, almost 80 % of the respondents stated that they would travel more, if they had higher income. Results were studied also by dividing respondents in segments formed on the basis of their attitudes. Less than one fifth of the respondents belonged to an environmentally aware segment. Practically all respondents who belonged to this segment considered protection of environment to be an important task of the society.

Almost four out of five respondents in this segment considered environment in their mode choice and left car home as often as possible, because of environmental reasons. However, almost 70 % of the respondents of the environmentally aware segment stated that they would travel more, if they had higher income. Approximately half of these respondents stated that flying was not environmentally friendly way to travel.

The ecologically unsustainable trend of growth in air travel will continue. On the other hand travel is a way to get familiar with new cultures and increase the understanding of the international world. Travelling also provides us with new experiences, possibilities to meet our far living friends and to escape from our everyday life. Therefore, many elements of holiday travel can promote achieving the sustainable society through social sustainability.

The population structure of Europe will age remarkably during the next decades. The median age in Europe was 29,2 years in the year 1950 and 37,7 in the year 2000. The median age in Europe is expected to rise during next 50 years and to reach 49,5 years by the year 2050. The median age in the world is expected to be 36,2 years in the year 2050. Both the amount and share of retired population in Europe will increase fast during the next half century. This trend will also have a strong impact on leisure travel.

Age is one important determinant of travel behaviour. Although the trip rate in oldest age groups is smaller than the average, these groups do not make much less voluntary trips than other age groups, especially before the age of 75-

80 years. The future elderly are expected to be healthier, economically more well-off and used to a life style which includes a car. The increasing group of relatively young retired persons will have a possibility to enjoy an active leisure time, travel frequently in everyday life, and also travel abroad.

Globalisation has a lot of divergent implications for transportation. New information technology and better telecommunication facilities have made the world accessible in many areas of life like trade, politics, consumption, and tourism. Globalisation also increases international and intercontinental travel, which is mostly done by aeroplane. Thus globalisation threatens ecological sustainability. On the other hand, if the slogan "Think globally - Act locally" is to be followed, the global concern of the environment may increase along with the globalisation.

Decreasing official work-time has been a long term trend already for almost a century. On the other hand, also a differentiation between the official work-time and realized work-time has been observed. Even if the official work-time in the future is decreasing, the realized work-time in some workgroups might increase. Additionally, work-times flexibility is expected to increase in the future. Even if the trend in decreasing work-time would end, the total amount of leisure time in European societies will increase because of the ageing of population structure.

The increasing amount of leisure time will probably have an impact on daily leisure travelling, but also on holiday travelling. Nijkamp et al. give an illustrative example of a recent trend in leisure travelling, which is partly caused by the increase of leisure time and income: "It is more and more common to make several short holiday trips per year in addition to the 'traditional' summer holidays".

One significant trend witnessed in the life styles and attitudes is individualization. Nijkamp et al. have listed some interrelated trends with individualization, which lead to major change of living patterns and also mobility. The trends are the increase of the number of one- and two-person households and the increasing participation of women in workforce, which increases the age at which women have their first child, which in turn change the traditional male and female roles. Individualization will probably also cause changes in everyday activity patterns and travel behaviour, and decrease the concern of environment from social view.

A mobile and materialistic life style has been generally adopted in developed countries. Leisure time activities and consumption define more and more who we are. Leisure time is expected to offer new experiences. In attitude survey in the city of Kajaani and Tampere Region 75 % of the respondents stated that they want new experiences from their leisure time. Particularly important this was to the youngest and oldest age groups. When the world is becoming more accessible because of faster modes of travel and better telecommunication facilities, it is highly probable that people look for experiences from further away. Already about 80 % of 15-29 years old Finnish consider it important to travel abroad.

Leisure time has become more individualistic. Every transparent effort to try to limit the freedom in leisure time is considered highly oppressive. During the leisure time people, feel that they should be free to do whatever they want and go wherever they want. Thus flexibility is highly valued quality of transport mode in leisure time travel. Freedom of movement is generally considered to be an important privilege.

Information technology gives us various different possibilities like virtual travelling, telework, teleshopping, new contacts via Internet, and virtual society. We are still in the phase of entering the information society and all its possibilities are not yet assessed. However, already in spring 2000 approximately 80 % of 15 - 74 year-old Finns owned a mobile phone and 60 % had an access to Internet at home, at work or at school. Approximately 80 % of Finnish school students had used computer at least once during the fall 1999.

Technology is not yet completely implemented and the future holds huge possibilities in this area. Whether virtual travelling is going to complement or substitute normal leisure travel is an open question at this stage. According to Grübler´s and Nakicenovic´s application of the life cycle theory to transportation a new mode of travel should be introduced around a year 2000, although air traffic will still increase its market share. The market share of this new mode will start to grow very fast. Nijkamp et al. assess that this new mode of travel could be high speed train or/and Maglev (electro)-magnetic leviation train. One possibility is also that the new mode of travel is virtual travelling.

The changes in the urban form and the travel demand in the Finnish cities by the year 2020 were studied by using three different social scenarios. The chosen scenarios describe the possible social conditions and the development leading to it. Telecommunications displace travel demand on various trip purposes. Life styles are technology orientated and technological applications are utilized on several social sectors significantly more than today. The migration to large urban areas continues to increase and the most popular type of housing is a large urban dwelling unit.

In the Eco-Society the economical growth is approximately 1 % per year. The Eco-Society represents a scenario of scarce resources, partly based on local network economy. The basis of the economy is traditional industry and new kind of primary production. Planning mechanisms are strongly regulated and taxation instruments are efficiently used. The life styles emphasize environmental awareness and time use at local environment or neighbourhood. The migration to urban areas decreases gradually. The most popular housing type is represented by urban relatively dense housing.

In the Virtual Society the amount of free time is increasing, partly because the work and free time are mixed. On the other hand the employment of time is strongly polarized - part of the population has plenty of free time and part almost no free time. The concept of time is syncronic and the society as whole is developing towards 'open 24 hours' society. The life styles orientate towards information society and technology-optimism.New technological applications are utilized at home, at work, at studying, in travel, and at leisure time.

In the Eco-Society the life styles are environmentally aware and critical towards new technology. Environmental assets are dominating all decision making and technology is geared to improve environmental conditions. Leisure time modes emphasize nature, ecology and health. Sports, outdoor recreation and eco-tourism are popular recreation activities. Walking and cycling are popular modes of travel due to their outdoor and motional character. Shopping, personal business and recreation trips are often done at neighbourhood. Small local shops, banks, post offices, day care centres and leisure services become increasingly popular.

Home based leisure activities, like cooking, baking, handicrafts, and home repair, are common. Households are not purchasing services as commonly as today and more leisure time is spent at home with family members or at local community. Consumption of commodities and services is decreasing. Most popular housing type is relatively dense urban housing, mainly dense detached housing.

In the Experience Society the economic growth increases the consumption and the ownership of for example several apartments and cars. The age of retirement decreases and the amount of free time increases more than in other scenarios. Emphasizingly consumeristic life style is encouraged by the economical growth. Leisure activities are exceedingly specialized and include remarkably much travelling. Leisure time is dominated by consumption of entertainment. Specialized sports and exercise are popular among all age groups.

The amount of daily trips has been relatively constant during the last decades, although there is significant differences between different age groups and sosio-economic groups. The changes in the age structure affect the travel needs directly - the demand for work and work-related trips will reduce. The reduction rate depends on the other hand on development of unemployment rates and retirement trends and on the other hand on the popularity of teleworking. The amount of work-related trips tend to increase while the work life specializes and new work forms become common. The powerful changes in the attitudes towards time use and leisure habits and the amount of free time can imply indirect effects on the daily number of trips.

Work-related trips, and trips to for example day care centres and to doctors appointments form a less regular demand group, in which the starting point of the trip is often bound, but the demand do not necessarily require daily travel and even the destination can vary. The third group contains shopping and other personal business trips, like trips to bank offices, hairdresser or tax offices. The trips in this group are necessary, but their starting point, frequency and destination can often be chosen.

In Virtual Society the daily number of trips is 7 % smaller than in the year 1997. In the Experience Society the development is the opposite - number of daily trips increases especially in the trip groups of leisure trips and shopping trips. The daily number of trips is 7 % greater than in the year 1997. In the Eco-Society the changes are relatively small and the number of trips is slightly lower than in the year 1997. The differences between the scenarios are more significant in the daily mileage than in the trip production.

The transport demand, measured both in number of trips and their daily mileage, increases most in the Experience Society. In the Experience Society the changes in the urban form, economic development, migration, and life style promote the increase in the transport demand. The mileage will decrease in the Eco-Society, especially in small urban areas. In the Eco-Society the trip lengths will decrease 10 - 25 % in the urban areas of different size. In the Virtual Society only the mileage of work related business trips and leisure trips increases. The mileage is almost the same as at the year 1997. In the Eco-Society all mileage groups decrease, the decrease is strongest at the leisure trip mileage.

Trends in Park Tourism

Nature-based tourism is a large and growing global industry. Nature-based tourism is travel dependent upon the attributes of the natural environment. Nature-based tourism is the travel and tourism activity dependent upon the destination attributes of the natural environment. This tourism is dependent upon two fundamental components:

1) appropriate levels of environment quality and

2) suitable levels of consumer service.

Nature-based tourism has become sufficiently large that submarkets are becoming apparent. Eagles suggests, using a motive-based methodology for segmentation, that the nature-tourism market contains at least four recognizable niche markets: ecotourism, wilderness use, adventure travel and car camping (Figure 1).

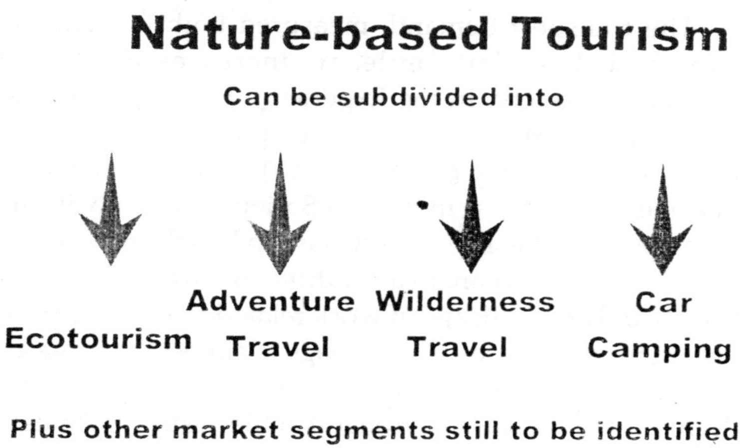

Figure 1: Submarkets of nature-based tourism

Ecotourism involves travel for the discovery of and learning about wild, natural environments. Wilderness travel involves personal re-creation through primitive travel in natural environments that are devoid of human disturbance. Adventure travel is personal accomplishment through the thrills of dominating dangerous environments. Car camping is safe, family travel in the interface between the wild and the civilized. This classification utilizes unique sets of social motives to identify the market segments. Each of the niche markets is at a different stage in the typical business cycle (Figure 2) using Butler's tourism life cycle analysis approach.

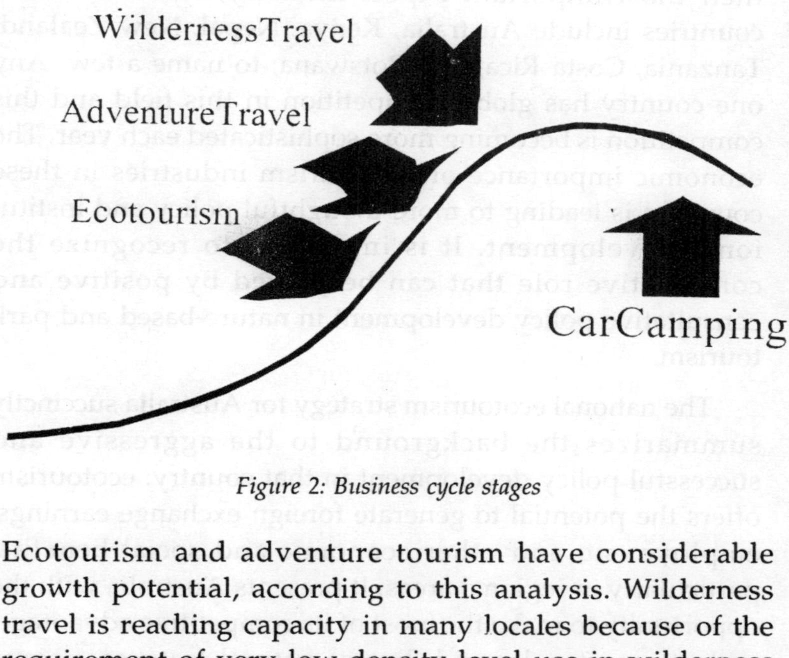

Figure 2: Business cycle stages

Ecotourism and adventure tourism have considerable growth potential, according to this analysis. Wilderness travel is reaching capacity in many locales because of the requirement of very low-density level use in wilderness destinations. Car camping is probably in decline, or soon will be, largely due to the peak population profile of the developed word passing beyond the ages in which camping is popular. All four of these market segments are visible in park tourism internationally. Given the different travel motivation sets in each submarket, it is important for planners and managers to be aware of the implications for park visitor management.

For example, the levels of social grouping, the level of desired service, the level of environmental quality and the desired environmental attributes vary amongst the four submarkets. Nature-based tourism is a large and growing component of international tourism. Several countries in the world have nature-based tourism as a key component of their most important export industry, tourism. These countries include Australia, Kenya, Nepal, New Zealand, Tanzania, Costa Rica, and Botswana; to name a few. Any one country has global competition in this field and this competition is becoming more sophisticated each year. The economic importance of the tourism industries in these countries is leading to more thoughtful policy and institut ional development. It is important to recognize the constructive role that can be played by positive and consultative policy development in nature-based and park tourism.

The national ecotourism strategy for Australia succinctly summarizes the background to the aggressive and successful policy development in that country: ecotourism offers the potential to generate foreign exchange earnings, employment, and other economic and social benefits, particularly in regional areas. It presents Australia with the opportunity to make the most of its competitive advantage, with its spectacular and diverse natural features, unique flora and fauna and diverse cultural heritage.

Ecotourism can also provide resources for environmental conservation and management and an incentive for the conservation and sustainable use of public and private land. To ensure the success of the national policy, the Australian government committed Aus.

$10,000,000 over four years for the implementation of the strategy. Tanzania has a draft national tourism policy document, an integrated master plan, and an infrastructure plan.

New Zealand has a very successful nature-based tourism policy that involves high levels of public and private cooperation in the protection of. landscapes, the management of protected areas, and the delivery of tourism services. These countries have government policy as the framework for a whole range of public and private activities, and this policy has helped foster a suitable environment for the development of nature-based tourism generally, and park tourism specifically.

Government policy plays a very important role in the development of tourism industries that are financially and ecologically sustainable.

Globally, the area of land covered by the world's parks and protected areas increased considerably from 1900 to 1996. By 1996 the world's network of 30,361 parks covers an area of 13,245,527 square kilometres, representing 8.84% of the total land area of the planet. This total land area occurs in 225 countries and dependent territories. The impressive growth of the world's park network is the result of the widespread acceptance of the ecological ethic and aggressive political action. It appears that the tourism activity occurring at these sites created a self-perpetuating phenomenon of visitation, education, and desire for more parks, visitation and education.

The global network includes a wide variety of types of protected areas, ranging from nature reserve through to protected landscape, within the International Union for the Conservation of Nature and Natural Resources' (IUCN) six-category system. The.management categories' system provides a common international standard for classifying the many different types of protected area designation in countries around the world, based on the primary management objective. This facilitates accounting and monitoring at national, regional and international levels.

Table 1 shows the global network listed by management category. All six categories are well represented in the network, but with national parks and resource management areas being the two categories with highest representation in the system. National parks, Category II, is a prominent and well-known land classification covering 2.67 % of the earth's land surface. A very significant amount of the world's most significant biodiversity conservation sites is located in Category I and II sites. However, all sites play some role. The name national park is closely associated with nature-based tourism, being a symbol of a high quality natural environment with a well-designed tourist infrastructure.

Table 1: Global Protected Areas Classified by IUCN Management Category

	Protected Areas Globally					
IUCN	Number Category	Percent	Total Area in km^2	Percent	Mean Area in km^2	Percent total land area of the world
Ia. Nature Reserve	4,395	14	982,487	7	224	0.66
Ib. Wilderness	806	3	940,344	7	1,167	0.63
II. National Park	3,386	11	4,000,825	30	1,182	2.67
III. Natural Monument	2,122	7	193,022	1	91	0.13

IV. Habitat Area	11,171	37	2,460,283	19	220	1.64
V. Protected Landscape	5,584	18	1,067,118	8	191	0.71
VI. Resource Management	2,897	10	3,601,447	27	1,243	2.4
Total	30,361	100	13,245,528	99	436	8.84

Eagles and Wind found that Canadian ecotour companies frequently used the name national park as a brand name to attract potential ecotourists to their sales offerings. With 30,361 parks in the world, and with 3,386 having the well-known name of a national park, it is clear that any particular political unit, such as one country or one province within a country, has a major task to get its sites recognized globally. There is a very large number of sites available for tourists.

Some countries, such as Canada, have the disadvantage of having many of their sites known as provincial parks, a name unknown outside Canada, and suggestive of a lower level of importance. Unfortunately, there is no global tabulation of park usage, as there is for park area. Therefore, it is not possible to comprehensively report on the total volume of recreational use in recent years or its change over time.

Eagles, McLean and Stabler calculated the total national and provincial/state park usage in North America. In 1996 there was an estimated 2,621,777,237 visitor days of recreation activity in the parks and protected areas of Canada and the US. Clearly, the outdoor recreation occurring in the parks and protected areas in Canada and the United States is a very large and impressive activity. With an estimated 2.6 billion days of use per year this activity has major economic, social and environmental impacts.

However, until there are international standards for park tourism data collection and management, and global tabulation of these data, this important international activity will suffer from a lack of co-ordination in data reporting and an associated void in public policy profile.

Economics is an important component of societal decision- making, but it is often given low priority in the parks' world. Usually in parks, the very strong emphasis given to ecology is seen by many park proponents as sufficient justification for public policy action. However, nature tourism is increasingly becoming important within sustainable development because of the potential of contributing to local and national economic development while also providing incentive for nature conservation and biodiversity conservation.

Most of the world's protected areas charge low entry and use fees. These fees typically cover only a portion of the cost of protecting the resource and providing the features on which the park visitation depends. This pricing policy developed during a period where resource protection was seen as the overwhelmingly important objective, a public objective that benefits all of society. If a public good benefits all, it can be reasonably argued that it should be paid for by taxes on society. However, this logic falters when applied to outdoor recreation in parks as only those who participate in outdoor recreation are beneficiaries.

In a time of widespread government financial retrenchment, it is increasingly difficult to justify public expenditure to subsidize the recreation of one segment of the population. Governments around the world are using this logic, in part, for the reduction or freezing of grants for park management. The reduction of budgets has been documented in Canada and the USA as has the development of new forms of park administration and new pricing policies.

The Parks Canada business plan summarizes this concept with the statement that "subsidies will be phased out on services of benefit to individuals, by transferring the operation to the nonprofit voluntary or private sectors, or these services will be stabilized on a full cost recovery basis". There are dramatic differences amongst the world's parks in terms of pricing policy, tourism income, and financial management.

A global study of biosphere reserves found that only 32 of 78 responding sites charged visitors admission fees. The fees ranged from less than $5.00 to $110 per person per day, in US funds, with the vast majority at the lower range. There was a statistically significant relationship between total direct income and the numbers of visitors for all biosphere reserves. Higher visitor numbers corresponded to higher budgets.

Generally, those parks with high levels of tourism clients gain higher levels of political power. This power is then translated into higher budget allocations. It is important to recognize that substantial management budgets are necessary in areas of high usage to avoid excessive damage to the natural environment of the parks. Parks often supply the most important part of the nature tourism experience, but typically capture little of the economic value of the stream of economic benefits.

The low entry and use fees in parks are the result of many factors, one being the effort of a centralized budget allocation process in many governments. With this form of government financial management, the park management does not keep earned fees within its internal financial.

structure, and therefore sees little benefit in comprehensive fee collection. This also contributes to a low emphasis on park visitor management. Such issues as retur n rates, length of stay, visit satisfaction and service quality all suffer when the financial return from the visitors is not tied directly to the financial operation of a park.

Many governments see nature-based tourism as an important tool for economic development. Unfortunately, most have not invested sufficiently in staff training, infrastructure or park resources that are needed to support nature tourism. This exposes sensitive sites to tourism-caused degradation. Most national tourism agencies do not keep statistics on market sectors, such as those associated with nature-based tourism and park-based tourism. Other management units, such as park agencies seldom fill this information void. As a result, important sectors, such as nature-based tourism, are not clearly documented for the benefit of policy determination.

Clearly nature-based tourism is one of the key elements of Canadian tourism. Filion et al. estimated that as much as one quarter of the tourism expenditures in Canada can be attributed to wildlife tourism, one of the elements of nature tourism. The Canadian Tourism Commission provides quarterly Canadian tourism figures to governments, business and the media. These data considerably raise the profile of tourism within the business sector. However, in Canada there is no system for the collection and distribution of information on nature-based or park-based tourism.

Therefore, the importance of nature tourism in the country is severely underrated due to lack of adequate information. The parks do not compare well to other economic generators, such as auto manufacturing or forestry, where the volumes and economic value of the products are carefully documented and reported within a continuous stream of information. This Canadian situation is common throughout the world.

The economic impact of park tourism is not well known, not well documented, and where known, not well communicated. This leads to a severe under-representation of the importance of park tourism within the fiscal sectors of government and business. Wells documented, globally, the economic studies available on nature tourism.

Eagles, McLean & Stabler compiled a national park- use database for Canada and the United States. They found that in 1996, the last year complete data were available, 2,506,451,728 visitor days of recreation occurred in the federal and state parks and protected areas of the USA, and an additional 115,325,509 visitor days of recreation occurred in Canadian federal and provincial protected areas.

The most recent economic benefits study for a park system undertaken in Canada was done for British Columbia. In 1993 the parks generated 5,300 jobs directly and 4,000 jobs indirectly. The 5,300 jobs created by parks are comparable to other industries such as newsprint (4,200), metal mining (3,800) and coal mining (3,000). In 1993 the BC provincial parks' system contributed about Can.$430,000,000 to the provincial gross domestic product. The park visitors reported significant benefits from recreational activities beyond the market transactions. These nonmarket benefits were estimated at Can.$670,000,000 beyond the cost of operating the system by the province.

British Columbia's provincial parks are a major economic force in the province. If the national parks' contribution was added to the BC provincial parks' contribution, then the benefits would be considerably enhanced. The Province of Alberta undertook an economic impact calculation of tourism in its provincial parks, following on the lead of British Columbia. The results showed an economic impact that was large and similar to the economic impact of forestry in the province. This is a common problem for park managers, interagency conflict that results in a suppression of data and resources with the goal of now allowing park tourism to gain the full public policy profile that it would otherwise enjoy. This is especially an issue when park management is within a broadly-defined resource management agency. This is least of an issue when parks are a stand alone agency or administration.

Coopers & Lybrand Consulting calculated that in 1993 British Columbia provincial parks produced total benefits of Can.$430,000,000. These benefits included direct benefits, and consumer surplus. In 1993 the parks had 22,300,000 visitor days of activity. In Canada there are several financial structures within the federal and provincial park agencies. Some are government agencies. Others function like crown corporations.

The recovery of management costs from tourist charges varies from only 1% in British Columbia, to slightly more than 50% in Saskatchewan This variation is largely due to government policy dictating the financial structure of the agencies, not to the volume of tourism nor to the amount of area being managed. Those with the lowest level of cost recover had very weak tourism expertise within the park agencies, with the result that most tourism income was earned by the private sector. Those with the highest level of cost recovery had revenue retention within the agency, and some form of corporate operations.

Goodwin et al. found in three parks in India, Indonesia and Zimbabwe that the income from tourism was between 7% to 24% of total expenditures. Clearly, most parks in this sample have the majority of their budget coming from sources other than tourism income. However, globally the trend is for government to demand that parks earn much higher amounts of their budget from tourism sources. Corresponding to this is the development of forms of management, such as parastatals, that allow for park agencies to function with the efficiencies of a private corporation.

Parks Canada has designed a management structure that encourages increasingly higher levels of cost recovery from tourists.

The Australian, American, Canadian, Ontario, and British Columbia studies show the significance of parks to economic life in those areas. However, generally there is a lack of national and provincial economic data on parks. This is a major inhibitor in public policy making across the world and in Canada. For park economics to have the policy impact that it warrants, there must be a continuous stream of up-to-date data provided. At the very least, yearly studies are required. However, quarterly figures provided to government, business and the media would be moreuseful and beneficial.

Park Pricing Policy

Typically, in most countries park pricing policy involves a flat fee for entrance, typically for a vehicle, or for facility use, such as for one campsite. In many cases no fees are charged, especially in low- use areas, in popular sites in the low season or in remote areas. The fees are modest and not subject to market forces. Recreation allocation is typically done by the first-come first-serve approach. In some parks fees are also charged by the park agency for specialized recreation services, equipment rental, accommodation, food services and souvenir sales.

Typically the income from tourism is well below the park budget, constituting a small percentage of the money used for management. Van Sickle and Eagles found in Canadian national and provincial park agencies that fees provided an overall average of 17% of the budgets, a very similar amount to the 18% found by Brademas and Readnor for the USA. Saskatchewan is the national leader in Canada, earning 52% of expenditures in 1994-1995. In contrast the British Columbia provincial parks' agency, with a very different administrative structure, recovered only 1% of revenues. Recent figures from state parks in the USA show that for 1998 33.8% of state park budgets were recovered from various types of tourism fees. These figures from the USA suggest that in this country state parks are successfully earning higher percentages of their budgets from tourism fees.

Globally, there is a trend of governments requiring parks to recover higher percentages of their budgets from tourist expenditures. Often the generation of small amounts of revenue provides little incentive for the central government to provide adequate levels of budget for management. Laarman and Gregersen point out that this situation leads to a vicious cycle of "low fees, inadequate revenue, and deficient public investment - followed by continued low fees, revenue and investment." The typical budget situation for parks is that of a central government body setting an annual budget, dependent upon the money available for the central treasury as well as various political and lobby group machinations.

Goodwin et al. found in studies of parks in India, Indonesia and Zimbabwe there was no direct relationship between park budgets and park tourism revenues. In these three countries the money was collected locally, then submitted to central government. In countries without a large tax-based subsidy for park management, tourism is often the largest source of income for park agencies. Throughout Africa, for example, the parks must earn much or most of their operating budgets from tourism. This has led to a level of innovation in pricing policy that is worthy of note.

South Africa has a booming tourism industry that has expanded dramatically in the past five years and is predicted to grow substantially in the next five years. Significantly, 60% of the 5.5 million tourists who visited the country in 1997 visited a national park or game reserve. The democratically elected government of South Africa has many social objectives calling for budget allocation. As a result all tax-based grants to the national and provincial park systems are being phased out, leaving the parks with the options of increasing income from tourism or cutting staff and services.

The parks are responding with impressive pricing and tourism service innovation. The South African National Parks (SANP) system is now at 80% budget recovery from tourism. SANP now operates an impressive array of tourism businesses in the national parks. It provides a range of accommodation, ranging from campgrounds through family cabins to hotels. All of the food and souvenir stores are agency operated. Many of the tours are park operated. Therefore, income is earned from entrance fees, lodging, food provision, product sales and tours.

In the future, licensing of intellectual property, such as logos and park names, is a possibility. Special promotional co-operation with associated industries, such as 4 by 4 vehicle companies, holds promise. This diverse set of income generators must be further utilized if the SANP is to gain sufficient income to reach the public policy goal of financial self- sufficiency. Differential fees are becoming more common. Foreigners pay more, and sometimes much more, than nationals do. At high demand times prices are sometimes higher.

Prices are becoming associated with service level, higher prices corresponding to more services. Those agencies that have parastatal status and have private sector involvement have a much higher diversity of pricing and servicing standards. South Africa is a good example of the development of a wide range of standards and pricing for accommodation in and near the parks. The parks typically provide three levels of basic accommodation services: personal tent camping, RV camping, and semi-permanent tent rentals, the latter of which typically are wood-floored, canvas tents. The parks sometimes also have three different levels of roofed accommodation, ranging from rustic cabins through cottages to hotels.

Many parks provide several levels of food provision, from restaurants, through fast. food outlets to grocery stores. Merchandise sales are common, typically for typical outdoor gear and souvenirs. In South Africa the private sector is heavily involved in the upper range market, providing two or three levels of highly priced accommodations and associated ecotourism services at private game reserves. The private reserves are often located adjacent to the parks, to take advantage of the wildlife and ecosystems of the parks as well as the already identified ecotourism profile of the location.

A few park agencies are experimenting with the licensing of intellectual property. The names and images of national parks are some of the most well-known and powerful in the world. Private corporations will often pay high sums for the use of these names and images. Cross marketing occurs when one product or organization advertises in concert with another. An example could be a park agency using one type of recreational vehicle, thereby advertising to all the visitors its special qualities in the park environment. In concert, the vehicle manufacturer would publicize the park as the point is made about the special features of a vehicle.

Table 2: Park Tourism Income Sources

Park Entrance Fees
Recreation Service Fees, Special Events and Special Services
Concessions
Accommodation
Equipment Rental
Food Sales (Restaurant and Store
Parking
Merchandise Sales (Equipment, Clothing, Souvenirs)
Licensing of Intellectual Property
Cross Product Marketing.

Australia is a typical example with most park agencies in the country relying on only a few of these sources of income, typically entrance fees, some recreation service fees and accommodation fees, usually for camping. Australia has a long tradition of free public access to na tural and cultural heritage assets, so much so that when the Great Barrier Reef National Marine Park proposed an increase from $1 to $6 for park visitors using commercial tourist operators a Senate parliamentary committee inquiry was launched.

In several countries dramatic increases in park use fees were introduced without proper client consultation, most specifically Costa Rica and Zimbabwe, resulting in vociferous objection.and subsequent roll-back of some of the increase. The lack of knowledge of pricing policy and the methods of price adjustment is common in parks, and is visibly evident in these two examples. There are implications for management of higher levels of income based on tourism (Table 3). Overall, park visitors will face higher fees and more increased opportunity where fees are charged. The biggest changes take place within the park agency. A business approach to management is necessary. This includes the ability to retain and utilize most if not all income.

Table 3: Implications of Tourism-based Income

Business-based Management
Increased Profile of Visitors in Management
More emphasis on Client Satisfaction
Service Quality Management
Enhanced Marketing
Independence from Government Grants
Higher fees

Given the need for income, the park visitors become more important. Their opinions on programs, their length of stay, their return rates, their facility and program needs and their overall satisfaction become important management variables. The managers become more aware of the need for marketing, that is the creation of a product that fits the market needs. Once the income becomes substantial park management has a higher level of independence from government grants, and from government in general.

Experience reveals many resistance factors from the move from a park agency dependent upon government grants, to an agency dependent upon tourism income. Nature is perceived as being universally-owned and requiring no human management. This concept of nature as a free good creates expectations that national parks and other forms of protected areas should provide free access. Over history this concept was reinforced with pricing for access well below the production cost.

In the USA national park use fees were prohibited by law for many years. The private sector in tourism usually objects to any fees, and especially to any increase in fees. In addition, it is obvious to many business people in tourism that substantial income can be earned by providing services to park visitors. These people therefore act like vultures, swooping into the political arena to seize the most important assets, such as accommodation and food provision. This denies the park management from important income sources.

Park agencies are typically not equipped to undertake business management. Their marketing, pricing policy, economics and financial expertise are usually deficient. This and other factors lead many park agency staff to vigorously object to a park agency operating as a business. It is common for important sectors of the public, such as environmental groups, to object to the business operation. This is often due to fears of over commercialisation. It can also be due to resistance to paying increased fees.

Competencies for Tourism Planning

All national parks and protected areas have some level of visitor use. This can vary from just a few to millions of visitors per year. Much of the visitor management is reactive, rather than proactive. The parks receive whatever visitor use that occurs, and then try to develop mechanisms to define and manage appropriate activities and levels of use. Often visitor management only takes place when some level of a problem is perceived. The parks usually provide "take it or leave it" levels of tourism service. In other words, a type of recreation program or facility and a level of service is provided, with the visitor free to accept this, or to not participate.

The majority of park agencies are weak in tourism competencies. Those that do occur are usually the result of resource managers learning on the job about visitors and tourism management. Very few agencies, and almost no parks, have professional expertise in leisure pricing policy, in tourism economics, in marketing, in tourism management, in social statistics, in service quality or in leisure studies. However, this situation is changing rapidly in several countries.

For example, Parks Canada is one of the leaders in the development of high levels of competency throughout the agency in tourism management. This increase is stimulated by the need of the agency to gain operational income from tourism. The low level of tourism competency occurs in park agencies where the emphasis is on resource protection and the budget comes entirely from a central government pot.

However, whenever a park agency starts to move to a tourism-based budget where income from visitor services provides the income, there is a much higher emphasis given to tourism management. Often the private sector operators in and near the parks have much higher levels of tourism market expertise than do the parks. In many parts of the world the private sector is the force behind the tourism in parks. It is the private sector that attracts the visitors, services their basic needs, and provides all of the tourism services. A pointed example of this is in Costa Rica, where the national parks and the wildlife refuges have low tourism competencies within the government agency. It is the private sector that has developed the internationally recognized, park-based ecotourism industry over the last 20 years.

A study found a very large ecotourism market in Canada and the United States. In the seven metropolitan areas studied, Seattle, San Francisco, Los Angeles, Dallas, Chicago, Toronto, and Winnipeg a market of 13.2 million potential ecotravellers was found. This was much larger than anticipated, and showed that a large market is now present in North America alone. The study found that the natural setting is the most critical factor in the determination of a quality product. The tourists showed increasing desire to find experiences in environments that were ecologically well managed.

Recreational activities were important and multiple activities were desired. Midrange accommodation was desired, and the experienced ecotourist placed much higher emphasis on the outdoor experience than on the accommodation. Competent guides and quality interpretive programs enhanced the quality of the travel product experience. The preferred trip was long, at seven days or more. Parks and the activities in the parks were found to be very important components of the ecotravel experience. Clearly, there is a large and growing ecotourism market in North America.

Travel trends throughout the world point to growing markets, especially in North America, Europe and Asia.

Given the large potential market size, the key issue becomes one of providing travel products that fit the market and ensuring that these products have positive economic and environmental benefits. Many parks are poorly designed for documentation of visitation levels. Parks are often large with many entry points, making it difficult to tabulate all entrances. Some park clients sneak in, to avoid fees. Many parks do not have staff covering all entrances at all times of the day and all months of the year. Shoulder season visitation is usually poorly documented.

Within.one agency there may be different data collection procedures in different parks. And in large parks there may be different data collection procedures at different entrances. However, the recent move in Canada and the USA towards parks retaining fee income is reversing this trend and placing much higher emphasis on catching as many of the clients as possible.

Every park system has its own, unique system of counting and recording its visitors. Some count all who enter, including recreationists, service vehicles, and vehicles just passing through. Some count only those who stay during the night, ignoring day visitors. Some count only those who pay. Some record the numbers of entrants, some the numbers of visitor hours, and others the numbers of visitor days. There is a need to standardize, in parks, in countries, and globally, the definition, the collection procedures, and the reporting of park tourism statistics. When this is done, the park movement will have new and powerful data for influencing public policy discussions.

Recently the World Commission on Protected Areas released the first-ever guidelines for the measurement of public use of parks and protected areas. Typically parks are managed by government agencies. In this situation most staff are government employees with a hierarchical form of decision- making. Budgets are provided each year from a central government allocation, with park income being returned to a central government pot. Often visitor services, such as accommodation, tours and consumer products, are provided by concessionaires who are licensed by the agency for a period of time.

Finance for Park Tourism

Park finance is ultimately dependent upon larger influences that affect park visitation, tourism, and management, it is important to consider the macro trends that impact on parks. The trends outlined should affect park management, worldwide, over the next 25 years. Growing demands for democratic forms of government translate into increased public participation and collaboration in park planning. Park planning and management developed into professional and bureaucratic forms as parks expanded in size and influence.

The limitations of these approaches started to become obvious as conflicts arose over diverging goals, as strong competitors for resource use arose and as park visitors and local communities became politically active. These influences and the global trend towards more democracy and accountability in government shift park management towards a more open style, with strong public participation and collaboration. Tourism is another pressure towards this approach, forcing park agencies to become more client-focused.

Increased accessibility of sophisticated technology and science means that visitors are knowledgeable about what opportunities exist and the consequences of management actions. Park visitors tend to be well-educated, urbane, well-travelled and open-minded. They are comfortable with advanced science and technology, somewhat strangely considering their strong interest in human-scale technology and human-powered activities in the parks. The average park visitor is well aware of the leisure and service opportunities available, both within parks and in other sites.

The visitor is aware of and interested in park management, and is capable of forming intelligent positions on a wide range of park management alternatives and actions. This type of clientele is both strongly advantageous to parks, in that they will easily seek out information and opportunities provided by parks, and challenging, as they will aggressively comment upon management actions. These people are sophisticated consumers, with a level of knowledge and savvy that will challenge most park management.

An aging population means that there will be significant demand shifts in what activities, settings and experiences visitors seek from parks areas. Throughout the developed world a revolution is underway in population demography. This area is entering a period with the highest proportion of retired and senior-aged people in history. These people are the healthiest and wealthiest older people in world history. They show strong interest in nature-based activities and travel.

They will be a very large potential market for the leisure experiences provided by parks and protected areas. They will not only be consumers of park activities, they may be a large pool of volunteer activity and donations. However, there are challenges. They are not very interested in camping, preferring roofed accommodation. They are less physically capable than younger people. Their ability to travel declines as age-related physical challenges develop.

As educational levels rise, demand for appreciative and learning opportunities associated with parks and protected areas will increase. In the vast majority of the world, educational levels of the population are rising quickly. There is an increasing participation rate in post secondary education. In the developed world almost 50% of all new jobs involve post secondary education. National park use is highly correlated with higher education levels. Higher education leads to higher service quality demands as well as higher educational service demands. Parks are challenged to provide services and programs that build on the education trend. However, since higher education levels lead to higher income levels, these people are able to pay for the services that they demand.

In the medium term, advances in the technology of travel and reductions in costs will result in increased demand for park and protected area opportunities distant from one's residence. For the last 50 years advances in airline technology, energy efficiency, information technology, human social welfare and education led to increases for long distance travel. Such travel affects many parks, and is a critically important export industry for many countries. This trend can be expected to continue in the medium term, for approximately the next 10 years. For most countries in the world park visitation increased, sometimes dramatically over the last 50 years. This increase can be expected to continue in the medium term.

Continued growing sensitivity to environmental, social, cultural and economic impacts of human activity lead to new and different roles of protected areas, often to multiuse sites similar to biosphere reserves. Private ecolodges and nature reserves develop, funded by tourism. As parks reach beyond the 10% level of the earth's terrestrial surface, their roles will continue to deepen and diversify. Tourism can adapt to a wide variety of situations, ranging for low-density wilderness to high density urban and resorts.

There is an emerging market for multi-use sites that provide a spectrum of opportunities within a geographically and conceptually-linked space, such as a biosphere reserve. Such a site can, in one place, provide ranges of experiences dealing with human use density, levels of physical challenge, ranges of accommodation quality and price and levels of interaction with nature from intense to casual.

Private ecolodges are developing strongly in many countries, typically exploiting the market for advanced levels of education and service. These sites vary dramatically in form as the industry experiments with this new type of travel destination. They are already having visibly positive environmental, economic and social impacts in many countries. Many of these sites will challenge public parks in the upper scale markets of nature-based tourism.

Growing knowledge about visitors, parks and their interactions lead to more sophisticated and effective methods of managing park-based tourism. As park tourism continues to develop, as parks recognize the need to compete for a finite tourism market and as park visitors demand more sophisticated services, park agencies must develop higher levels of tourism management competence. The key areas include:

— Understanding visitors' needs and wants

— Service quality management

— Leisure pricing policy

— Leisure marketing

— Tourism and resource economics

— Finance

— Tourism management

The global increase in park area, number of parks and park visitation outstrips the capability of many park management institutions. The ecology imperative is also a cultural imperative in much of the world. As a result societies place increasing amounts of land into parks. However, equivalent amounts of money for the effective management of these lands are not forthcoming from taxpayers.

Clearly, the new parks, the increasing area to management and the increasing visitation leads to new management challenges. Some of the outcomes of this trend include:

— Financial needs exceeding the current money supply.

— Paper parks.

— Environmental quality degradation.

— Increased emphasis on tourism income.

— Increased use of NGO, volunteer, profit sector management.

Park management shifts gradually from government agency structures, with centralized financial control, to parastatal forms, with financially flexible and entrepreneurial forms of management. The typical government park agency is designed to make the park visitor into a problem. Such an agency is an expenditure unit with a fixed budget. The agency gets no direct benefit from the visitor and sees the visitor as a drain on that fixed budget. Increases in visitation are problematic with a fixed budget. New areas to manage, increasing numbers of visitors and increasing societal roles for parks all stretch the government agency management model to the breaking point.

Government and policy innovators look for alternatives to the government model. Three are three models. One is privatizing all of the tourism services to the profit-making sector of society. This brings efficiency, but not necessarily effectiveness and little equity. Another is privatizing many of the tourism services to the non-profit sector, such as Community and Friends Groups. This can provide efficiency, effectiveness and some equity. Another is privatizing within government, the use of the parastatal form of management. The model is increasingly used, often in concert with the non-profit sector. This approach may be the best model to provide the most balanced mixture of efficiency, effectiveness, and equity. Examples of park agencies using the parastatal model include the park agencies in the following areas:

— Ontario Provincial Parks (Canada's oldest and biggest provincial park system)

— Parks Canada (National Parks, National Historic Parks and National Canals)

— TANAPA (Tanzania National Parks)

— SANP (South Africa National Parks)

— Kenya Wildlife Service (Kenya National Parks)

Park management funding increasingly shifts from government grants to park tourism fees and charges. This results in higher levels of visitor focus in management. It is reasonable to propose that since all people benefit from the ecological and cultural values of parks and protected areas, that all people, through public taxes, should pay for such benefits. However, only park visitors benefit from a trip to a park, and increasingly there is resistance to public funds being spent on such private benefits. Therefore, a substantial portion of park management funding is shifting from taxes to park tourism fees and charges.

Parastatal forms of management are particularly effective in handling with this shift. For example, in the 8 years since Ontario Provincial Parks moved from a government agency to a parastatal the agency's cost recovery moved from 32% to 82%. This shift moved the agency more strongly into a client focus, and moved it away from a government hierarchy focus.

Park agencies develop increased sophistication in their understanding and management of park visitation and tourism. The level of sophistication for park management within park agencies is rapidly increasing. Increasing numbers of visitors and the move to revenue retention stimulate this. Strong innovation occurs in areas such as pricing policy, service quality, accommodation, and food and beverage provision.

For example, Kruger National Park in South Africa provides many levels of accommodation within the park. There are at last 6 pricing levels with the park, 3 in camping and 3 in roofed and lodge accommodation. The private ecolodges on the western side of the park provide 3 more levels, typically at the more exclusive levels. Such innovation allows this nature-tourism industry to capture the maximum level of financial return with this broad range of service provision.

Increasing globalization of information, business and government results in increasing international cooperation amongst park agencies, park visitors and non-governmental organizations. Globalization affects parks in many ways, two of which will be following here: digital convergence and professionalization.

Digital convergence results in the rapid, inexpensive and effective global transfer of information. Very soon park managers and park visitors alike will be able to utilize advanced computer power, instantaneous access to data bases, Geographical Positioning Systems (GPS) and Geographical Information Systems (GIS) anywhere on the earth's service at any time.

The impact on parks can be enormous. For example, a person so equipped could record a bird in the field, transmit that sound to a central computer that identifies the bird to species, records the location geographically and records the data into a database. Simultaneously, the visitor may download maps of the site, a summary of all the records of this species and a status report. The activity of wildlife observation becomes profoundly enhanced. Such technology will affect all aspects of park tourism. It is probable that many park visitors will carry such technology with them throughout all areas of the parks they visit.

Park management is vitally important profession that will gain much more influence and recognition as the protector and interpreter of the world's environmental and cultural inheritance. This professionalization will strengthen over time. There will be a much more widespread generation and exchange of knowledge. The World Parks Congress here in Durban is an example of such an exchange. The huge attendance at the Congress is a visible signal of the demand for such knowledge and the many speakers a willingness to share this knowledge. Exchange programs will flourish as a way of sharing knowledge and professional development. As this field develops, there will be more specialized programs in park management in colleges and universities. The USA and Canada lead in this area now, but many other countries can be expected to develop such programs.

Foreign aid and grants from NGOs will increasingly fund biodiversity conservation and sustainable tourism development in developing nations. Increasingly foreign aid and bilateral aid funds biodiversity conservation and sustainable development with the goal of providing both conservation and economic benefit. Sustainable tourism has the potential of providing on-going conservation and economic benefits.

Increasing demands for resource exploitation, such as oil, gas, minerals, water, and wood, place stronger pressure for the exploitation of park resources. As renewable and non-renewable resources outside parks become scarcer, the demands for exploitation within parks increase. Healthy park tourism provides one counter balance with its politically relevant benefits. However, it is vitally important that these benefits are accurately calculated and effectively communicated.

A substantial number of parks and their tourism will be destroyed by war, famine and civil unrest, especially in Africa and Asia. Some countries will see a decline in park tourism, typically when social unrest is given widespread coverage in the press. Countries with recent tourism declines due to widely-reported social unrest include:

— Zimbabwe (Nature Tourism, both consumptive and appreciative)

— Uganda (Nature Tourism)

— Indonesia (Cultural and Nature Tourism)

— Israel (Religious Tourism)

International travel will increase until decreasing supplies of inexpensive light oil result in large increases in cost between 2010 and 2020. As the energy costs increase, international travel will decline. Substantial pressure will take place on many parks and protected areas. The world annual oil production will peak some time between 2005 and 2015. This is known as Hubbert's Peak. After this peak, there will be substantial impacts on the global economy and on tourism.

Global climate change will affect most parks and most park tourism. Global climate change will continue to affect many parks. The impacts on park tourism are unclear, however some obvious impacts could include:

— Increasing drying and droughts leading to water stress, droughts and fires. Travellers involved with summer outdoor recreation may move into cooler climes to avoid heat stress.

— Substantial changes in snow-based activities with reductions of snow cover. Substantial changes in tourism as weather changes typical climate-based recreation seasons (i.e. periods of drought, heat and coolness shift).

— Much higher risk exposure with increases in fires, winds and erratic storms.

Future Trends

A variety of far-reaching and globally effective changes in society and economy have lately created a significant change in both leisure and tourism behaviour. Many regional and local suppliers of tourism and, in the wider context, leisure services failed to adapt to these new market parameters. It was not until then that science, popular science and practice started to think about the new tourist and new leisure trends. Subsequently, research became increasingly concerned with leisure and tourism trends.

Tourism destinations, particularly alpine tourism destinations, have over the last 3-4 years faced a difficult phase, as of late there have been new markets, products and tourism segments which suggests that the leisure and tourism industry have realised the necessity to adapt to these new competitive forces.

Popular publications have now gone so far as to argue that the crisis in the tourism and leisure industry has been ultimately overcome. In (the case of) Austria, it seems that suppliers partially adapted to these new leisure and tourism trends through quality enhancement programs, more customer orientated product development (e.g. all inclusive packages, family products, reengineering of old products such as bush walking, events and theme parks) as well as improved promotion and marketing activities (e.g. marketing co-operations, more focussed promotion, use of IT for new marketing and sales strategies, etc.). However, there are several considerations and observations which apparently have been left out:

— Product life cycles replace each other in shorter and shorter sequences. As a result, changes now occur at an accelerated but variable pace and previous adaptations can not be considered as final and/or optimal.

— A number of adaptations, especially in tourism, followed the rule of "thoughtless imitation" or "imitation instead of understanding". This means that certain global changes are replicated without considering local or regional positioning, thus without adding local authenticity.

— With many trends occurring simultaneously, it can be said that the real trend is that there is no mainstream trend, according to the rule "Anything goes".

These statements or hypotheses suggest a common thread: trends become postulated and replicated without a thorough understanding of the deeper underlying social and social psychological determinants. Moreover, postulates are often only applied with respect to a limited number of leisure areas, such as tourism behaviour. Quantitative and qualitative changes in leisure behaviour (an thus implicitly also work behaviour) have however a much stronger and prior effect on the leisure and tourism industries due to the diffusion and/or dynamics of multiplier effects.

"Leisure Futures" aims at exploring the underlying determinants and dynamics of future leisure trends and does so both from a conceptual (theoretical) and practical perspective. Both scientists and practitioners are invited to participate, including firms involved in the shaping of the future tourism and leisure industry.

Bibliography

Bernier, C., "Occupational map of tourism and leisure job titles", in E. Laws (ed.), *The ATTT Tourism Education Handbook*, London, Tourism Society, 1997.

Bernthall, R., "Designing curriculum: will industry participate?", *paper presented to, International Conference for Tourism Educators*, Guildford, University of Surrey, 1988.

Berry-Lound, D., Batersby, D., and Parsons, D., *Jobs in Tourism and Leisure: A Labour Market Review*, London, British Tourist Authority, 1991

Borocz, J., "Leisure migration: A Sociological Study on Tourism", Pergamon Press: UK, ISBN 0080425607 HB 110 Dutch Guilders, 1996.

Bosselman, R. H., "Issues of accreditation in hospitality and tourism education: the value controversy", Tourism Recreation Research, 21(2) pp.31-35, 1996

Collins, M.F. and Cooper, I.S. (eds) 'Leisure Management: Issues and Applications', *CAB International: UK*, HB, ISBN 0851992153 stlg40.00, 1997.

Davies, J., "Language skills in the leisure and tourism industry", *Tourism*, 102: 20, 1999.

Foley, M., Lennon, J. and Maxwell, G. (eds) 'Hospitality, Tourism and Leisure Management: Issues in Strategy and Culture', Cassell: UK, PB, ISBN 0304332399 stlg16.99, (1997)

Groves, D., "A framework for the analysis of leisure-based academic and certification programs in travel and tourism", *Hospitality and Tourism Educator*, 8(1): 54-56, 1996.

Horner, S. and Swarbrooke, J. 'Marketing Tourism Hospitality and Leisure in Europe', ITBP: UK, PB, ISBN 1861523033 stlg21.95, 1996.

Kemp, K. and Pearson, S. 'Leisure and Tourism: GNVQ Intermediate', Addison Wesley Longman: UK, PB, ISBN 0582304105 stlg13.99, 1997.

Krippendorf, J., 'The Holiday Makers: Understanding the Impact of Leisure and Travel', Butterworth Heinemann: UK, PB, ISBN 0750604417 stlg22.99, 1989.

Owen, G., 'Accounting for Hospitality, Tourism and Leisure', Longman: UK, PB, ISBN 0582312957 stlg20.99, 1998.

Persic, M., "Training of tourism professionals in Croatia", *World Leisure and Recreation*, 40(3): 19-25, 1998.

Sharpley, R., 'Tourism and Leisure in the Countryside', Elm: UK, PB, ISBN 185450245X stlg11.95, 1996.

Swarbrooke, J., "Tourism and leisure education in the United Kingdom", in G. Richards (ed.), *European Tourism and Leisure Education: Trends and Prospects*, Tilberg, Netherlands, Tilberg University Press, 1995.

Torkildsen, G., 'Leisure and Recreation Management', Spon: UK, PB, ISBN 0419167609 stlg19.50, 1992.

Tribe, J., 'The Economics of Leisure and Tourism: Environments, Markets and Impacts', Butterworth Heinemann: UK, PB, ISBN 075062342X stlg20.99, 1995.

Veal, A.J., 'Research Methods for Leisure and Tourism: A Practical Guide', FT Management: UK, PB, ISBN 0273620525 stlg19.99, 1997.

Watt, D., 'Event Management in Leisure and Tourism', Longman: UK, PB, ISBN 0582357063 stlg17.99, 1998.

Youell, R., 'Leisure and Tourism: Advanced GNVQ', Longman: UK, PB, ISBN 0582278422 stlg16.99, 1995.

Index